to *know* and
nurture
a reader

to *know* and *nurture* a reader

Conferring with Confidence and Joy

Kari Yates & Christina Nosek

Foreword by Kim Yaris & Jan Burkins

Stenhouse
PUBLISHERS

PORTLAND, MAINE

Stenhouse Publishers
www.stenhouse.com

Credits
Figure 2.3 Diagram informed by Vygotsky's zone of proximal development
Figure 3.2 Informed by Vygotsky's zone of proximal development
Figure 7.2 Informed by Collins and Glover (2015)
Figure 7.4 Informed by Fountas and Pinnell (2016a)
Figure 7.6 Informed by Fountas and Pinnell (2016a)
Cover design, interior design, and typesetting: Alessandra S. Turati

Library of Congress Cataloging-in-Publication Data
Names: Yates, Kari, author. | Nosek, Christina, author.
Title: To know and nurture a reader : conferring with confidence and joy / Kari Yates and Christina Nosek.
Description: Portland, Maine : Stenhouse Publishers, [2018] | Includes bibliographical references.
Identifiers: LCCN 2017058113 (print) | LCCN 2018010965 (ebook) | ISBN 9781625311733 (ebook) | ISBN 9781625311726 (pbk. : alk. paper)
Subjects: LCSH: Reading (Elementary) | Individualized instruction. | Children--Books and reading. | Children's literature--Study and teaching (Elementary)
Classification: LCC LB1573 (ebook) | LCC LB1573 .Y36 2018 (print) | DDC 372.4--dc23
LC record available at https://lccn.loc.gov/2017058113

Manufactured in the United States of America
24 23 22 21 20 19 18   9 8 7 6 5 4 3 2 1

PRINTED ON 30% PCW
RECYCLED PAPER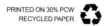

To every child we've had the honor
to know and nurture as a reader

contents

Foreword...viii

Acknowledgments xi

Introduction: *conferring with courage and commitment*................................. 1

PART 1 Interactive Moves: *the how of conferring* 7

    Chapter 1 Wonder: Bringing Curiosity and an Open Mind to Every Conference........11

    Chapter 2 Affirm: Celebrating Effort, Strategy, and Emerging Work 26

    Chapter 3 Extend: Nudging Readers Forward.. 38

    Chapter 4 Remind: Ensuring Transfer Beyond This Conference....................................51

PART 2 Intentional Directions: *the what of conferringv* 63

    Chapter 5 Confer to Support Book Choice 68

    Chapter 6 Confer to Develop Healthy Habits 94

    Chapter 7 Confer to Strengthen Strategic Process 116

    Chapter 8 Confer to Support Authentic Response 144

PART 3 Organizational Moves: *behind the scenes*..167

    Chapter 9 Gather Materials: Getting Ready for Teaching and Learning On the Go 169

    Chapter 10 Make a Plan: Creating Time to Confer with All Students 173

    Chapter 11 Take Note: Holding On to Thinking to Help Pave the Path Ahead........... 185

Putting It All Together: *the art of decision making*..194

Appendix 217

References 229

Index...234

foreword

By Jan Burkins and Kim Yaris

In the process of reading *To Know and Nurture a Reader*, we have come to the realization that most of our exchanges with people can be described as conferences. When our children come home from school and we inquire about their day, this is a conference. When we talk with our spouses about the pickup and drop-off schedule for after-school activities, this is a conference. When one of us, as writing partner and best friend to the other, takes on the risk of nudging the other to stretch into uncomfortable parenting or writing or teaching domains, this is a conference. Thus, any book about conferring is a book about getting better at the whole of your life, and this, dear friends, is not just any book about conferring.

While we were reading *To Know and Nurture a Reader* together, we were also reading *Moments: Why Certain Experiences Have Extraordinary Impact*. In it, brothers Chip and Dan Heath explore the emotional, psychological, and intellectual alchemy that turns even ordinary experiences into life-defining moments. They offer four pathways for anchoring moments in hearts and minds: (1) **elevate** the moment so that aspects of it are unexpected, (2) **connect** deeply in the moment to build relationships, (3) provide opportunities for **insight** in the moment, and (4) build **pride** in the process or product.

As we read these two books simultaneously, we were struck, chapter by chapter, by how Kari and Christina replicated for the classroom what Chip and Dan Heath were working to do for the general public.

First, *To Know and Nurture a Reader* elevates conferring experiences for students by immediately breaking the script of traditional student-teacher interactions. This book teaches us to start each conference by giving ownership of both the reading experience and the exchange to the student, asking permission to interrupt and engage. This disruption of traditional student-teacher hierarchies demonstrates trust in students' learning intuition, which immediately elevates conferences. The elevation is sustained as unselfish teachers listen and respond in ways that demonstrate their trust in the reader in front of them, as well as trust in themselves to follow that reader's lead.

Second, through their language and their classroom examples, Kari and Christina teach us how to build personal connections by quieting our minds around a single, face-to-face moment with an individual child. They demonstrate the posture and presence required to affix our gaze on the best in all students, thus truly seeing our students. This presence, of course, creates deep personal connections in ways that turn moments into experiences.

Third, Kari and Christina show us how to set students up for insight. They teach us how to focus and facilitate a conference in ways that create pathways for students to discover and claim their most important learning in that moment. This graceful support lifts the conferring "moment" to the level of "experience," as students discover both immediate Ahas! within their work and also their own power.

Finally, Kari and Christina model for us how to build students' pride or confidence, which gives them energy and courage to continue the work. They don't build students up through traditional teacher stroking, but by naming students' moves as readers and learners, and by giving students opportunities to rise into these expanded identities.

As readers, we are particularly drawn to books that show us how to refine our language, and we are super nerds about studying them. As we read Kari and Christina's deftly crafted manuscript as a precursor to drafting this foreword, we were delighted to find ourselves enveloped in the consuming self-reflection that comes from reading a book and letting it change you. *To Know and Nurture a Reader* teaches us how to be better teachers by changing our words.

The amazing thing about books that give us better words—words that are precise, words that empower, words that give ownership, words that name, words that affirm, words that stretch, words that engender confidence—is that as we practice the better language, it seeps into all the crevices of our lives. Even more significant, the improved language has the potential to lead us to more open conversation. It creates opportunities to see our loved ones in new ways, and for them to see themselves in new ways.

For example, it is not uncommon for us to talk about what we love or appreciate in each other as writing partners and best friends. But, when Kari and Christina reminded us that "I statements" are limiting, we immediately began practicing the phrases they offered as substitutes: "You are the kind of partner who is brave and intentional when giving feedback" and "You are the kind of friend who becomes a student of your companion's needs and brings your best self to support them." This shift in language, from feedback that takes power to feedback that gives power, required our attention and extra effort because revising language involves interrupting habits long entrenched by neural pathways and muscle memory. But the result of being bathed in reminders of who we are, rather than reminders of how our accomplishments make someone feel good, is that we develop more confidence and become more present with ourselves.

Of course, these language shifts spilled into our conversations with our families. Kim finds herself saying to Craig, "You are the kind of husband who looks for ways to support the people he loves." And Jan finds herself saying to her son Victor, "You are the kind of friend who takes care of your friends even when it is hard."

But not only do our better words better support those whom we are nurturing, they diminish our need to be the center of the universe. By saying "I love it when you. . ." less and less, and by simultaneously saying "You are the kind of person who. . ." more and more, we begin to recognize how filtering our identity through our students and our children (and everyone else in our lives) diminishes our experiences of them and of ourselves—not to mention their experience of our time together.

Rich conferences, like the ones Kari and Christina describe within the pages of this book, become transformative events, not only for students, but also for us as teachers. So, it only feels fitting that we should close this foreword by asking permission to confer with you. You, of course, can decline by turning the page.

We want you to know that we—and Kari and Christina—see you. You are the kind of teacher who looks for better ways to know and nurture the readers in your charge. We want to assure you that you have come to the right place. You will find that Kari and Christina's attention to their writing craft will elevate your experience of reading their work. You will also find that, on each page, they are present and vulnerable teachers, available to connect with you and poised to support you as you discover your own insights into your interactions with students and others. Kari and Christina have crafted this wise and beautiful book from love and experience to know and nurture you, the reader. In fact, we know that this sweet and powerful book can change your words, which can change your relationships, and that, dear reader, can change your life.

acknowledgments

Just two years ago we had no idea we'd be writing a book together. How could we? We hadn't even met! Christina was living and teaching in the San Francisco Bay area and Kari was 1,784 miles away in a school in Moorhead, Minnesota. It was after following each other's blogs, connecting through Twitter, and finally meeting in person at the National Council of Teachers of English Convention in 2015 that our writing partnership was born.

Because of the ways it contributed to our finding each other, we begin by thanking Amy Brennan, Jenn Hayhurst, and Mary Howard for having the insight, the courage, and the stamina to put #G2Great into the world. You've created a safe and welcoming place for educators to come for connection, renewal, growth, and continual learning. What you do every Thursday night is a gift to educators, to our profession, and most important to the children we serve.

Online communities, like #G2Great, have had a ripple effect in our lives, helping us both find our people in ways that have been life-changing. These connections have lead us into a supportive virtual, and now personal, network of literacy education professionals from across the country. So, it is with boundless gratitude and love that we thank a group of people that we first knew as fellow educators on social media but later came to cherish as a family of sisters, brothers, and cousins: Trevor Bryan, Jan Miller Burkins, Dani Burtsfield, Jill DeRosa, Justin Dolcimascolo, Donna Donner, JoAnn Duncan, Lisa Eickholdt, Julieanne Harmatz, Fran McVeigh, Cornelius Minor, Erica Pecorale, Susie Rolander, Margaret Simon, Tara Smith, Jennifer Sniadecki, Kathryn Hoffman Thompson, and Kim Yaris. These people have shared our joys and our struggles, our laughter and our tears. They have fueled our passion for this work and therefore our courage to pursue it. They have not only influenced our practices but also helped stretch our thinking in entirely new ways. Because we've been part of this family, we know we are forever changed.

To our editor, Tori Bachman, we extend a huge hug of gratitude. You believed in our book from the beginning and gave us the space and encouragement we needed to make it truly our own. You provided reassurance when we doubted ourselves, smart suggestions to make the book better, and confidence that what we had to say was something teachers of the world need to hear. Thank you.

To the entire Stenhouse family, we say thanks for betting on us and our book. For your care and attention to detail, giving this book the TLC it needed, we are forever grateful. We are humbled and honored to have been invited to share in your journey, as you keep searching for ways to support hardworking teachers everywhere.

There are a few giants in the world of literacy education on whose shoulders we humbly stand. Our work as educators and this book would not be possible without your words, texts, example, and unwavering passion on behalf of all children. Your ideas and work, both written and spoken, a collective call to action, continually encourage us to be reflective, attuned teachers, who respond to the nuances of every individual reader. For this, we are so grateful. Carl Anderson, Nancie Atwell, Kylene Beers and Bob Probst, Lucy Calkins, Marie Clay, Irene Fountas and Gay Su Pinnell, Gravity Goldberg, Kelly Gallagher, Ann Goudvis and Stephanie Harvey, Amanda Hartman, Peter Johnston, Penny Kittle, Lester Laminack, Donalyn Miller, Zoe Ryder-White, Jennifer Serravallo, Vicki Vinton, and Grant Wiggins, your immense contributions to the field have influenced not only our own thinking but also that of teachers around the globe. Our gratitude to you extends far beyond the boundaries of this text.

From Kari

As this project ends, I look around me and realize my heart is full and my blessings are many. Every word I write is simply a reflection of the gifts, opportunities, and experiences that I've been fortunate enough to have in my lifetime.

To all the children in my circle of love—Anni, Bode, Caden, Zach, Rumor, Macy, Ridge, McKinley, Breck, Lucas, Carsten, Tegan, Claire, Anna, Charley, Sydney, Sawyer, Olivia, Forest, Nate, and Victor—thanks for being a constant source of joy and inspiration. You drive me to do whatever I am able to make the classroom a better place for you and for children like you everywhere. May your days be filled with wonder and possibility.

John, my partner in all things, you know this work wouldn't exist if not for you. From keeping me supplied with dark chocolate, ginger ale, and clean clothes to fiercely believing in everything I set out to do, propping me up when I stumble, and always helping me to see the lighter side in things—my every day is better because of the big and small ways you love me. Erika and Briana, I'm not sure how it is possible, but it seems that just the blink of an eye ago you were wee ones taking my breath away with the funny, empathetic, and insightful things you then said as we shared books together. Suddenly you are these huge-hearted, strong-minded women, taking my breath away with the ways you live lives of passion and courage. You are now, and have always been, my most persistent and inspirational teachers.

To my mom for teaching me to work hard and to be kind; to my dad for teaching me to dream big; and to Jim, my bonus dad, who asks with sincere interest and listens with genuine care, I send my love and gratitude.

To Kathy Fisher, my "bestest bud" in all the world, you know every one of my flaws, fears, and faults, and still cheer me on wildly at every corner. More than three decades later, I can't believe my good fortune. To Jan Miller Burkins, who keeps helping me stretch into a better version of my former self. To Joan Moser for your generous gifts of time, encouragement, and feedback as the earliest drafts of this work came together. To the staff of the Moorhead Area Public Schools whom I learn from every day. Thanks for sharing your thinking, your time, your celebrations, your struggles, and your students with me. I couldn't be prouder to call you my colleagues.

And, finally, to my writing and thinking partner, Christina Nosek, who has hung in there through all the bumps and bruises and twists and turns of this project. You've taught me so much about conferring, but more importantly, you've taught me new lessons in collaboration and partnership. Thanks for saying, "Yes!" I am forever changed because of the time we've spent together giving life to this text.

From Christina

I first learned the true spirit of knowing and nurturing from my family: Mom, I am the strong woman and advocate for the underdog that I am today because of you; Dad, by always providing for us and showing us how to provide for ourselves, you planted the seeds of commitment and perseverance that have grown and stayed with me throughout the course of everything I've set out to do; and Tommy, your passion to help others and to do what's right no matter the cost is a gift to our world, and you are a gift to me. No sister has ever been more proud and grateful. Aunt Terri, Uncle Joe, Heather, and Kyle, I'm so excited to share the love of reading with Emma Grace! Thank you for always believing in me.

I'm also grateful for my entire village of support across the country. Katie, Robyn, Jenni, and Jenny, I'm so lucky to have unbelievably supportive friends who I also call family. I'm looking forward to many years ahead of reading and conferring with your kiddos. Mary, Emily, Leigh, and Gayle, our dinner discussions have given me the laughter and humility I needed to help guide my way. Laura, Katie, Marie, thank you for all that you give me daily.

Michelle Haughney, Katie Kinnaman, Jim Meininger, and Jennifer Aza Allan—what a lucky teacher I am to have taught alongside you and to have learned from your dedication, humor, and honest example. Angie Lew, your conferring know-how and knowledge of books continue to be a constant source of inspiration. Katie Wears and Alissa Reicherter, I continue to consider myself truly lucky to have watched you in action in classrooms so many times. Dr. Marva Cappello, I hope you know that you were the very first person to ignite what has become a full-blown, fierce fire. Thank you is simply not enough.

To my supportive colleagues and our amazing kiddos at Lucille Nixon Elementary School, thank you for your openness to grow, learn, and laugh with me as I balance teaching and writing. To our leader, Mary Pat O'Connell: We are so lucky to be led by someone who always puts the needs of kids above all in a place where "we all teach all the children." Truly, Nixon is my teacher home.

Finally, Kari—yes, let's write a book! Who knew a simple handshake would launch something so wonderful and truly life changing? I've learned immense lessons through this entire process for which I am forever grateful. Thank you for believing in my words—both spoken and written—and inviting me into this wonderful journey.

introduction

conferring with courage and commitment

We Are Called

We are called to teach,
to nurture, to nudge, to persist.
And we are called to learn,
to be still, to be silent, to watch, to wonder.

We are called to celebrate,
to uncover gifts, to see hearts,
to polish stones, and to water seeds.

We are called to inspire courage, curiosity, and joy,
for children and for ourselves.
Yes, we are called to shape young lives.
But, also to be shaped by theirs.

Such a magnificent calling this is.
What a privilege to answer . . .

One child.
One moment.
One brave act at a time.

With unwavering determination, an open mind, and a brave heart, we believe every teacher can learn to confer with confidence and joy. That's why we're here. That's why we've written this book. We want to help you fall in love with conferring just as we have. We want to help you build a practice that is purposeful, effective, and authentically yours.

What Is Conferring, Anyway?

At its simplest, conferring is the act of pulling up alongside a reader to engage in a one-to-one learning conversation. At it's best, conferring is the daily choice we make to give our wholehearted and undivided attention to one reader at a time, intentionally noticing, celebrating, and moving their reading life forward. Ultimately, it is a commitment to students, aimed at empowering them to become more agentive, independent, and joyful readers.

When we confer, we go to our students, meeting them wherever they are, physically, academically, and emotionally. We use keen observation, thoughtful inquiry, and attuned listening to explore and respond. We honor self-selected book choices, recognizing and encouraging their own preferences and interests. We celebrate growth and build on strengths. We tease out challenges. And we nudge readers forward with next steps uniquely situated within their own zone of proximal development (Vygotsky 1962).

Conferring doesn't unfold by following a script, a checklist, or a curriculum resource. Rather, it unfolds by following our hearts, our minds, and our curiosity in order to understand and respond to what is happening with each of our readers, in real time, moment to moment, day to day.

Why Confer?

We confer because we believe in a purpose as teachers that is so much more significant than helping students learn how to read. And it's so much more far-reaching than preparing kids for success on "the big test." The most critical work of a reading teacher is to prepare students for what Donalyn Miller (2013) refers to as "reading in the wild." This means supporting them to build sturdy and vibrant reading lives that will far outlast their short time with us. And so, we confer.

We confer to build an intentional bridge between reading in the classroom and reading in the world outside of the classroom. We confer to help students reflect on their own habits and learn to set meaningful goals, stretching and challenging themselves. We confer because we believe that each child's learning world is worthy of exploring and understanding more deeply. We confer to uncover the kinds of practical information about readers that fancier formal assessments never could. And we confer because these tiny moments fill our own hearts with joy, refueling, refreshing, and sustaining us, reminding us why we teach in the first place.

Simply put, conferring is our tool of choice to:

- Spread a love of reading

- Strengthen relationships with each and every student

- Gather a constant flow of real-time information on which to base teaching decisions

- Understand and plan for the diverse needs of each individual reader

- Notice and celebrate effort, approximation, agency, and strategic decision making

- Offer small bits of new teaching to make a big impact

- Nurture our teacher souls

So, if you aren't conferring with your readers yet, get ready. It's going to change your teaching practice. If you're already conferring, we're glad you're here to take a fresh look at conferring with confidence and joy.

Making the Commitment to Nurture a Joyful Conferring Practice

Waiting for the thing that cannot be improved (and cannot be criticized) keeps us from beginning. Merely begin.

—SETH GODIN

Before we start we want to assure you that you don't need to have all the answers to begin. All you need to get going are three small but powerful commitments to yourself. We encourage you to start with your conferring practice wherever you are and build your expertise as you go. These three commitments are the foundation on which a thriving conferring practice is built. They don't take any special training. They are simply promises you make to yourself and to your students to show up every day with a caring heart, intent on making the most of every moment as you learn alongside your students. The three commitments include:

1. **Confer to learn.** This means you come to a conference first to learn and only later to teach, and that you keep pushing yourself to grow each step of the way.

2. **Confer with tenacity.** This means that you confer every day, as much as you are able to, saying no to distractions, and resisting the temptation to throw in the towel when things get tough. And they will get tough. That's normal. Tenacity involves choosing to move forward despite difficulties or roadblocks.

3. **Confer from the heart.** This means you give yourself permission to make your conferring practice truly your own, trusting yourself to respond to your students in meaningful ways. It's not helpful to be hard on yourself, so give yourself a little love. When you do, you'll have even more to spread around to your students, making it easy to create positively joyful interactions along the way.

We believe in you and we believe that by making these three commitments you can transform your conferring practice from uncertain to unstoppable, starting right now.

The Decision Making Map

Whenever we visit a new museum, an unfamiliar shopping mall, or a new city, we're always somehow reassured when we find a map at the entrance or at major crossroads—the kind with big yellow arrows saying, "You are here." These strategically posted visuals help us get our bearings, see what's nearby, and make sense of the signs around us. They don't tell us precisely which way we must walk or which path we should take. They don't bark step-by-step directions at us like a GPS. Rather, they simply empower us with the information we need to do our own navigation. Which direction to go? Which moves to make? Maps leave these important decisions to us.

The Decision Making Map (shown inside the front cover) is this same type of tool. It shows the lay of the land within a conference, reminding you where you are so that you can decide which direction to proceed and which moves to make along the way. This book is a bit like a guidebook, designed to help you navigate a reading conference by consulting the Decision Making

Map with know-how and confidence. Beyond this introduction, the book is divided into three parts and a final chapter.

Each of the chapters in Part 1 takes an up-close look at one of the versatile teacher moves for conferring. The moves are the ways you interact with readers, leveraging language to build strong relationships and impact learning. These chapters include practical advice about how to make the moves happen, sample language, language frames, and video examples. You can think of moves as the *how* of conferring. The four interactive moves include:

- Wonder

- Affirm

- Extend

- Remind

Part 2, is aimed at helping you develop a deeper understanding of each of the four intentional directions for conferring. You can think of the directions as the *what* of conferring, each of them representing a collection of strategies, skills, mind-sets, or motivations that readers need in order to thrive. In each chapter of Part 2 we'll deeply explore one of the directions, sharing signs to watch for and ways to interpret what you see in order to decide when to spend more time in one direction over another. We've also packed these chapters with scenarios from classrooms and tips and tools to enhance your work with students once you decide which will be your direction of focus for the conference. The four directions for conferring include:

- Book choice

- Healthy habits

- Strategic process

- Authentic response

Part 3 includes a few short but practical chapters focused on behind-the-scenes moves. These are the moves for getting and staying organized with this fast paced, one-the-go teaching. Think of these moves as your practical guide to organization, preparation, and planning, the stuff you do before you head out and the notes you take to help yourself remember what's important. Behind the scenes moves include:

- Gather materials

- Make a plan

- Take note

Finally, in the final chapter, it's time to pull everything from Parts 1 through 3 together with both flexibility and intention. Here, we'll revisit our two guiding questions for every conference—What's going on? and How might I respond?—weaving the teaching moves, or the how of conferring, together with the directions, or the what of conferring. We'll do this through considering full-length conference scenarios, coaching support, and more videos of us conferring with students.

Throughout the book, you'll discover we've posted copies of the Decision Making Map in key locations. We've labeled each with handy little "You are here" arrows. Our hope is that the maps will orient and guide you, becoming an indispensable tool as you gradually and systematically build your confidence for both the *what* and the *how* of conferring.

Please keep in mind, the Decision Making Map is simply a framework. It's not a checklist, rulebook, or formula. There is not one right or wrong way to do this work. So, loosen up, have some fun, and, when in doubt, trust your instinct to follow your students.

Sten.pub/
KnowNurture

As you read, we hope you'll also dig into the *To Know and Nurture a Reader* Online Companion Site, Sten.pub/KnowNurture. There, you can watch dozens of video clips of conferring in action with students of different ages and easily access downloadable resources from throughout the book.

We are so glad you've joined us for this journey. How lucky we are to spend our days getting to know and nurture young readers. Let's begin!

the how of conferring

Learning to confer is learning how to teach responsively, to pay close attention to where readers are and what they are doing, so that you can follow their lead and respond accordingly. This kind of teaching requires in-the-moment decision making in response to what the student beside us reveals. We can't know where a conference will take us, and this can feel intimidating to say the least. Will we know what to do? Will we know what to say? Where should we focus our attention?

In Part 1 we'll help you stock your conferring toolkit with a collection of interactive teaching moves aimed at taking some of the uncertainty out of these questions. These dynamic moves are proven and predictable ways of responding to students. They are the *how* of conferring, helping you leverage thoughtful teaching language to empower students and impact learning. The moves position you to meet readers wherever they are, recognize the great work they are already doing, and nudge them forward.

Best of all, the moves we offer in Part 1 are extremely versatile. Once you know a bit about them you can make them your own, using them in many different combinations, whichever direction you decide to take the conference. These interactive moves include:

- Wonder

- Affirm

- Extend

- Remind

The Decision Making Map is designed to help answer two critical questions that are on our minds in every conference. One of them guides us to better know readers, the other guides our decision making about how to best nurture readers.

The KNOW Question: What's going on with this reader?

The NURTURE Question: How might I respond?

As you study the map, you'll see these questions presented in thought bubbles. Together, these two questions are the driving force behind all responsive teaching, pushing us to understand each student on a deeper level and to be more reflective in response to what we observe. Everything else on the Decision Making Map supports you in answering one of these two questions as you confer.

Ahead, in Chapter 1, we tackle the Know Question—"What's going on with this reader?"—with the first of the interactive moves, Wonder. Once we've learned to use Wonder to prioritize a direction for the conference, we move on to The Nurture Question—"How might I respond?" This second question is answered using any combination of the remaining interactive moves: Affirm, Extend, and Remind. These moves are the focus of Chapters 2, 3, and 4.

If conferring is new to your students, we want to offer you a few special words of advice. In our experience, sometimes all of this up-close attention and questioning can feel uncomfortable to students at first. They may wonder, "What's happening? What is my teacher doing? Am I in trouble? Why is she here talking to me like this?" So, when conferring is new, we recommend letting your students in on the goals and routines right from the start. Consider teaching a mini-lesson or providing a fishbowl demonstration to let them know what conferring is all about. Let them know you're going to be spending time every day visiting with as many of them as possible to talk about their reading lives. Let them know they can help to make the most of the experience by sharing honestly about the things that are going well for them as readers and what's not going so well. Let them know you're there to join them as a partner, willing to roll up your sleeves to help make reading the best it can possibly be. As you patiently but persistently work to learn the moves of conferring and become more intentional with your language, children will become more comfortable with their role in this new partnership, too.

We also want to assure you that you don't need to master—or even try—all the interactive moves to get started with conferring. You can jump in and get going with just a couple of them. You can learn and practice any of the moves individually, with the ultimate goal of using them all seamlessly and in varying combinations for different purposes and situations.

So let's get moving. Figure P1.1, Teacher Moves for Conferring: A Simple Guide to Get You Going, shows all the moves at a glance, including the Interactive Moves we're about to explore in Part 1 and the Behind the Scene Moves that we introduce later in Part 3.

Figure P1.1
Teacher Moves for Conferring: A Simple Guide to Get You Going

TEACHER MOVES FOR CONFERRING

MOVES FOR PARTNERING WITH STUDENTS			
Move	**Icon**	**Purpose: To Know or Nurture**	**Questions**
WONDER		To get to know a reader by learning more about what's happening right now in order to make decisions about what this reader might need	What's really going on with this reader at this moment? Book choice? Habits? Process? Response? What will I choose as an intentional area of focus for the conference?
AFFIRM		To nurture a reader by noticing and naming strengths, effort, approximations, and emerging skills to build confidence and consistency	What is worthy of affirmation? What appears to be a new or emerging skill? What do I want to encourage more of?
EXTEND		To nurture a reader by helping the reader extend themselves in the area chosen as priority. Selecting learning that is within reach, right sized, and transferrable.	What learning is within reach? Most urgent? Transferable to any text? How will I teach offering the lightest support possible?
REMIND		To nurture a reader by clearly reminding the student how to transfer this learning to other books and situations	How can I make sure this learning really sticks? What will I say/do to remind the student to apply this strategy in the future?
MOVES FOR STAYING ORGANIZED			
Move	**Icon**	**Purpose**	**Questions**
GATHER		Gather what you'll need for teaching and learning on the go	What do I need during conferences with students? What will I carry with me?
MAKE A PLAN		Make intentional plans for conferring with students	Who will I decide to meet with? How often will I return?
TAKE NOTE		Keep track of important notes to inform future teaching	What notes will help me remember what's happening now in order to plan for next steps?

1

wonder: bringing curiosity and an open mind to every conference

❓ WONDER MOVE AT A GLANCE	
Why choose this move?	To discover "What's going on?" in one or more of the four directions for conferring in order to prioritize next steps
Guiding questions	What's going on in one or more directions for conferring? • Book choice? • Healthy habits? • Strategic process? • Authentic response? Which of the four directions will I prioritize as an intentional focus for the rest of the conference? Into the future?

Peek in any dictionary and you'll see the word *wonder* is defined as both a verb (desire to *know something*; *feel curious*) and a noun (*a feeling of amazement and admiration, caused by something beautiful, remarkable, or unfamiliar*). We read these definitions with a smile and a nod, because both the noun and the verb so beautifully describe what is possible when we use Wonder in each conference.

Wonder is a versatile and dynamic conferring move built on a foundation of curiosity and openness. Wonder can have a profound effect on absolutely everything else that unfolds in the conference. You might even say that Wonder is the champion of all conferring moves.

Wonder is a search for the strategic, the remarkable, the new things each student is doing in the moment, as well as a search for potential next steps to help them grow. It's a relentless desire to better understand what makes each reader tick. It's a daring honest look at what's really working and what's not. It's a hunger for information that will position us to become more responsive, not just during the conference but also across the entire literacy framework. It's a longing to know each child in new and consequential ways so that we can nurture each child's growth in deeper more meaningful ways.

Wonder is a commitment to watch, to ask, to listen, and to notice. Wonder is the move that helps us answer the driving question at the very top of the Decision Making Map (Figure 1.1), the Know Question: "What's going on?"

Making It Happen

When you approach each conference with a sense of Wonder, you intentionally leave your teaching hat at the door, trading it in for one of a curious learner, fascinated and ready to discover all that you can about the topic of your inquiry: this reader at this moment in time.

The following suggestions are provided to help you use the Wonder move efficiently and effectively, getting the information you need to prepare for an informed next step as you zoom in on an intentional focus.

1. Step back to see the big picture.

2. Set the tone.

3. Explore in more depth.

    - Observe up close.

    - Ask exploratory questions.

    - Be an engaged listener.

    - Listen to reading.

Figure 1.1
Decision Making Map: Wonder

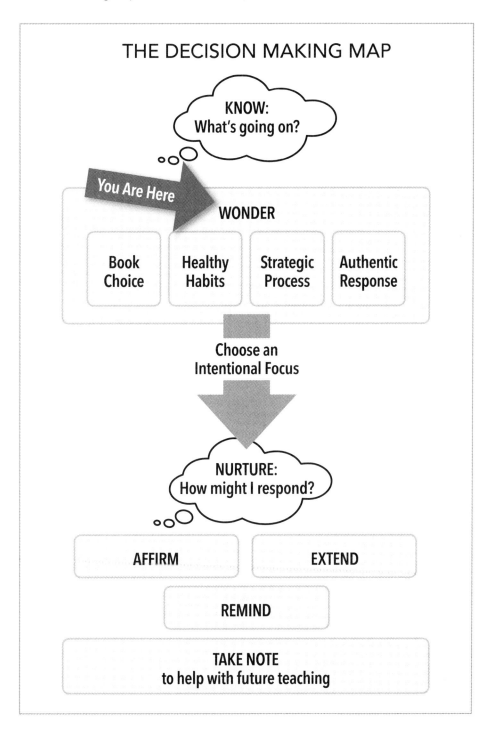

Step back to see the big picture.

Many times, rather than jumping right in with individual conferences, you might start your conferring routine by stepping back to see the big picture of independent reading in your classroom. Observation or, as Yetta Goodman (Owocki and Goodman 2002) calls it, "kidwatching," is a powerful and underappreciated means of formative assessment. Intently watching a whole class of readers to see what reveals itself is the perfect starting point for the Wonder move.

So, grab a clipboard, notebook, and pen or digital note-taking method and find an out-of-the-way spot. From here, you can spend a few moments systematically observing each of your readers, considering as objectively as possible what you notice. It's amazing how much you can discover about the reading habits and engagement levels of students in a few short minutes, when you simply slow down enough to really see what's going on. You'll probably see a few things that tempt you to jump back into teaching right away, to redirect students or to fix things. But, if you want an honest appraisal of how independent reading is going for your students, treat this observation as formative assessment, and leave readers alone to show you a true picture. Use this time to jot a few notes about what you see. The time for action will come soon enough.

When you step back to wonder from afar every week or so, you'll be able to spot reading behaviors worthy of celebration, opportunities for strategic scaffolding, and tidbits to think about. Figure 1.2 lists some lenses to look through while observing readers from afar.

Most important, your observations from afar will reveal any disengaged readers. These students, often easy to spot from a distance, are not yet reaping the benefits of their independent reading and likely need to be bumped to the top of the list for some conferring attention. Conferences with these readers will allow you to learn more about what's really getting in the way so that you can consider what next steps might be most helpful.

Set the tone.

Pulling alongside a reader to confer is like knocking on someone's front door. Sure, you could barge through the front door with your positional teacher power (like a police officer with a warrant), asking interrogative questions and demanding to know what's going on. But to make the most of the Wonder move, we suggest entering with the good grace of a guest. Approaching the conference like a friendly visitor in the child's learning space can help you achieve trust and partnership with readers. To be a gracious guest, you'll want to:

- Be gentle and kind in your tone. Start with, "May I interrupt?"

- Approach the conference as one reader who has a genuine interest in how things are going for another reader.

- Believe in the capacity of every learner, and expect to find things to admire and appreciate about their efforts.

- Trust students to take the lead, expertly teaching you about their reading lives.

- Believe in the ability of whatever unfolds to take the learning in a meaningful direction.

- Avoid overstaying your welcome; this student has important reading work to get back to as soon as possible.

- Extend your appreciation and gratitude, by thanking the child for their time.

Figure 1.2
Some Lenses to Look Through When Observing Readers from Afar

- What is there to celebrate or affirm?

- How are readers spending their time?

- What evidence do you see of deep engagement?

- What evidence do you see of disengagement?
  What might be getting in the way?

- What evidence do you see of the routines you've taught? What might need to be refined?

- What patterns do you notice?

- Who appears to be most urgently in need of a conference?

- What might you explore in more depth up close?

When we approach each conference as a gracious guest, maintaining an inviting and respectful tone (Yates 2015), we increase the likelihood that students will engage in honest and meaningful conversation, will take risks in our presence, and will welcome and look forward to subsequent conferences.

Explore in more depth.

Whether you've known a student for six minutes or six months, the goal of every conference is the same: you're there to harness your curiosity in the service of better-informed teaching decisions. To do this, you come with curiosity and openness, ready to follow where the child leads. You'll watch. You'll ask. You'll listen. You'll look for clues. All of this so that you can clearly understand, "What's going on?"

To get you started, we offer a set of essential questions in each of the directions of conferring, which you'll learn more about in Part 2. These essential questions will serve as guideposts, bringing a greater sense of clarity and purpose as you work to decide what's worthy of more attention right now. Figure 1.3 highlights the essential questions for each of the directions of conferring. We'll explore each in depth in Part 2, but for now, we simply encourage you to keep them in mind as lenses for exploration using the Wonder move.

Figure 1.3
Essential Questions for Each of the Directions for Conferring

As You Wonder About . . .	Essential Question to Keep in Mind . . .
Book choice	Is the reader consistently finding texts that lead to high levels of engagement?
Healthy habits	Is the reader making intentional decisions that result in lots of time spent reading both in and out of school?
Strategic process	What strategic actions is the reader taking to solve problems and make meaning of the text?
Authentic response	How is the reader using reflection, connection, or action in authentic ways?

Observe up close.

Sitting shoulder to shoulder, up close at the point of real reading, you'll want to be on the lookout for physical evidence of how things are really going. Body language and artifacts are two important kinds of evidence to consider.

Body language. Readers often give clues through body language. For instance, we might notice a mismatch between what childen are saying with their words ("Yes, I'm really enjoying this book.") and with their nonverbal communication (slumped shoulders, lack of animation, flat affect).

Artifacts. We might also glance through artifacts, such as book boxes, sticky notes, tools for keeping track of reading, response journals, or other artifacts that contain clues about children's reading life. Figure 1.4 provides suggestions about the clues you may gather through observation of artifacts in a conference. These observations ground us in the here and now, at the same time as they drive forward both our understanding and our curiosity about readers.

Figure 1.4
Observation of Artifacts During a Conference

Artifact.	What You Might Learn.
Book box, bag, or stack	What texts is the child selecting? Type? Topic? Readability? Variety?
Tools for keeping track of reading	How much is the child reading each day? What patterns can be seen? Genre? Pace? Abandonment?
Sticky notes	What does the child find noteworthy? Big ideas? Details? Can the child use the notes effectively to identify ideas worth thinking, talking, or writing about?
Notebook	What does the reader find worthy of consideration through writing? Does the writing show a connection with the themes and ideas of text? Are the reader's own thinking and ideas about their reading reflected in their writing?

Ask exploratory questions.

The success of the Wonder move hinges largely on learning to ask worthy exploratory questions, the kind that will get students talking about their reading lives in honest and helpful ways. You're not there to quiz kids on the contents of their books, you're there to find ways to help them thrive as readers. Figure 1.5, Four Square Conferring Questions, provides example questions to help you start using Wonder to get to know readers in any of the four directions. These questions can also be found in Appendix D as a single printable page for you to carry with you on the go as you confer. The topic of each quadrant is the focus of an entire chapter of its own in Part 2.

Figure 1.5
Four Square Questions for Conferring

Book Choice Is the reader consistently finding texts that lead to high levels of engagement?	Healthy Habits Is the reader making intentional decisions that result in lots of time spent reading both in and out of school?
• What are you reading right now? How is it working for you? • What kind of books do you most/ least like to read? • Does this book feel like a good choice for you? Why or why not? • What makes you like (or dislike) this book so much? • I'm curious, what made you decide to choose this book? • Does this book seem more like relaxed reading, stretch reading, or somewhere in between? What makes you say that? • What's the best book you've chosen recently? What made it such a good choice? • Have you recently chosen a book that didn't work for you? Why do you think that was? • What part of our library do you visit most often? Why? • What's the best book you're reading right now? How did you find it?	• What goals or plans do you have for yourself as a reader? • What else might you do to help yourself grow as a reader? • What habits are you most interested in developing as a reader? • When is reading the best for you? When is it most challenging? • How do you help yourself make the most of reading time? • How is this spot working for you? What else could you try? • How much reading are you doing each day? In school? Out of school? What do you think about that? • How might you help yourself get even more reading minutes? Outside of school? • What can we celebrate about your life as a reader right now?

Strategic Process What strategic actions is the reader taking to solve problems and make meaning of the text?	**Authentic Response** How is the reader using reflection, connection, or action in authentic ways?
• May I listen in as you read aloud? You can choose a part you'd like to read aloud or read aloud from where you left off. • How can you help yourself? What could you try? What else? • Are you right? How can you check? • What did you notice about your reading? • What are you thinking about (or learning) as you read? • What is the book mostly about? • What challenges do the characters face? What are you learning about the characters? • What questions do you have as you read this book (part, chapter, etc.)? • How might you summarize the part you just read? • What predictions are you making based on what you know so far?	• In your reading, what's worth thinking more about? Talking about? Writing about? • Does this text call you to action in any way? • What other reading does this book make you think about doing? • What questions do you have? How might you find answers? • What big feelings has this book made you notice? • How has this book changed you? What will you take away from it? • How might you respond to a book like this? • Who might you like to tell about this book? Why? • How might you let others know about it? Talk? Draw? Write? • It seems like this book is really important to you. What next steps are you considering as a result of having read it?

These sample questions are a starting point. But like any conversation, you'll need to get comfortable thinking on your feet during the conference to keep the exchange moving forward productively. To get students talking about their thinking and decision making as readers, and less about every minute detail of the book they are reading, try to keep your questions focused on the reader rather than on the text.

Yet even the most skillfully crafted questions won't get you the information you long for if students feel under the microscope or suspicious of your intentions. If students sense you've come to check up on them, they may put up their defenses and give short tell-her-what-she-wants-to-hear-so-she'll-leave sort of answers. This, of course, isn't helpful.

In many cases, the tone of a question can be shifted dramatically by inserting what we call a "Wonder clause" at the beginning. The simple addition of words such as "I wonder," "I'm curious," or "I'm interested to know" on the front side of a question may help to communicate that you're not here to interrogate, scold, or quiz, but rather because you have a genuine desire to know more about how things are really going. For example, rather than asking, "How did you decide to choose this book?" you might say, "I'm curious, how did you decide to choose this book?" Transforming questions with a Wonder clause can be especially helpful in the opening moments of a conference as we work to put students at ease. Figure 1.6 has some examples of questions transformed with a Wonder clause.

Figure 1.6
Inserting a Wonder Clause at the Beginning of a Question

Basic Open-Ended Questions	Questions Transformed with a Wonder Clause
How did you choose this particular book?	*I'm wondering* how you chose this particular book?
What are you reading?	*I'm interested* to know what you're reading.
What are you working on as a reader, today?	*I'm curious to know* what you're working on as a reader, today.

Discovering the true picture of what's going on with a student's reading life requires practice, patience, and persistence. A single question rarely uncovers the depth of information you need to identify an area of focus so you can prioritize next steps. A few conferences may unfold effortlessly with a question or two, but most are much messier than that.

Figure 1.7 demonstrates various paths a conference might take in the dance between questions and their responses as you prioritize an area of focus. Sometimes, student answers are vague or confusing, and clarifying questions are required as a follow-up. Sometimes, what the child says triggers you to wonder in a different direction, and your questions change course altogether. Sometimes, what is revealed immediately points you in a specific direction for deeper exploration. All the while, you're on the lookout for clues that will point you toward your next move.

Figure 1.7
A Flowchart for Using Wonder to Identify an Intentional Focus

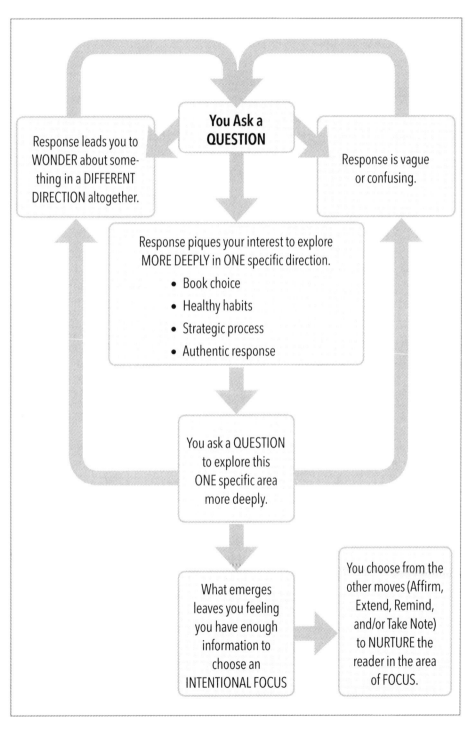

Be an engaged listener.

It's hard to learn about your students while you're doing most of the talking. So, ask a question, then bite your tongue, and try to really listen. We offer three essential strategies to help you listen more completely while showing your students you're genuinely interested in hearing what they have to say.

- **Provide generous wait time**—Letting students truly have the floor can be challenging for us as teachers. Too often, we jump in, move on, rescue, or, worst of all, change to a different question when there is even a tiny bit of hesitation or silence from our students. But, even if it makes your heart pound a bit in the beginning, silence is not something to fear. When we quietly wait, we communicate to students our belief that they have something worthy to say. We show them we expect they will answer and that we are so interested in hearing from them that we'll patiently wait while they get their thoughts together. Sometimes, we might even reassure them (and ourselves) by saying, "It's a good idea to take your time. Please don't feel rushed." If wait time feels difficult to you, you might practice doing some slow counting in your head during the silence. This will both occupy your thoughts while you wait and will likely surprise and inform you as well. What may feel like an eternity of wait time often turns out to be less than ten seconds. Although the silence may feel awkward to us, often it is the gift students need to ponder ideas and articulate their thoughts.

- **Use nonverbal gestures**—When students talk, you can demonstrate you're listening by using intentional nonverbal communication. Let your face and body do the work of showing interest in what the student is saying. You might lean in, nod your head, smile, show surprise, or even raise your eyebrows. Of course, you don't want to do these things in exaggerated or unnatural ways but, rather, in ways that genuinely encourage and reassure students that we're following them and we care enough to give them a few minutes of our undivided attention.

- **Acknowledge the reader's thinking**—By simply restating your students' big ideas, you can acknowledge their thinking without judgment. This says to the reader, "I hear and understand what you're saying" rather than, "You gave the right (or wrong) answer."

Listen to reading.

Another important inquiry tool to help with the Wonder move is listening while students read a short segment of their current text aloud. Listening to reading can provide direct evidence and observation of a child's interactions with a text, especially with regard to strategic process. In Chapter 7, "Confer to Strengthen Strategic Process," we offer specific ideas about how to make the most of listening to reading.

I've Used the Wonder Move, Now What? Moving Forward with an Intentional Focus in Mind

The Wonder move is critical for getting to better know *what's going on* with each reader, using a combination of observation, conversation, and listening to reading when we are trying to explore within one or more of the four directions for conferring. But it isn't the questions, observations, or listening that will make a difference for readers. It's how we learn to sift through what is revealed, piecing things together, and searching for those seeds that seem most worth watering. As we wonder, our goal is to discover information that helps us envision and prioritize our next moves. We watch and listen intently, learning to sort through what is uncovered. This in-the-head and in-the-moment decision making allows us to move confidently from Wonder to the remaining moves, with an intentional focus in mind. Deciding on an intentional focus encompasses both the heart and the art of conferring. What you choose to prioritize for your next moves is not an exact science, nor should it be viewed as a formula. Rather, it is based on your own obser-vations, perceptions, experiences, and context. So, trust your instincts and learn as you go.

If you take a look at the Decision Making Map (Figure 1.8), you'll see the marker we've left to help you get your bearings as we transition from Wonder into the remaining interactive moves: Affirm, Extend, Remind, and Take Note. Poised here, with an intentional focus in mind, you're ready leave the Know question, "What's going on with this reader in this moment?" and move on to the Nurture question—"How might I respond?" In response to this question, you'll use one or more of the remaining interactive moves to nurture the reader in whichever of the four directions for conferring you've selected as your area of focus.

Figure 1.8
Decision Making Map—Choose an Intentional Focus

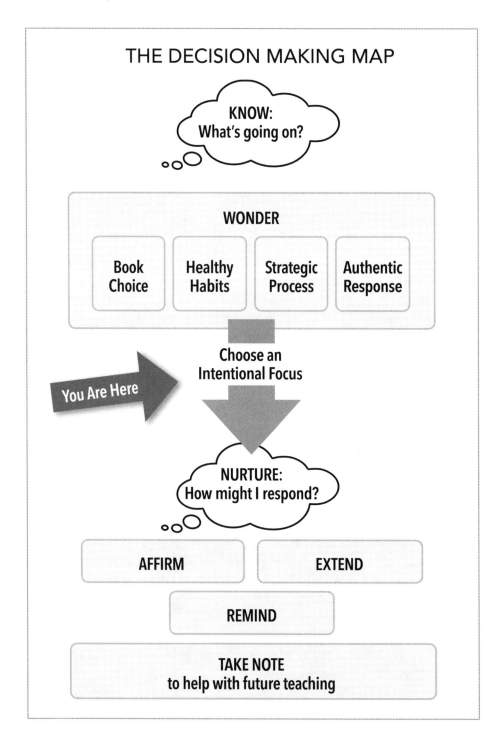

Let's Explore the Wonder Move in Action

Let's watch the Wonder move in action in the classroom. As you watch the video clip(s) of teachers engaging in the Wonder move with readers, you may wish to reflect on the following questions:

CLOSE READING OF THE WONDER MOVE
VIDEO CLIP EXAMPLE(S)

What do you notice about how the teacher establishes rapport?

- What open-ended questions does the teacher ask?
- What do you observe about wait time?
- Are there other methods, besides questioning, that the teacher uses to gather information in the conference?
- What did this example leave you wondering?
- What might you choose as an intentional focus for the next stages of the conference?

Sten.pub/
KnowNurtureWonder

2

affirm: celebrating effort, strategy, and emerging work

👍 AFFIRM MOVE AT A GLANCE	
Why choose this move?	To notice and name strengths, effort, approximations, and emerging skills to build confidence and consistency
Guiding questions	What is worthy of an affirmation? What appears to be a new or emerging skill? What do I want to encourage more of?

As we move around the classroom, pulling up alongside readers with a genuine sense of curiosity and wonder, we quickly begin to make oodles of observations about *what's going on with this reader.* And because we are teachers by trade, we also see all kinds of places our teaching services may be called for. We want to dig in and start to fix what we see needs fixing. But, wait! Let's first take a step back. Vitally important work must be done before we do any new teaching.

Before you show your readers one more new thing or something from the past that they aren't yet transferring to their independent reading, we encourage you to take a closer look to recognize what they are doing right now. The Wonder move uncovers lots of possibilities for what we can affirm in our students, reflecting back to them what they are currently doing that is strategic and helpful for them as readers. The Affirm move (Figure 2.1) is a chance to say, *Hey, look at what you did right here!*—nurturing each reader by affirming the strategic work they are already doing.

By taking the time to polish up our admiring lens (Goldberg 2016), we approach each conference with kindness and respect, determined to shore up both the reader and the relationship by pointing out what's working. This fierce determination to notice what's right, right now, before we set about with other teaching, helps our students move from, "Oh, no, here comes the teacher" to "Oh, yes! It's my turn to learn more about myself as a reader." Learning to notice and name what's working not only helps us get more of what we hope for from our readers but also builds teacher and student confidence simultaneously. All readers are doing strategic work regardless of where they are in the process of learning to read. Every student deserves to know what they are already doing well as readers. Once they know, it is more likely they will repeat or build on these strengths to continue their growth.

Believing that you must go into every conference on a mission to find "something wrong" and "fix it" would be a complete energy drain for you and your students, not to mention a lot of unnecessary pressure. But the Affirm move of the conference can be a bit magical in the way it allows you to actually create positive energy through the art of celebration. Many before us have written about the power of affirmation. Peter Johnston coined this critical work as noticing and naming (Johnston 2004). The Teachers College Reading and Writing Project refers to these celebrations as *compliments* (Calkins 2015a and b), while Gravity Goldberg (2016) calls it *mirroring*, reflecting back to the student the good work they are already doing.

Noticing and naming, complimenting, mirroring, or affirming are not simply to prepare for or to replace teaching; they are actually important learning opportunities all on their own. Each time we thoughtfully affirm what a reader is already doing, we provide a specific kind of feedback, pointing out how the reader can continue to grow and stretch as they move along the path to becoming a lifelong reader. An affirmation is much more than simply telling a reader what it is we like about their reading. It is an intentional learning message—helping the reader understand what they are already doing well so they will leverage it time and time again.

Figure 2.1
Decision Making Map: Affirm

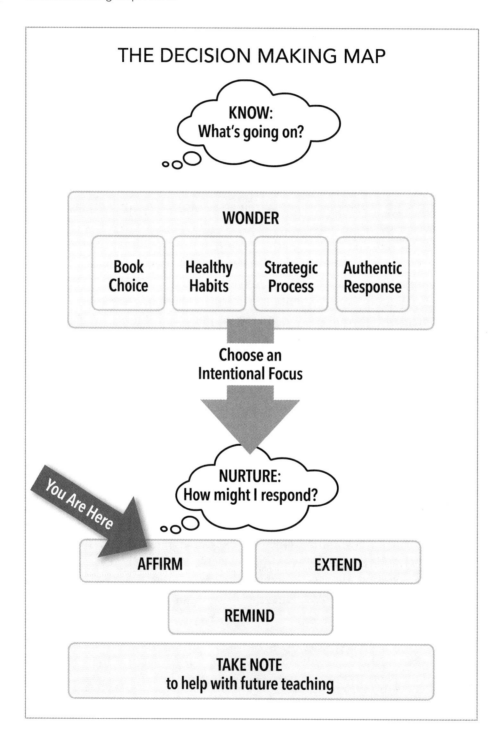

Making It Happen

The Affirm move of the conference is a celebration that teaches by illuminating what we see the reader strategically doing. To succeed with the Affirm move, consider the following steps:

- Use thoughtful and intentional language to deliver an affirmation.

- Recognize effort and traits worthy of affirmation.

Use thoughtful and intentional language to deliver an affirmation.

As Lucy Calkins (2015a and b) reminds us, reflecting back what we see is a gift to children.

To start using the Affirm move effectively and immediately, we've provided a simple but essential language frame. Once you're comfortable with this frame, you'll quickly find ways to make it your own.

Step 1—Let the reader know an affirmation is coming.

Step 2—Tell the reader specifically what strategic or helpful thing they are doing.

Step 3—Make the affirmation stick by clarifying how this behavior will be helpful now and into the future.

When you string these three parts together, it may sound like this:

Wow! You're doing something really helpful as you talk about your reading.

(Pause. Eye contact.)

As you shared your thinking, you used the text to help you, referring back to certain places that were important to you.

*You can use specific parts of the book in this
way anytime you want to back up your thinking,
whether it is in conversation or in writing.*

So, let's break this apart, slowing down to think about what's happening in each of these steps.

Step 1. Let the reader know an affirmation is coming.

This first step is a straightforward but essential one. You simply want to create a moment for the student to realize that an affirmation is on its way. Without this moment to pause, the important gift you're about to give the reader might breeze right by without notice. So, go ahead and build the anticipation a bit. Let the reader know you've noticed something worthy of mentioning. Then smile, and pause for just a second. Chances are, the child's eyes will light a bit with anticipation, pivoting toward yours. We humans, it seems, can never get enough of this positive and productive feedback from others. This might sound like:

- *Wow! May I share something strategic you're doing as a reader?*

- *Let me tell you what you did here as a reader!*

- *You were doing something so important in your reading just now.*

- *You're doing something that's so important to continue. Would you like to hear about it?*

Step 2. Tell the reader specifically what strategic or helpful thing they are doing.

When working to master this step, there are two considerations:

- **Use student-centered versus teacher-centered language.**
  Working to become more intentional about our language in this move will increase the likelihood the readers repeat the strategy to help themselves and not to simply please the teacher. So, working to break the habit of using teacher-centered language such as "I like . . ." (Do this to please me, your teacher) and shifting to using more student-centered language such as, "As a reader you are . . ." (Do this to help yourself as a reader) is essential to nurturing indepen-dent and agentive readers.

- **Name the behavior or trait that was helpful.** Allow your readers to see what you see. Shine light on things you want them to value and repeat as readers time and time again.

When we reflect back to readers what we've noticed in this way, it might sound like:

- *As a reader, when you came to this tricky part you tried several different ways to solve the unknown word.*

- *You're clearly the kind of reader who takes time to find books that you are deeply interested in.*

- *When you were talking about the character in your reading just now, you described how her actions affected another character and how this made you feel. Did you notice you were doing that?*

- *Right here [point it out to the reader], when something didn't make sense to you, you went back and reread. Going back to reread is a strategic move you're making to help yourself as a reader.*

Step 3. Make the affirmation stick by clarifying how this behavior will be helpful now and into the future.

Affirmations are like fertilizer for readers. They build confidence. They increase the likelihood that these productive reader actions and traits will be repeated enough to become habits. So, the final step of the affirmation is to state explicitly how and when this strategy or trait can help the reader into the future.

- *If you continue to do this again and again as a reader, it will help you_____   .*

- *Don't forget, this is something you can do each time you read.*

- *Next time you_____, you can do this again to help yourself problem solve.*

This same language can be used after teaching something new. The Remind move, which we'll explore in Chapter 4, is all about ways to help readers carry their successes forward into future reading.

Recognize effort and traits worthy of affirmation.

As you work to find the good in every reader and to draw attention to it, it's important to note that not all affirmations are created equal. Some have much greater impact on the reader than others. And you're going for high impact, right? So, you'll want to sharpen your own ability to recognize and point out actions truly worthy of affirmation.

Affirming behaviors that a reader has already been doing for a long time usually have little impact on their growth. But carefully watching for sprouts of growth positions us to nurture readers by pointing out their new or developing attempts. Think of it like this: We clap and cheer when a baby takes his first steps, but once a child has been walking for awhile we don't fuss over it anymore. Instead, we shift our attention to their attempts at learning to climb stairs or pedal a tricycle. Your readers need the same from you. Figure 2.2 shows a few examples of language we may use to affirm the emerging work (new news) rather than focusing on behaviors that are already consistent (old news).

When we're watching for evidence of emerging work, it's more likely that we'll be able to meet students in their zone of proximal development (Vygotsky 1978). This is the most fertile ground for affirmations and new teaching to take root and grow. The arrow in Figure 2.3 marked Confer Here will help you to visualize the effort and strategies most ripe for our attention with readers.

You can spot behaviors to affirm by being on the lookout for effort, approximations, inconsistencies, and transferable strategies using the Wonder move.

Be on the lookout for effort.

Traits worthy of affirmation are often found by simply looking for signs of effort, such as ways students are trying to become more independent, more resilient, and more strategic as readers. To nurture a growth mind-set (Dweck 2007) in your students, pay attention to effort and process at least as much as outcome or product. Affirming effort happens by noticing readers' intentional actions, regardless of whether they are completely successful. For example, you might affirm a student's attempts to work through a tricky word, even if they don't completely solve it in the end. Noticing and naming those attempts increases the likelihood that the student will continue to put forth this effort.

Finding efforts to name and affirm is usually accomplished in one of two ways. The first is simply watching for actionable steps students take to help themselves solve problems, achieve goals, and make meaning from text. The second is asking, "So what have you done to help yourself?" This question

Figure 2.2
Language Focused on Noticing New Reading Behaviors

What You Observe	Noticing "Old News"	Noticing "New News"
Kindergarten student reading who has had consistent one-to-one matching for many weeks but has not been cross-checking between picture and word at point of difficulty.	"You pointed to each word and made it match."	"When you came to the tricky word, you looked at the picture and the word. You thought about what would make sense and look right. This is something you can continue to do when you come across a tricky word."
Second-grade student who fluently reads many pages at a time, but spends little time stopping and thinking about the story, except when asked.	"You're reading the words smoothly."	"Did you notice when you stopped and mentioned what you thought about the character's words right here (point to the dialogue in the text), rather than rushing on to the next page? Doing this is one way you can continue to help yourself better understand what's happening."
Fourth-grade student who quickly settles in during independent reading time but often becomes distracted when sitting near friends in class.	"You grabbed your book and started reading right away. That's going to help you to get more reading minutes each day".	"Today, you made a strategic decision as a reader. You chose to sit in a spot away from distractions so you could settle into your book. If you do this each time you read, you'll read more and more, and distractions won't stop you."

is an especially powerful one because of the way it reminds readers they are empowered to help themselves and demonstrates the teacher's confidence that they have been working to do so.

For example, after reading a novel about space exploration, Stephan was hungry to learn more. He followed his interest into an informational text on the topic. Although this new text turned out to be challenging for him, Stephan was determined to persist. His teacher asked, "How have you worked to help yourself with this challenging text so far?"

After a moment of reflection, Stephan said, "I looked at the back cover and the inside cover and I read through all of the parts of the table of contents."

Figure 2.3
Conferring "In the Zone"

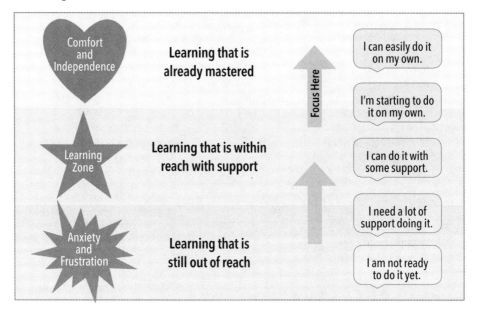

His teacher responded by affirming his efforts, "Taking your time to study the text features in a book like this is a strong move as a reader. All the parts can work together like pieces of a puzzle. You can use this same strategy throughout an entire book like this, taking time to deeply study not only the words, but also the pictures, captions, headings, and other text features that the author has embedded in addition to the front and back cover and table of contents."

Be on the lookout for approximations.

Approximations are those brave but imperfect attempts that readers make to try out new behaviors. Clay (1993) defines approximations as evidence of behaviors over which the reader has partial control. When we focus on their willingness to attempt new work, regardless of how spindly or imperfect the attempt, we help the sprout take root (Bomer 2010). This means recognizing students trying out new strategies, even if they haven't quite mastered them yet. Consider this conference between Hamida and her teacher:

Hamida is preparing for a book club discussion. She has been using lots of sticky notes to mark points of potential interest for conversation, but has not figured out how to organize them and seems to be uncertain about how to use them constructively in the book club discussion. Her teacher, Ms. Carlisle, can see that Hamida is clearly attempting to use sticky notes as a tool, however imperfectly, and decides to affirm her attempt: "Hamida, you are doing something strategic to help yourself get ready for your book club meeting. You're taking the time to mark things in the text that are worth coming back to. Anytime you want to find your way back to things in a book worth spending more time on, you can use a sticky note to help yourself do this." This affirmation reinforces what's happening right now, while at the same time it positions Ms. Carlisle to help Hamida extend this strategy to the next level by offering some teaching on organization, when the time is right.

Be on the lookout for inconsistencies.

Inconsistencies are those strategies or behaviors that the student relies on sometimes but not others. Notice in the conference example that follows how it is possible to use an affirmation to nurture a student toward more consistent use of the strategy:

When Tanner comes to the word carpenter *in his reading, he carefully studies the word, looking for parts he knows and eventually piecing it together. However, when he comes to the word* electrician, *he simply shrugs his shoulders and says, "I don't know that word." He is inconsistently using the strategy of looking for known parts within a tricky word to help solve the word. His teacher, Mr. Sieu, draws attention to the success with* carpenter *as a nudge toward more consistent application of the strategy. "Wow, Tanner, look at the work you did when you came to the word* carpenter. *You looked across the word and found parts you knew to help*

*you solve the whole word. You can use that same
strategy with any tricky word."*

Be on the lookout for transferable strategies.

You'll want the affirmations you choose to be bigger than the current
moment. You'll want them to provide the child with a narrative about what
he can do every time he is in a similar situation in the future. So, for example,
rather than choosing to affirm a train-loving reader on finding a book about
trains, you might turn the affirmation into one that can be extended to every
time she is looking for a book: "Wow! As a reader you are really using what
you know about yourself to find books that will hold your interest. Every
time you are looking for a book you can ask yourself, 'Is this a topic I really
care about?'"

Let's Explore the Affirm Move in Action

Figure 2.4 offers some examples of the Affirm move, using the three-part
language frame in each of the Four Directions for Conferring.

As you watch the video clips of teachers engaging in the Affirm move
with readers, you may wish to reflect on the following questions:

CLOSE READING OF THE AFFIRM MOVE
VIDEO CLIP EXAMPLE(S)

- How does the teacher let the student know an affirmation is coming?
- How does the student physically respond to the affirmation?
- What is the focus of the affirmation?
- Which of the four conferring directions does this affirmation support?
- What did this example leave you wondering?

Sten.pub/
KnowNurtureAffirm

Figure 2.4
Example Affirmation Language Across the Four Directions for Conferring

Direction	Step 1: Indicate that an affirmation is on the way.	Step 2: Use reader-centered language to tell what you noticed.	Step 3: Clarify how this is helpful now and into the future.
Book choice	"Wow! You just said something that will be so helpful."	"You said, 'Whenever I hear a friend talking about a book they love, I write it on my list.'"	"Keeping track of the books you hear about from friends will help you inform your reading choices in the future."
Healthy habits	"As a reader, you've made a really powerful choice today."	"You grabbed your book box and immediately settled yourself in with a book in your hands."	"Getting started right away like this will help you get the reading minutes you need to keep growing as a reader."
Strategic process	"May I tell you what you did right here that you'll want to keep doing as a reader?"	"When you came to this tricky part, you tried three different things. (1) You studied the picture for clues, (2) you reread the sentence, and (3) you tried the word more than one way."	"Every time you come to a challenging part on any page or in any book, you can help yourself by trying many things like you just did here."
Authentic response	"As a reader, you just did something really important."	"You stopped to take a moment to think more deeply about what you just read. You thought and offered a wondering about why the author chose to describe the scene in this way. Did you realize you just did that?"	"As you continue to read, you can keep doing this from time to time to help you become more connected with the story and how it is having an effect on you."

3

extend: nudging readers forward

EXTEND MOVE AT A GLANCE	
Why choose this move?	To help the reader extend in the area chosen as priority, and select learning that is within reach, right sized, and transferable.
Guiding questions	What learning is within reach? Most urgent? Transferable to any text? How will I teach offering the lightest support possible?

The Wonder move empowers you to actively explore one or more of the directions for conferring: book choice, healthy habits, strategic process, or authentic response. The Affirm move positions you to notice and highlight the powerful or strategic actions that a reader is already taking. And although in some conferences you'll use just those two powerful moves, Wonder and Affirm, other times you'll decide to stay a bit longer, taking the learning a step further. This decision to teach something more in the conference is what we call the Extend move (Figure 3.1).

Figure 3.1
Decision Making Map: Extend

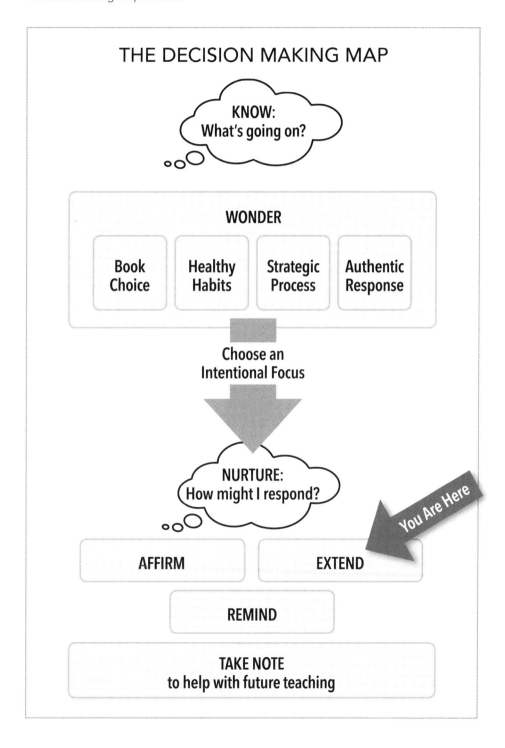

You choose to make this move, not because you *must* teach something new in every conference, but because in this conference, you've identified something you believe could expand the reader's success and open up more possibilities for the reader. You've decided to help a student extend in order to become more agentive during independent reading—solving problems, making meaning, carrying out plans, and getting the most out of their reading when we're not around.

This teaching you do in the conference will likely follow many of the same tenets as the teaching you do in other instructional formats; you'll clearly name a strategy, demonstrate or show examples, and get students actively involved in trying things out. However, conference-style teaching is short, sweet, and focused—lasting only a few minutes.

Making It Happen

The Extend move provides a chance to do what you love to do—teach. In this move, you'll take what you've learned about the reader's readiness and offer a next step, nudging them gently forward. We offer a sequence to help you succeed with the Extend move:

1. Thoughtfully select a focus.

2. Offer your partnership through conferring.

3. Teach with the lightest support possible.

4. Get the reader involved.

Thoughtfully select a focus.

Guiding question:
What might I teach, right now, today, that will help the reader take the next step up toward engagement or independence?

Once you've decided which direction you want to go to help the reader become more independent, successful, or engaged you'll also want to make sure the teaching you offer is within reach, right sized, and transferable.

- **Within reach**—Spotting within-reach work has many of the same characteristics as spotting work worthy of affirmation (Chapter 2). In fact, some of the most powerful teaching you can do in a conference will happen when you pivot directly off of the affirmation into teaching. Spotting partial understandings, inconsistencies, or approximations draws you into the child's zone of proximal development (Vygotsky 1978), setting you up to affirm what the reader is doing (partially doing, trying to do, or doing sometimes but not others) and then immediately offer teaching that scaffolds the reader, helping the reader to step up to the next level. Figure 3.2 shows where we might position our teaching within the conference.

Figure 3.2
Conferring "In the Zone"

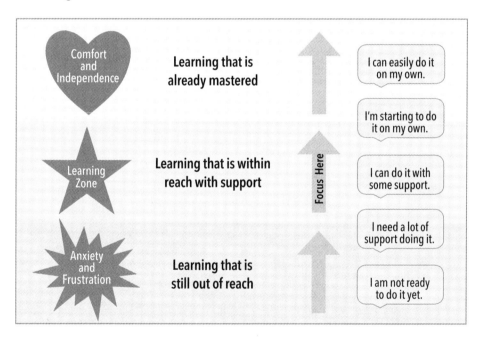

- **Right sized**—In the conference the right-sized teaching is usually bite-sized teaching. When conferences are too long, exceeding six or seven minutes, it's often because we've tackled teaching that is too big for the moment. Keeping conferences short allows the reader to get back to reading and you to spread your time to other readers as well. Occasionally, if a student's needs are very different from the other readers in the class, you might use the conference for bigger chunks of teaching. However, quite often the teaching in a conference is more like a nudge forward, an extension, or an adaptation of teaching that has already happened in a more efficient format, such as whole-group or small-group teaching.

- **Transferable**—Choosing a transferable focus means choosing a step that will help the reader now and into the future, enabling them to become more agentive and independent, solving problems and initiating actions for themselves. Transferable strategies are high-utility strategies because they can be used again and again, not just right now but in future reading and future books. This type of strategy instruction is the pot of gold in teaching. In a 2012 blog post, Grant Wiggins (2012) wrote that "transfer is the point of education." We agree. There is no better way to teach for transfer than to choose those high-utility skills and strategies that fall within students' zone of proximal development (Vygotsky 1978). Figure 3.3 provides examples of how an affirmation might pivot directly into helping a child lift what they are already doing up to the next level.

Figure 3.3
Examples of Building On an Affirmation in the Extend Move

Example of Affirming the Reader	Example of Using Extend to Build On the Affirmation
"You backed up and reread from the beginning of the sentence when you got stuck. Rereading a sentence allows you to think more about it and try something else."	You might offer a strategy the reader can use as he approaches the tricky words, such as thinking what would make sense and getting his mouth ready for the first sound.
"To help yourself get started today you went back and reread the last couple pages from yesterday. That helped you get 'back into' the story, jogging your memory about important ideas or details."	You might nudge the student toward taking time to review her most recent sticky note jots as well before jumping back into reading.
You have made note of some wonderings and confusions about this story. When you have questions as a reader, it can deepen your interest in a topic and give you a reason to explore more deeply."	You might decide to show the reader how to create a notebook entry dedicated specifically to tracking his thinking about a question of high interest.

The in-the-head work of learning to select a meaningful teaching focus while the conference is unfolding is a complex skill that takes time and experience to develop. Here, two commitments for conferring are critical to keep in mind. First, confer from the heart. Trust yourself to choose a meaningful focus for Extend and go with it. Second, confer to learn. You'll make some mistakes. Sometimes, your teaching focus will be magically right on, and other times, it might be a bit of bungle. The important thing is that you keep working to refine this skill and learn as you go.

Offer your partnership through conferring.

To keep the conference feeling like a safe conversation between readers, there is a simple step we use before diving into the meat of our teaching—offer the teaching, rather than insist on it. Offering partnership toward a next step ensures the conversational tone of the conference won't take a turn from collaborative to completely teacher controlled. This offer of support often comes right after an affirmation and may sound like:

- May I offer a suggestion?

- You're ready for your next step as a reader. Would you like to hear it?

- I noticed that you're trying to . . . May I show you something that works for other readers?

- Some readers do this a different way. May I show you?

You get the idea, right? Taking a moment to offer your assistance rather than thrusting it on the reader allows the student to come along as a true partner in reading, making a proactive choice to extend in some way.

Worried about students turning down your offer? No need. Some students may be more low key in their acceptance of the offer to extend themselves than others, but the kids we've known have been consistently open to learning when they trust us. Kids want to learn, and they appreciate being respected enough to be asked. So we ask. The offer is not some kind of trick to get buy-in. Instead, it is a way to set a collaborative and anticipatory tone for the teaching that is to come.

Teach with the lightest support possible.

Teaching within the conference can take on lots of different looks. The type of teaching you select will be driven primarily by the level of support you believe the student needs to extend, or take the next step as a self-directed, independent reader. Your goal is to teach with a light touch in the conference, offering the least amount of support needed to get the job done.

All day long and in all curricular areas, you already move skillfully up and down the scale of gradual release of responsibility (Pearson and Gallagher 1983), deciding whether students need a higher or lower level of support. The reading conference allows you to tailor the degree of support you offer based on individual student needs. Using a range of supports (explicit demonstration, guided practice, example, explanation, or prompting to try something) you can support different readers in different ways or help the same reader with decreasing levels of support across time. Figure 3.4 shows how the various types of teaching you might offer within the conference provide more or less support to students. Depending on the student and the situation, your conferences across time will likely include all of these levels of support.

- Watch while I show you step by step how to do this.

- Let me remind you of an example from the past.

- Let me explain how to do this.

- How do you think you could help yourself with this?

Watch while I show you step by step how to do this.

This type of teaching includes a high level of support in the form of a demonstration. You model for your students by doing the work right in front of them as they watch. You make the strategy visible, often pairing demonstration with think-aloud. Choose this level of support when the work is new to a student or you think they need a more heavy-handed approach. Demonstration often sounds like:

- Take a look as I try this out on the next page.

- Watch. I'll show you what I mean.

- Listen as I read this part, and pay attention to how I pause at punctuation.

Figure 3.4
Varied Levels of Support for Teaching Within the Conference

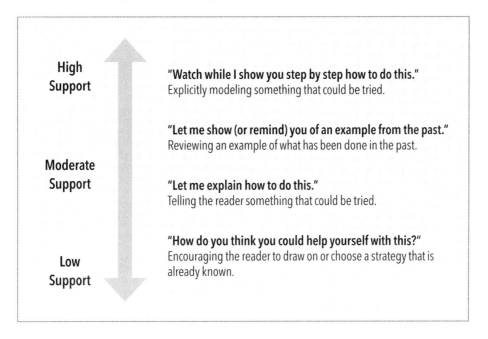

Let me remind you of an example from the past.

In this type of teaching, you are showing an example, drawing the reader's attention to something that has already been done. Sometimes we choose to use examples as a reminder of past teaching to jog the memory about a strategy that has already been taught but is not being consistently transferred to independent reading. Sometimes, we choose to use an example because we believe the reader is capable of piecing together the steps without the more heavy-handed approach of the demonstration teaching.

- Do you remember during the read aloud when . . .?

- May I show you something you did to help yourself on the previous page?

- The chart we made yesterday has an example of this. Let's take a look.

Let me explain how to do this.

This type of teaching includes telling the student how to use a strategy through thoughtful explanation, rather than demonstrating. This method of teaching provides a lower level of support to the student. Often it is used to restate or remind a student of what has already been taught on another day or in another format.

- When selecting a reading spot, think about a place where you will be free from distraction before making your choice.

- To read with a smoother voice, try scooping up a few words at a time. These words can be read together instead of one by one.

- Before you start reading the next chapter, you might try to pause to recall your wonderings from the previous chapter. This will help your understanding as you move forward.

How do you think you could help yourself with this?

This type of teaching is actually a form of encouragement for students to initiate their own problem solving in response to a challenge. This is the least scaffolded method of teaching. When we ask students, "What can you try?" we are turning the teaching table on them, calling on them to come up with an idea or strategy to support themselves. While at first glance this may not seem like teaching, it can actually be a powerful instructional tool. In some cases, students will come up with strategies they've already learned but hadn't yet tried. Other times, students will actually come up with new ideas of their own. If you try this approach and a student has trouble coming up with something to try, you can always transition into one of the more scaffolded teaching methods:

- What do you think you can do to help yourself when choosing a new book?

- How might you be able to figure out what this word means?

- Think about what you might be able to try to help yourself remember what you've already read.

Figures 3.5–3.8 show example language demonstrating varying levels of teaching support in each of the directions for conferring.

Figure 3.5
Example Language Demonstrating Varying Levels of Support with Book Choice

Book Choice–Finding Books of Interest	
Watch while I show you step by step how to do this.	Watch as I look through this basket of books, considering carefully which book covers appeal to my interest or make me curious in some way.
Let me remind you of an example from the past.	Let's look back at a book that worked really well for you in the past and think together about what made it such a good choice.
Let me explain how to do this.	Before you start to search through the baskets, think about a topic you might be interested in reading about.
How do you think you could help yourself with this?	What is something you can try to help yourself find a book you really love?

Figure 3.6
Example Language Demonstrating Varying Levels of Support with Healthy Habits

Healthy Reading Habits–Organizing Space to Maximize Time	
Watch while I show you step by step how to do this.	Watch as I work to organize my reading space for the day. First, I take all the books I plan to read and put them in a stack to my right. Next, I take one book off the top, place it in the middle and start to read. Then, when I'm done reading it, I put it in a stack on the other side. Now it's time to do the same thing again.
Let me remind you of an example from the past.	Let's take a look at how Jackson has organized his books. Look he's made one stack of all the books he plans to read today. He takes the one on top and puts it in front of him, so he can read it. Then look what he does. When he finishes, he puts the book in a different pile on the other side. This is a pile of the books he's done reading. These stacks make it easy for him to keep reading the whole time.
Let me explain how to do this.	To make the most of your reading time, you can make one stack of books that you plan to read and one stack for books you've finished. When you finish one book, you'll know just which one to read next.
How do you think you could help yourself with this?	Is there a way you think you can organize your books before you start reading that will help you always have your next book ready to go?

Figure 3.7
Example Language Demonstrating Varying Levels of Support with Strategic Process

Strategic Reading Process–Tackling Multisyllabic Words	
Watch while I show you step by step how to do this.	Watch while I try looking for little parts I know within a bigger word. When I see the big word I stop and look carefully across it. Oh, here I see the little word *at*, here I see the word *ten*, the last part I see is the word ending *-tion*. I'm going back to put it all together. *At-ten-tion.*
Let me remind you of an example from the past.	Do you remember at the guided reading table yesterday, when we broke apart the big word *attention*, looking for smaller parts that we knew? That's the same strategy you can use when you are reading independently.
Let me explain how to do this.	One thing you can try to solve a tricky word like this is to look for parts of the word that you already know.
How do you think you could help yourself with this?	What else could you try when you come to a big word like this?

Figure 3.8
Example Language Demonstrating Varying Levels of Support with Authentic Response

Authentic Reader Response–Taking Note of Big Feelings	
Watch while I show you step by step how to do this.	Sometimes readers pause to think or write about big feelings. Watch while I show you. So, I'm reading this part in *Each Kindness* where the kids are refusing to let Maya play with them at recess, and I can feel my heart start pounding. I realize I'm feeling really angry. It's a big feeling, so I am going to stop and take the time to jot a note about. This is something I might want to talk or write more about later.
Let me remind you of an example from the past.	Do you remember in the read-aloud this morning when we came to the part about kids refusing to let Maya play with them at recess? That was an example of a time when we just stopped reading and took a moment to jot a note about how each of us was feeling. You can do that same thing in your independent reading. When you find yourself having big thoughts or feelings, you can stop and jot some short notes for yourself about it, and later you might decide to write or talk to somebody about it.
Let me explain how to do this.	When you notice that you are experiencing big feelings or emotions when reading, it's a good time to stop and jot it down on a sticky note.
How do you think you could help yourself with this?	What might you try to help yourself remember these big feelings and come back to them when you're discussing the book?

Get the reader involved.

Teaching within the conference will be strengthened, and more likely to stick, whenever it is followed by an immediate opportunity for the student to get involved, trying the strategy while you're still there to provide productive feedback. In this stage of Extend, we say, "Here, you try it out. I'm here to help if you need me." Figure 3.9 shows possible teacher language encouraging active involvement.

Figure 3.9
Example Language Encouraging the Reader to Actively Try Out the Learning

Direction of the Conference.	Language to Encourage Reader Involvement
Book choice	"Here, you try it. Look through this shelf of books, stopping to spend more time with those that are appealing to you."
Healthy reading habits	"Go ahead and try it out. Gather up all the books you intend to read today and put them together in a neat stack to your right. I'm eager to see what you'll choose."
Strategic reading process	"You try it. Keep reading. When you come to a big or tricky word, stop and take time to look for parts you might know. I'll watch and listen."
Authentic reader response	"You can do it. Go back to the part you said made you feel so _____ . Read it one more time and think about how you might like to help yourself remember that so you could come back to write or to talk more about it."

This step is a critical bridge to helping students make a strategy their own, transferring it to their reading lives beyond this conference. As the student tries a strategy, we are there on standby, watching and thoughtfully providing a just-right amount of feedback to ensure success. We act as a coach, there on the sidelines, watching the play on the field and choosing strategic moments of feedback, such as a simple nod of encouragement, a reminder prompt, a redirection, or an affirmation.

Let's Explore the Extend Move in Action

When you use the suggestions in the chapter to thoughtfully select a teaching focus, offer your partnership with varying levels of support, and get the reader involved, you'll be able to turn small slices of interaction into powerful teaching moments, helping readers Extend to new possibilities for success and independence along the way.

As you watch the video clips of teachers engaging in the Extend move with readers, you may wish to reflect on the following questions:

CLOSE READING OF THE EXTEND MOVE
VIDEO CLIP EXAMPLES

- Why might the teacher have chosen this particular teaching focus?
- What might make this a right-sized piece of learning?
- Is there evidence that the teaching comes from an observed approximation or partial behavior? If so, how?
- How does the teacher present the learning as an invitation?
- Does the teacher use demonstration, example, or some other teaching technique?
- How does the teacher actively engage the student?
- What did this example leave you wondering?

Sten.pub/
KnowNurtureExtend

4

remind: ensuring transfer beyond this conference

🖉 REMIND MOVE AT A GLANCE	
Why choose this move?	To clearly remind the student how to transfer this learning to other books and situations outside of the conference
Guiding questions	How can I make sure this learning really sticks? What will I say/do to remind the student to apply this strategy in the future?

It happens to all of us at one time or another. We're working with a student and suddenly think, *Hey, wait. I've already taught this. He should know this. He should be able to do this already.* And it's probably at least partially true. We likely have taught this already. But, for one reason or another, it hasn't stuck, not with this student, anyway. Often referred to as lack of transfer, teaching that doesn't stick is really no different than teaching that hasn't happened.

With the Remind move we actively work to ensure that what happens in the conference *doesn't* stay in the conference. With the Remind move (Figure 4.1), our teaching lives on, actively helping a child become more engaged or independent as a reader. After all, we didn't come to the conference to teach a book or a strategy. We came to nurture a reader by offering solutions that they can use again and again even when we aren't beside them.

Figure 4.1
Decision Making Map: Remind

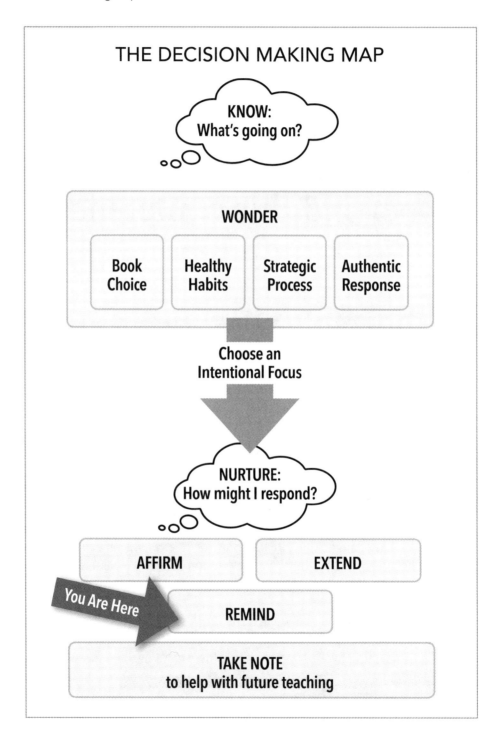

In this chapter, we offer simple but critical mechanisms you can use to make learning stick by closing the conference with intention. When you remind, you sum up for readers in clear and memorable ways the high points of your time together and leave them with a clear plan of action that will help them apply the learning throughout their reading lives.

Making It Happen

The Remind move consists of the purposeful actions you can take, usually at the end of a conference, to help the student realize the strategies you've taught can be applied repeatedly, moving them from the strategy of the moment to forever strategies. To succeed with the Remind move, you have a few options. You may decide to:

- Use the language of transfer.

- Leave a visual reminder behind.

- Plan for follow-up teaching.

- Spread the word.

Use the language of transfer.

The first tool at our disposal for making learning stick is the language we choose to use, especially as we close the conference, summing up and reminding the reader of what we've taught. Peter Johnston points out the critical importance of intentional language saying "when we are teaching for today, we are teaching into tomorrow" (2012, 7). To help yourself consistently use the influential language of transfer with readers, teaching for both today and tomorrow, we offer a simple frame: name the strategic action that has been taught, and remind the reader how it can be used again and again, across time and across texts.

- So remember, anytime you _____, you can help yourself by _____.

- Whenever you are trying to _____, you'll be able to help yourself by _____.

Does this language sound familiar? We hope so. It's the same thoughtful and intentional language we want to use with the Affirm move. And whether we're using this language to follow up an affirmation or a newly taught skill, the language of this move reminds students they can harness the power of the strategy they just used or learned forevermore. Using each of the Directions for Conferring as a possible focus, we've provided examples of language aimed at showing how to use Remind to making learning stick (see Figure 4.2).

Figure 4.2
Examples of Language Aimed at Making Learning Stick with the Remind Move

Focus of the Conference	Example Remind Language at the End of a Conference
Book choice	Don't forget, anytime you're unsure whether a book is a good fit, you can help yourself by trying out a few pages to see how it goes. This is something you can try each time you are looking for a new book.
Healthy habits	Before I leave you to your reading, don't forget that anytime you find yourself in a reading spot with lots of distractions, you can take charge of your own reading life. You can use what you know about yourself and your preferences to find a spot that will allow you to enjoy your chosen book for a longer period of time.
Strategic process	So, remember, whenever you come to a tricky part, you can help yourself by backing up and taking another run at it. This will help your brain start to think about what would make sense and look right. This is something you can possibly try each time a tricky part arises as you're reading.
Authentic response	Whenever you sense yourself feeling a strong emotion like you just did right now, you can stop and leave yourself a note in the book. By remembering to do this, you'll be able to find your way back to things that are worth thinking, talking, or writing more about. This is something you may decide to do whenever a strong feeling arises.

Leave a visual reminder behind.

A second way we increase the likelihood of students using the strategies we've taught, eventually making them part of their day-to-day repertoire, is by leaving visual reminders, or temporary scaffolds, behind. This might include:

- **Sticky notes**—The most versatile leave-behind tool we know is a simple sticky note. We often carry a variety of sizes and shapes with us while conferring, making simple reminder notes with icons or keywords to remind students of the new possibilities they are exploring. These notes should be concise, simple reminders that can be made on the go. See the examples in Figure 4.3.

Figure 4.3
Examples of Sticky Note Reminders

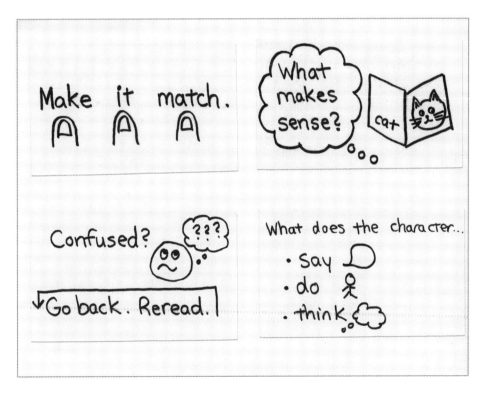

- **Bookmarks**—Simple white paper cut into bookmark-sized strips makes the perfect blank slate on which to create visual scaffolds, representing strategies taught. With a simple sketch and a few keywords, either teacher or student can create these. In *DIY Literacy: Teaching Tools for Differentiation, Rigor, and Independence* (2016), Kate Roberts and Maggie Beattie Roberts include a chapter dedicated to ways to support students in creating these bookmarks.

- **Anchor charts**—Many students benefit from having a personal-sized copy of a classroom anchor chart close by to help them practice and internalize its steps. To create mini anchor charts, simply take a photo of a class-made anchor chart and print personal-sized copies. Younger students can keep these mini-charts in their book bags or boxes, while older readers might keep them in a folder or glue the charts into their reading notebooks.

- **Student-created reminders**—Sometimes in the conference you might encourage a student to take a moment and create a visual tool for themselves. This can be especially important when it comes to helping students select goals to extend themselves as readers. You might say, "If you were to create a reminder for yourself, what words or pictures would be most helpful?"

- **Individualized strategy sheets**—In some cases, it might be helpful to create an individualized reference tool that lists a number of strategies taught to support a broader goal (Serravallo 2015). For instance, if partnering with a student to make stronger book choices, you might title the page *Book Choice Strategies* and add a new sticky note to the page each time you introduce a new strategy on this topic. Figure 4.4 shows an example of a collection of strategies taught over time to support a student who wants to read at home more each day.

Plan for follow-up teaching.

Another component of the Remind move is to make sure that this time together is not an isolated, stand-alone event but, instead, that it becomes part of a chain of connected interactions. The Remind move is versatile in that it can happen both as part of the conference and then at some point in the future after the conference is over.

Think of this like an annual visit to the physician. The visit likely begins with some follow-up on the conversation or suggestion she made the last time you were together (Have you been getting more exercise?) and ends with making plans for the future. These plans might include additional assessment (blood work, mammogram, etc.), strategies to try (use more sunscreen, eat more fruits and vegetables), ways to find more information (a pamphlet or a website address). The annual checkup is not a stand-alone event, rather it is part of an ongoing chain of events, connecting past and future.

Figure 4.4
Example of Strategy Reminders to Support a Specific Goal

The same feeling of connectedness is a hallmark of an effective conferring practice. It can be achieved in our conferring practice any time we begin a conference with a previous focus in mind or end a conference with a plan for the future. Plans for follow-up include a wide range of possibilities:

- **Future conference**—What we learn about our students during each conference will help us decide how quickly we need to check back with another layer of conferring. Whether a student needs a check-in before day's end or you decide they can wait until your next planned conference in a week or so, getting in the habit of planning for follow-up before we leave today's conference is not only a huge planning timesaver but also strengthens the links on the chain. This is especially true for a conference during which focused teaching has happened. Without a plan for follow-up, our efforts are too often lost. Planning for follow-up can be as simple as jotting a note on our calendar and saying to the student, "Let's get back together next week (tomorrow, in a few days) and see how this is going for you. Will that work?" Once again, the mere act of asking the student's opinion ends the conference on a note of respect, student empowerment, and partnership, just as it began.

- **Small groups**—You are likely to start noticing patterns in the types of support that students might need. These observations may lead you to decide to form or adjust small groups in order to make follow-up teaching more efficient. For instance, after dedicating several conferences to helping kids strengthen their book choice skills, you may decide to form a short-term group with book selection as the common goal for a group of four to six students. Figure 4.5 gives examples of the types of follow-up that may be successful in small groups as a result of conferring. In many classrooms, especially in the primary grades, students may already be participating in small-group work, so follow-up in that format is often a natural next step. In intermediate classrooms, strategy groups may be more flexible and short term, making it easy to adjust them according to the real-time needs observed during conferring.

- **Whole group**—There will be times when the patterns you observe will inform your whole-group instruction. As a general rule of thumb, if you discover a pattern of need that affects at least half of

Figure 4.5
Using Conference Observations to Inform Future Teaching in Other Formats

Direction for Conferring	What You've Observed	How You Might Respond
Book choice	Many of your students have come from classrooms where book choice was rigidly controlled by requirements to choose from specific reading levels only. Your students are having difficulty judging which books will be a good fit for readability.	Because many students exhibit this same need, you decide to start with a few whole-group lessons demonstrating specific strategies for choosing books. If some students need additional support, you will likely form a small group that meets in the library once a week, where they can continue to learn and apply book selection strategies.
Healthy habits	Several students have not shown any evidence of at-home reading on weekends or evenings.	You decide to create a small group for these students. Your focus will be helping them plan for and create routines outside of school that increase their time spent reading. This group will meet every few days to follow up on how the created routines are working. As out of school habits develop, some students might leave the group, needing less ongoing support, while others continue to meet.
Strategic process	A number of early stage readers seem to focus only on the print at the point of difficulty, and appear in need of more support with strategically cross-checking pictures with word predictions. (Does it make sense and look right?)	You already have guided reading groups established for your emergent and early level readers. You decide to revisit this as a teaching point in the groups that these students are part of.
Authentic response	Three of your students are reading books that are quite challenging, but still engaging. They are struggling with some of the vocabulary.	You decide to pull together this group of three once a week to provide work focused on strategies for noticing and determining the meaning of unfamiliar vocabulary words.

the class, it will be much more efficient to teach a couple whole-group lessons in that direction than it will be to try to accomplish the teaching through conferring or even small-group work.

Spread the word.

When we publicly acknowledge and celebrate the good work of one student, the whole community of readers benefits. Purposefully spreading the word about the good work we observe readers doing is another powerful way to utilize the Remind move. As we find ways to draw attention to the work of one student, we reinforce and encourage that student while encouraging others to follow suit. This can be accomplished through:

- **Public affirmation**—The public affirmation takes the Affirm move a step further, sharing the celebration with other students as something they might try to replicate. Public affirmations can be shared in the moment with the students sitting closest to where the conference is happening, during a future small-group lesson, or even during a whole-group lesson or share session. The public affirmation is an opportunity to let a student's effort or example become a teaching point for others, encouraging them to try the same thing in their own reading. It might sound like this:

    Readers, I have to share with you the thing I just observed Lucinda doing. When she picked up her book today, she made the choice to begin by taking time to review the jots she made to herself on sticky notes, thinking a bit about each of them before she started to read. This helped her get her mind back into the story before she began to read. This is something that may help some of you as well, using your sticky notes to restart your thinking, remembering the important ideas you'd noticed in the past. You might choose to try this out when you begin reading again at home tonight.

    Never mind that you explicitly demonstrated and scaffolded this very work for Lucinda during your conference today. The public affirmation is a way to boost the confidence of one reader while spreading the same information to others.

- **Partner work**—We learn when we teach. So, why not set your kids up to deepen the strategy they have been learning by teaching others about it? One of the simplest ways to do this is to suggest that a student demonstrate a strategy for another student. If you already have a structure for reading partners in place, it's easy to plant the seed in a conference:

  > *So today, during partner reading, you could demonstrate this strategy—look for smaller parts you know inside a bigger word—to your partner. You could use this sticky note to help you remember if you like. You might even show your partner a few examples of where you've tried it.*

- **Teaching assistant**—Every teacher wishes they could duplicate themselves at times, and this strategy does just that. Taking partner teaching one step further, you can create purposeful opportunities for students to remind others about smart and strategic work they are doing as readers. The set up might sound like this:

  > *If you are still having trouble _____ you might like to learn from _____. You could (ask him, use the sign-up sheet on the wall, join us at the table right now).*

Of course, students might need some support in thinking about how to be most effective in this teaching of peers, and using a gradual responsibility, you might scaffold success with modeling, visual reminders, and rehearsal.

Let's Explore the Remind Move in Action

As you come to the close of each conference, you can make sure the teaching you've offered doesn't fizzle in the moment. By using the language of transfer, leaving a visual trail of learning, planning for follow-up teaching, and spreading the word about the new strategies students are using, you are leveraging the Remind move to help your readers grow and thrive beyond the conference—you're increasing the chances that the day's work will live on long beyond your time with students.

As you watch the video clip(s) of teachers engaging in the Remind move with readers, you may want to think about and discuss with colleagues the following questions:

CLOSE READING OF THE REMIND MOVE
VIDEO CLIP EXAMPLES

- What language does the teacher use to help make the learning transfer?
- Were any visual reminders left behind? If so, what were they?
- Was there any evidence of follow-up planning? What follow-up might you consider in a similar situation?
- How might this student's learning be publicly affirmed in ways that would benefit other learners as well?

Sten.pub/
KnowNurtureRemind

---

the what of conferring

Even with the interactive moves in our tool-kits, the limitless possibilities for *what* to focus on in a conference can still leave many conferring teachers feeling unsure and unde-cided. We know. We've been there ourselves. Of course, we love spending one-on-one time with students. What teacher doesn't love to talk to kids? Of course, we want to teach responsively, tuning in to and responding to the unique and individual needs of each student. But time is precious. Every minute matters. To keep our own conferring from feeling unfocused and ineffective, we longed for a systematic way to help ourselves organize our thinking about each reader. We wanted a reliable process to help ourselves move from overwhelming possibility to purposeful and intentional focus.

Our daily lives are simplified and enhanced by dozens of systems of organization. We organize our closets, we organize our pantries, our file cabinets, our silverware drawers, and even our desk drawers. We organize by sorting things out, prioritizing, and grouping like things together. In doing so, we bring a greater sense of clarity and calm to our thinking.

Without some sense of organization, we potentially experience confusion, anxiety, and a loss of precious time. When our closet is in disarray, we feel the frustration of lost time every morning. When our desk is piled with stacks of unfiled papers and projects, we often feel the drain of energy as we enter the room, uncertain where to begin. When our thinking about readers is jumbled and chaotic, we begin to doubt the value of our work.

And so, it was out of a desire to organize the thinking in our own busy brains as we sat next to readers, that we developed the four directions for conferring:

1. Book choice,

2. Healthy habits,

3. Strategic process, and

4. Authentic response.

These four directions are simply ways of sorting the work we were already pursuing with our students in order to nurture their thriving reading lives. We offer them hoping they will be helpful to you as a means of systematically organizing your own thinking during the conference. However, we want to be crystal clear that these four directions are not offered as a checklist, a curriculum, or a sequence for teaching reading. They are simply a format for organizing all the complex and boundless possibilities, in a way that allows us to tidy up our thinking and proceed with more clarity and intention.

Figure P2.2 gives a quick overview of the four directions, including the intentional focus of each, and the essential question to help guide your thinking about your readers.

Figure P2.1
Decision Making Map

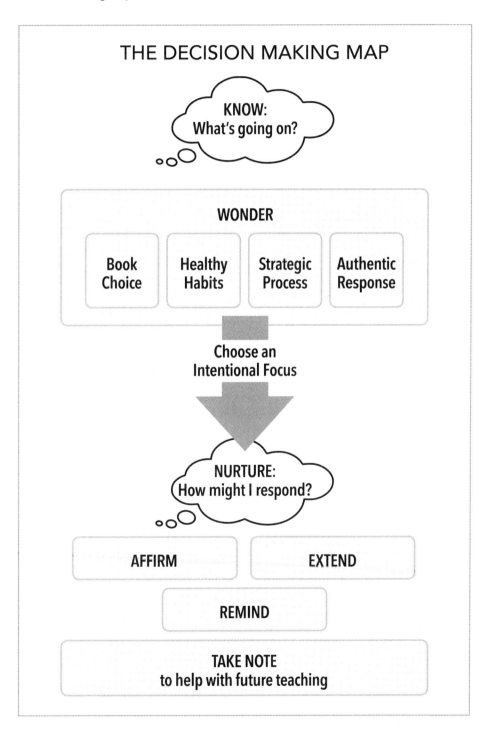

Figure P2.2
Overview of Four Directions for Conferring with Readers

Direction	Purpose	Essential Question
Book choice	When we confer with students on book choice, we are focused on helping them develop their ability to consistently find texts that lead to high levels of engagement; texts they *can* and *want* to read.	Is the reader consistently finding texts that lead to high levels of engagement?
Healthy habits	When we confer to help students develop healthy reading habits, we are empowering them to take charge of their own reading lives by being intentional about choices, routines, plans, and goals that will help them develop and sustain joyful and purposeful reading habits throughout their lifetimes.	Is the reader making intentional decisions that result in lots of time spent reading both in and out of school?
Strategic process	When we confer with students to build strategic reading process, we equip them with strategies and skills for problem solving and meaning making that will open up even more possibilities for them as readers. By doing so, we prepare them to tackle increasingly diverse and complex texts with confidence.	What strategic actions is the reader taking to solve problems and make meaning of the text?
Authentic response	When we confer toward authentic reader response, we support readers in doing the things that readers in the world outside of school naturally do in response to reading: think, feel, question, wonder, talk, and take action as growing readers and deep-thinking, contributing citizens of the world.	How is the reader using reflection, connection, or action in authentic ways?

With these four directions to guide you, we believe your conferences have the potential to become more focused than ever before. Better understanding of the directions will enhance and intensify the power of the moves. And as you learn to consider the essential questions both routinely and systematically, you'll start to see readers in a new light, spotting patterns, sorting through observations, and confidently committing to an intentional focus in one of these directions for each conference.

Using the four directions as its organizational structure, Part 2 has a chapter dedicated to exploring each direction in more depth. Our goal is to help you develop comfort and confidence as you navigate in a conferring direction with a reader by your side. Each chapter is organized in the same way:

- **Why does this direction matter?** In this section we'll help you better understand what each direction is all about, why each is so essential on its own, and how each is inextricably linked to the others.

- **Signs a student might benefit from a conference focused in this direction.** In this section, we'll look in on conferences where students are showing signs that indicate they might benefit from the conference moving in this particular direction. We'll help you learn to spot some signs and offer ideas for response. Here we'll also invite you to hone your skills for thinking like a conferring teacher, bringing your own instincts, experiences, and approaches to the table.

- **Some important tools and tips.** Think of this section like advice from a trusted colleague. It provides strategies and suggestions to help save time, anticipate bumps, overcome common challenges, and develop new skills for moving a conference in this direction.

- **Conferring Reference.** This tool summarizes key reader behaviors for the priority area that has been the focus of the chapter. It is designed to help you consider what students might already be doing in this direction as well as what some important next steps might be.

5

confer to support book choice

An intentional focus on book choice is a commitment to helping readers learn to consistently find texts that lead to high levels of engagement—texts they can and want to read. To inform your work in the direction of book choice, we offer the following essential question:

Is the reader consistently finding texts that lead
to high levels of engagement?

Take a moment to think about the last book you read that you absolutely loved. Perhaps it was something you carefully picked out after searching an online site or a book store for a topic of interest. Maybe it was a recommendation from a good friend or on a best sellers list. However you found this book, we hope it was one that was hard to put down—one that you looked forward to settling in to read every moment you had the chance. This feeling of loving a book is exactly what we want for each of our readers. This level of high engagement in a book is something every reader in our classrooms deserves.

It's easy to spot classrooms in which self-selected book choice is valued and nurtured. You'll see it in the high engagement levels of the students. When it's time for independent reading to begin, there's no scrambling to the classroom library or rummaging around in desks for something to read. Students of every age know right where to find their book boxes, bags, or

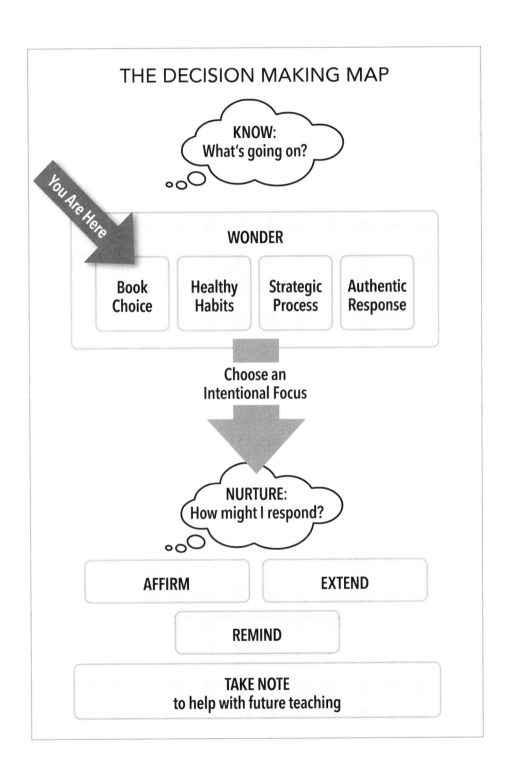

current reads. These personally curated collections of books are a bit like the piles any of us might have on our bedside tables—texts of all shapes, sizes, types, topics, and purposes; texts that will engage, inform, entertain, and stretch us as readers. Daily independent reading time is dedicated solely to this appealing collection of books that our young readers care about and want to read. Engaged readers are eager to get started and often reluctant to stop.

When we confer in the direction of book choice, we are equipping readers to find one good-fit book after another, in school and beyond, throughout their lifetimes. To do this, we must support them in learning to thoughtfully consider interest, readability, and variety, and to reflect and adjust based on both their hits and their misses.

Why Does Book Choice Matter?

Helping a classroom of students develop the skills to maintain a personal collection of engaging independent reading materials is no easy task, however. Everyone doesn't hit the jackpot every time. Our students don't always come to us knowing how to find texts that they can and want to read. Developing the skills for finding books they care about and can read may take time, patience, planning, and even some temporary scaffolding on our part. So, we encourage you to claim this work as worthy of your time and attention, never apologizing or worrying about spending too much time here. If we are serious about nurturing lifelong readers, we must take seriously the work of book choice.

No factor has more influence on motivation, meaning making, joy, and overall growth than allowing students to choose books for themselves. As Allington and Gabriel (2012, 10) tell us, "The research base on student-selected reading is robust and conclusive: Students read more, understand more, and are more likely to continue reading when they have the opportunity to choose what they read." Time and again, this claim has been proven.

Scholastic Reading Report (2017, 10) reported that 89 percent of children, ages six to seventeen years old say, "My favorite books are the ones that I have picked out myself." Research by Guthrie and Humenick (2004) showed that when students follow their individual interests, they pay closer attention, persist longer, learn more, and show more enjoyment. Hidi and Harackiewicz (2000) found that offering choice results in higher levels of motivation, engagement, and reading gains. And Pressley (2003) found evidence that the reverse is also true; a lack of student choice is a primary factor in undermining both motivation and achievement.

So, before we can expect students to develop healthy reading habits, build stamina, read with independence, or respond to texts in deep and meaningful ways, we must wholeheartedly commit to helping them learn to consistently find worthy texts. Without engaging texts in their hands, everything else will be that much more difficult to achieve. But with interesting and worthwhile texts, readers are much more likely to grow and thrive. Motivation matters and motivation comes from choice.

Helping Readers Find Books They *Can* and *Want* to Read: Considering Interest and Challenge

So, what makes a self-selected text a good fit and why does good fit matter so much? We believe the answer to both questions is the same: engagement of the reader. A good-fit text is one that engages the reader, a text that the reader cares about enough to invest the time and energy it will take to read it.

We worry when we hear of teachers limiting choice purely by text level, since this is not authentic (we certainly don't choose by level at the public library or bookstore), and we don't believe it's good for readers.

Ultimately the quest for an engaged reader hinges on finding good-fit texts. As a general rule of thumb, the higher the interest, the higher the level of engagement and the more likely students will thrive with a range of readability levels.

We have created the Book Choice Reflection Tool (Figure 5.1 and Appendix A) to help you teach about and assess book choice. To get started using this tool, select a single student and a single self-selected text and then follow these three simple steps:

1. **Consider level of interest in the text**. How interested/motivated is the child in reading this particular text? Choose a representative location on the left axis, ranging from high interest to low interest. The higher the placement, the more likely the engagement. Ideally, most choices will land in the upper half of the grid. If a student is falling into a pattern of choosing texts that they'd place in the bottom half of the grid, you'll want to confer with them to support selecting higher interest texts.

2. **Consider degree of challenge.** How easy or challenging is the text
    for the student? Choose a representative location across the top of
    the grid, from low challenge to high challenge. Most thriving readers
    choose a healthy balance of relaxed reading and stretch reading.
    Texts closer to the center are more likely to encourage sustained
    engagement (stamina) and growth. With text choices on the outside
    edges (very low challenge or very high challenge), pay close attention
    to patterns over time. If readers regularly choose very-low-challenge
    texts or very-high-challenge texts, they may benefit from a confer-
    ence or a series of conferences in developing their skills for recog-
    nizing what makes some texts more or less challenging.

Figure 5.1
Book Choice Reflection Tool

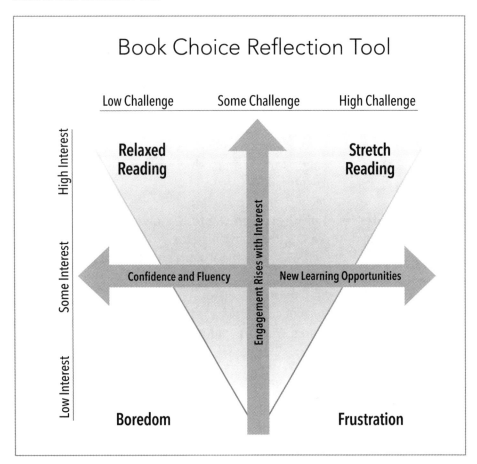

3.   **Find the place where interest and challenge meet on the grid**.
Make a real or an imaginary dot at the intersection of the interest and
challenge. Which of the four quadrants does the book fall into? We
have used the terms *relaxed reading*, *stretch reading*, *boredom*, and
frustration to describe the reading conditions that result from various
combinations of interest and challenge.

Relaxed Reading—These choices are high interest and range from
low to moderate challenge. With these books, students will be able do the
important high-success reading work that Allington has found to be so critical
to reading development (Allington and Gabriel 2012). These texts support
both fluent and accurate reading, allowing students' cognitive processes to
be freed up to focus on deeper content. Some teachers worry that, if the
books students choose are too easy or have been read before, students won't
grow enough as readers. But rereading and spending time with easier texts
is something that all readers do and benefit from (Allington 2009a, 2012).
Most of adults' self-selected reading is done with an extremely high accuracy
rate. Take, for example, the text in your hands at this very moment. We're
pretty certain that you could comprehend a text with a much more challenging readability level than this. Yet, we hope this is a good-fit text for you,
not because of your precise reading level but because of your high interest in
the topic of conferring. And, even though the text itself might be easy for you
to process (there is probably not a single word that you can't read with ease),
that doesn't mean the text is not worthy of your time and attention. You may
even choose to reread certain chapters or sections in the future. Rereading
is a powerful tool for going deeper with both fiction and informational texts.
Reading a book once doesn't necessarily mean you are done with it. So, as
long as texts are of high interest, we encourage teachers to make room for
choices that lead to more relaxed reading.

Stretch Reading—These choices are high interest and range from
moderate to high challenge. These texts offer readers the greatest opportunities to stretch themselves, developing new skills and strategies. An important
key to success with challenging texts is reader motivation; and usually when
student interest is high, so is motivation. This is why readers so often surprise
us with these more challenging texts. Of course, even if they struggle, the last
thing you want to communicate to a determined reader is, "Sorry. You can't
read this book. It's too hard for you." We especially don't want to say things
like, "The level of this text is too hard for you. It's a level O. You're a level
M." Students aren't levels, of course. They are readers. When they choose

stretch reading, we are presented with rich opportunities to use conferring to nurture their growth mindset (Dweck 2007), their strategic reading process and their skills for reflecting on book choice. One go-to strategy we rely on in helping readers navigate challenging texts is learning to chunk the time spent into smaller pieces, alternating time spent reading stretch texts with time spent on more relaxed texts from their collection.

Boredom—These choices are both low interest and low to moderate challenge. Although these texts may be easy enough for the child to read, the child has little interest in reading them. Texts that lack both interest and challenge quickly lead to boredom and disengagement. Low-interest book selections often result from limited access to texts. Either the classroom library is not well stocked or organized, or student choice is strictly limited by level or category. In classrooms where students are asked to make all of their book choices from a few baskets of books at "their level," we're likely to find lots of low-interest book choices that result in disengaged readers. Conferring provides the opportunity to reinforce an interest-first approach to book choice.

Frustration—Frustration results from low-interest, high-challenge book choices. When a reader is neither interested in nor able to read with accuracy, engagement is likely to suffer significantly. Texts like these can be especially detrimental because they feed students' negative perceptions of themselves as readers. For some students the unfortunate truth is that much of what turns out to be frustration reading for them has been assigned by a teacher. In some cases, the first step toward less frustration reading is allowing more student choice. The next step is making sure that students have access to a wide selection of worthwhile texts they can and want to read.

Handing control over to students to navigate this dance between interest and challenge is not always easy for them or for us. So many students with so many varied skills, preferences, and choices inevitably lead to some imperfect and mismatched choices between students and their books, just as it does with adult readers. Figure 5.2 gives a number of suggestions for using the Book Choice Reflection Tool in your day-to-day practice. Keep in mind, however, some of your bravest teaching will depend on trusting your students once you've empowered them with meaningful strategies for choosing their own books. You likely know the proverb, *Give a man a fish and you feed him for a day. Teach a man to fish and you feed him for a lifetime.* We believe the same is true of book choice: *Give your students a great book and you engage them for a day. Teach your students to find great books and you engage them for a lifetime.*

Figure 5.2
Ways to Use the Book Choice Reflection Tool for Assessment and Instruction

- **Create an anchor chart of the grid.** Use it to teach a series of mini-lessons about book choice. After helping the students understand both axes, place sticky notes on the anchor chart with the names of books you have read that were in each of the quadrants. Next, have each student prepare a sticky note with the name of a book they are currently reading and place it on the chart. When Christina did this with her class, she shared how a few books in her reading life fall into each of the four quadrants. Her students were surprised to learn that a popular book about Minecraft fell into the frustration-reading quadrant for her! This book fell into other quadrants for some of her readers. One book can bring a different level of interest and challenge to different readers.

- **Carry a copy of the visual with you as your confer with students.** As you confer with students about the books they are reading, offer the visual as a tool for them to consider where their texts fall along the continuum of interest and challenge. Use the labels of each quadrant to help students understand the strengths and challenges of reading in each of the quadrants and coach them to seek more balance between relaxed and challenge reading. Christina has a copy of this visual taped to her conferring clipboard for easy access.

- **Provide students with a copy of the grid.** Encourage them to document the books they are currently reading. Support them in using the information to consider patterns and set goals for themselves. Students can glue a copy into their reading notebooks or folders. Or, it can be copied onto cardstock and placed in each student's book box or bag.

- **Use a copy of the grid as a tool for jotting notes about book choice while you confer.** Keep a blank grid with your conferring notes. Each time you confer with a student, jot the name of the book and the date in the appropriate quadrant. Over time, this will help you to consider patterns and possibilities for supporting the reader.

- **Use the grid to teach parents about book choice.** Help parents start to use the same language with their students by bringing this tool into parent education events or conferences. We think sharing this grid and teaching parents about book choice at Back to School Night or early on in the school year will be highly beneficial. Parents have the potential to be our partners in conferring when given the appropriate tools.

Signs a Student Might Benefit from a Conference Focused on Book Choice

Essential question:
Is the reader consistently finding texts that lead
to high levels of engagement?

Because engaged reading requires that readers find texts they deem worthy of reading, the essential question for book choice should be foremost on our minds in each and every conference. Whether the answer to this essential question is yes or no, every book choice tells a story, about both the reader and their book-finding skills. Deciding to spend time exploring in the direction of book choice will help you:

- Understand what led the reader to make this choice.

- Consider what can be learned from this choice to effectively support future choices.

Because book choice is so essential to the overall success of independent reading, it is likely to be the focus of a number of conferences with every child in your classroom throughout the entire school year. When in doubt, you simply can't go wrong by using conferring time to explore a student's book choice. Students will always benefit when you choose to affirm the new and strategic book-choosing behaviors you observe. In addition, there are also some specific times a reader might benefit from a conference to support book choice. These might include:

- When you're getting to know a reader

- When a reader isn't settling into engaged reading

- When a reader requires extra care with book selection

- When a reader seems frustrated with a book choice

- When a reader is frequently abandoning books

- When a reader seems to be in a rut

In the sections that follow, we share classroom scenarios that illustrate each of these signs, suggestions and considerations for each scenario, and an invitation for you to think about how you might respond as a conferring teacher, drawing on the interactive moves from Part 1 paired with your experience and instincts.

When you're getting to know a reader.

> *Ms. Fontell will want to learn many things about each of the fourth-grade readers in her class this fall. Before anything else, she wants to know what kinds of books will light them up as readers. So, even though it's the first day of school and the classroom library isn't open yet, she's set out many baskets of what she knows to be high-interest books for her readers to choose from. During this first day of school and their first session of independent reading, she confers with seven different readers, having quick informal conversations with each student about the books they've chosen, favorite books and topics from the past, and even interests outside of school. A single day of conferring helps her get to know about a quarter of her readers well enough to begin to make some intentional adjustments to the current baskets. (Kira loves horses, Mateo is learning to play soccer with his uncle, and Thomas is itching to read the newest book in the Land of Stories series.) On the third day of school, she sprinkles in more books about soccer and animals, which seem to be popular. By the end of the first week, she knows enough about the reading preferences of each of her students to strategically consider which library book bins and sections might be most important to introduce first.*

In the first few weeks of the year, when all of your readers are new to you, using conferring to explore and support book choice with each and every child is essential. Conferring provides windows into both what makes your students tick and what frame of reference they already have to guide their book choices. What you learn in these early conferences will help you identify interests, patterns, and needs. You'll also be able to take what you learn and use it to help you to focus for your whole-group and small-group teaching, consider books you may choose to highlight through book talks, and make plans for the gradual and strategic introduction of the classroom library.

One student at a time, you'll be able to leverage conferring to start to develop a clearer sense of who has the skills for consistently finding engaging texts and who needs more support. For those who are successfully finding engaging books, the focus of your conferring may shift to other directions for conferring: healthy habits, strategic process, or authentic response. But for some students, you will continue to confer with an intentional focus on book-finding skills, persisting for weeks or even months into the school year until each of your readers know the joy of finding a book they just can't put down.

As the school year progresses, new students will possibly join your classroom community, and again you will be able use conferring as a platform to begin to get to know them as readers and book finders. With new students, conferring allows you to build strong relationships from day one, while gathering formative assessment data in an authentic and natural way. Figure 5.3 shows examples of language you might use in these early conferences.

Now, think back to how Ms. Fontell chose to learn about each of her readers at the beginning of the school year. What are some ways in which you can get to know your readers' book choice selection skills, regardless of time of year? Or, what are some ways that you can affirm what they are already doing or offer next steps through conferring?

When a reader isn't settling into engaged reading.

Between conferences, Mr. Aquino, a first-grade teacher, often scans the room using engagement as his lens. He doesn't worry at the first sign of an unsettled reader. He knows that many of his young readers need periodic brain or body breaks. But when he notices a pattern, someone who is consistently struggling to settle into focused reading, the first thing he begins to wonder about is book choice.

Figure 5.3
Examples of Conferring Language for Book Choice

WONDER When learning about a reader, you may ask . . .	AFFIRM Language for noticing evidence of the book choice strategy	EXTEND Language to move a reader toward intentional book choice
What kinds of things do you do when you're not at school?	You used what you know about yourself outside of school (you love soccer) to guide your book choice.	One way you can find good-fit books is by thinking about what you like to do or study (soccer, dinosaurs, etc.). Let me give you an example . . .
In the past, how have you helped yourself find good books?	You helped yourself find a good-fit book by repeating what worked for you the last time (going back to the same basket, reading the book jacket, asking a friend).	You can help yourself find good-fit books by thinking back and repeating what worked for you the last time. For instance, you found this book you love by . . .
I'm curious to know what led you to choose this book?	You took your time and searched for a book by thinking about your interests and taking time to sample the pages to see how challenging they seemed.	Readers make thoughtful choices about books, taking time to look for topics of interest and then by trying out a part of the book to see how it goes. Let me show you . . .
What books have you loved reading in the past?	You named the thing you loved about a past book to help yourself use it to find another book like it.	When you really love a book, you can take time to think deeply about what it was that made it so special to you. Once you can name what you loved, you can use it to search for other books. Let's try this together . . .
Are there any books you are hoping to read this year?	You've been paying attention to the recommendations of others as a way to help yourself make a plan for future reading.	Readers make plans. When they hear about a book or get a recommendation that interests them, they add it to their list of books to check out in the future. Let me show you the list I keep inside my notebook.

We believe books are the magic fairy dust of engagement in the reading classroom. When readers aren't engaged, our first suspect is not stamina, attention problems, or purposeful misbehavior. Instead, our first suspect is the absence of texts worthy of the reader's attention. Sure, sometimes it might turn out that a reader is off track because they're simply tired, have an earache, or are so busy thinking about their birthday party that there's not room for anything else. More often, book choice is the culprit. And even when there are other factors, the more engaging the text in the hands of the reader, the more likely the reader will be able to settle in. Therefore, anytime a child is regularly struggling to settle in during independent reading, you'll likely want to start by exploring their book choices. Some possible conferring phrases may include:

- *I notice you're having trouble finding a book. May I join you in the library to talk about a few book-finding strategies that may help?*

- *Think about the last time you remember loving a book. Talk a little more about that book and why you think you might have loved it so much.*

- *What can you try to help yourself find books that you really want to spend time with?*

Take a moment to think about a few steps you might take when you notice readers in your classroom having difficulty settling in to engaged reading. How might you offer to confer with them to help find books that lead to engaged reading?

When a reader requires extra care with book selection.

Before today's conference, Ms. Han has gathered some books that she thinks might present new possibilities for Jameel, a fifth grader who reads on a second-grade level. "I was thinking about you," she begins. "I brought some things that I thought you might be interested in trying out. I noticed you had lots of interest in Jackie Robinson last week, so I brought a few informational picture books. One is about Jackie Robinson, and one about

*the Brooklyn Dodgers, which was Jackie's team."
Jameel immediately takes the Jackie Robinson
book and smiles as he starts to page through it.
After a moment, Ms. Han continues. "I know you
said chapter books seem really long sometimes,
but I've been wondering if you've ever tried out a
graphic novel. There are two of those in the stack
as well, and they're both about baseball! Graphic
novels look a bit like comic books, and to really
understand them, you read the words and study
important details in the pictures. Would you like to
try one out?"*

While some readers almost effortlessly find a steady supply of good-fit books, others require extra care and attention with discovering books that really work. Some readers just have not been able to figure out what it is they really want to read. A few have very specific but uncommon or hard-to-find interests. A few are reading at levels not widely represented in the classroom collection. And some are simply overwhelmed by having too many options.

We may provide extra care to these readers, such as explicit instruction on book-finding strategies, more guided practice, or visual scaffolds, including shopping cards or mini anchor charts (Figure 5.4). Some students' interests make us aware of the need to expand our collections in order to provide access to texts that will engage them. Some students benefit from conferences that can be thought of as book shopping lessons, taking place right in the classroom library. Or you might come to the conference with a hand-selected pile of possibilities that reflect the student's interests like Ms. Han did in the example. She selected books that made her think of Jameel. This is what Donalyn Miller (2009) refers to as offering a book stack. Some possible conferring phrases may include:

- *I've brought a stack of some books that made me think of you. Would you like to try on a few to see if anything feels like a good fit for you?*

- *May I join you in the library to figure out how to find some books that feel right for you right now?*

Now, think about a reader like Jameel in your own classroom who may require a little extra care. What are some ways you can respond to provide the support they need? Are there interests you can affirm through a stack of books? Is there a next step you might invite this reader to try? Or, perhaps you'll need to do a little more exploration to learn about this reader's interests and background. We agree with Annie Ward and Stephanie Harvey that truly the best intervention is a good book (2017). What do you think?

Figure 5.4
Mini Anchor Chart of Book Choice Strategies

When a reader seems frustrated with a book choice.

> *Mr. Jaxson knows that Margot has chosen an extremely challenging text but one that she was excited and determined to try out. Today, Margot's furrowed brow and slumped posture tell Mr. Jaxson a different story. So, he decides to sit down with Margot for a conference. The simple greeting and questions, "Hi Margot, may I join you? How's your reading going today?" create space for Margot to confirm her frustrations. "I thought this book was going to be a good one. I really want to read it, but it's so hard!"*

When readers become frustrated with the texts they've chosen, it's time to take action, not to rescue them from their choice but to offer our support through conferring to decide whether to continue on or to consider abandoning the book. Sometimes readers simply need the assurance that it's okay to change your mind about a book and move on. We can use the conference to help them reflect on the choice that didn't work, hoping to help them find something in the experience that can be used to improve future choices. For example, sometimes readers realize they've chosen books without really trying them out; these readers can benefit from coaching on how to sample pages for readability and understanding before settling on a book. Sometimes, readers suspect that texts are going to be too challenging, but they so desperately want to pursue a topic or specific title that they don't listen to their instincts. These readers will likely appreciate help finding similar texts (topic, genre, style) that are a better readability match.

However, despite the uphill climb, some readers will be determined to continue with a text regardless of the fact that it may seem to fall in the frustration quadrant of the Book Choice Reflection Tool (Figure 5.1). In these cases, you might need to get more creative. Offering specific reading strategies, such as multiple reads of the same content, alternating short chunks of the challenging text with more relaxed reading, offering an audio recording, or exploring with the student whether there is someone at home who could partner with them to read the text aloud might all be options. The most important role we can play with frustrated readers is not that of book choice police but, rather, that of supportive reading partner who helps consider the options and make a plan. Some possible conferring phrases may include:

- How's the reading going?

- Every book we choose doesn't turn out to be the good fit we'd hoped, and that's ok.

- Sometimes readers decide to set a book aside until later. Other times readers decide to be done with a book altogether.

- What were some of the things you remember considering when you chose the book?

- What can you take away from this book that will help you when you consider other books?

Let's take a moment to think about Margot. What might you try to support Margot as a reader? Is there an affirmation that may be a good way to start? Perhaps learning more about what Margot is thinking by gently stating, "Tell me more," might be a good option. Or, maybe you can remind Margot of something she has successfully done to help herself in the past, extending it into a next step.

When a reader is frequently abandoning books.

> *Ryan spends only a few short minutes in the library choosing books for the week to come. He peeks inside a few of the books he chooses, but mostly seems to choose based on the appearance of the cover. When it comes time to read these texts, it turns out nothing really seems to hold his attention. Because she's seen the speed with which Ryan chooses his books, Ms. Cohen decides to invite him into the library for a book-shopping conference aimed at helping him slow down his decision making to become more reflective about his choices.*

Chronic book hopping can be a problem for kids at all stages of reading development. Yet, for many of them, the root problem is the same: they aren't taking enough care in choosing their books in the first place. They need mentoring and support with slowing down the book selection process. They will benefit from learning to become more thoughtful and aware as they consider what will make a book a truly good fit. If you have several students with needs in this area, don't hesitate to gather them up together for one or more group conferences, focused on book selection strategies. You may even choose to meet in the classroom library where you can easily demonstrate and students can apply thoughtful strategies, such as browsing in high-interest book bins, carefully paging through books to explore the pictures or features, trying out a page or two, or reading book jacket information. Some possible conferring language may include:

- Tell me more about how you choose your books?

- Of all the books you have right now, which feels like it's a really good fit? Which book or books have not really worked out the way you hoped? Let's make two piles.

- What can you learn from the books that haven't worked out as well? What can you learn from the books you've most enjoyed?

Thinking back to Ryan, what might he benefit from at this moment? What are some specific actions Ms. Cohen might take to support him in this important work of making choices about the books he reads?

When a reader seems to be in a rut.

> *Joshua has read every one of the twenty or so Elephant and Piggie books in the classroom library at least once—most of them more than once. The Mo Willems book bin is always his first stop on his book shopping day. His teacher, Mr. Ramirez, has not seen him read any other books in the past few days. He decides he wants to have a conference with Joshua to learn more about his choices as a reader.*

Occasionally, you might worry that students have fallen into a rut with book choice, but step lightly here. Sometimes the pattern isn't a rut, it's a passion that motivates and engages the reader. Sometimes, though, you start to see evidence indicating that same, old standby series or genre isn't engaging a reader as it once did. Sometimes, you simply want to nudge a child to spread his wings with more challenging or varied texts. Readers like Joshua can benefit when we pair what we know about what interests them with our knowledge of other texts, genres, or series that might stretch or engage them in new ways. Sometimes, we will focus our conferring toward healthy reading habits, emphasizing that growing as a reader requires a balance in the reading diet.

But, again, we suggest caution here. Being in a reading rut is rarely a reading emergency and is best approached with patience, presenting new possibilities over time. It's unlikely that Joshua will stick with only Elephant and Piggie forever, but for now, he's likely better off reading a whole lot of Mo Willems books rather than being forced into other texts that don't engage him in the same way.

Book talks, partner shares, read-alouds, book displays, and reorganization of the classroom library book bins can all help students break out of a rut. Sometimes teachers put together baskets specifically targeted toward stretching kids in new directions. For instance, "If you liked Captain Underpants, you might consider trying these books." Once the book bin is established, anyone can make contributions. Some possible conferring phrases may include:

- What patterns are you noticing about your reading right now?

- If you were to try something new as a reader, what do you think it might be?

- Have there been any recent recommendations from other readers (book, series, genre, author) that sound interesting?

What might you say in a conference with Joshua? Would you benefit from learning more about why he is consistently choosing certain books? At this moment in his reading life, both an affirmation and a next step for growth could greatly benefit him. What would you say to affirm some of his choices? How might you deliver a next step to help him grow as a reader?

What Are Some Important Tools and Tips to Support Book Choice?

To add to the strength of your conferences focused on book choice, we offer the following tools and tips:

- Nurture students' desire to read with frequent read-alouds.

- Adopt a multitext approach.

- Make room for more than one kind of reading.

- Avoid using text levels as the primary means of student text selection.

- Cocreate an anchor chart with students focused on book selection strategies.

- Curate the classroom library.

- Keep growing your own awareness of great children's books.

- View imperfect book choices as formative data.

Nurture students' desire to read with frequent read-alouds.

In Kari's first book, *Simple Starts* (Yates 2015), she identifies three factors that contribute to successful book choice. The first is a student's desire to read in the first place. In other words, successful book choice doesn't start with choosing books; it starts with students deciding that reading is an endeavor worthy of their time and attention in the first place.

One of the most important ways to grow each student's desire to read is through a rich daily read-aloud. When you read aloud, you invite children into the world of reading; you become a living billboard for great books and show students the ways that books can make our lives richer and more wonderful. During the read-aloud, you show time and time again that hard work to become a reader is definitely work worth pursuing. And, of course, read-aloud isn't just for the early years; readers at every age and stage deserve and benefit from the rich rewards of read-aloud.

Adopt a multitext approach.

Having readers choose multiple texts, rather than just one at a time, equips them with options that increase the likelihood they'll be able to engage in long stretches of daily reading. By having a bag, box, or stack of many texts, varying in length, challenge, and content, readers can move smoothly from one text to another as they finish reading or as they find they need a change of pace based on challenge, mood, or time. Figure 5.5 provides a sample of independent reading text types and numbers for various grades.

Figure 5.5
Suggested Number of Independent Reading Books by Grade Span

K–2	3–5
8–12 Texts Readers in the early grades need a wide variety of self-selected texts, including a balance of fiction and information texts, that allow them to read conventionally and texts that will be read in other ways, such as reading pictures and retelling.	3–6 Texts 1–2 Chapter books or novels 1–2 Informational books 1–2 Short-length texts, such as picture books, magazines, or poetry.

Make room for more than one kind of reading.

Readers outside of the school walls don't just decide what to read, we also decide how we will read. We don't read every book, magazine, or newspaper word by word, page by page, cover to cover. We read in many different ways. We skim headlines and choose sections that appeal to us. We dip into chapters. We flip through books, stopping to study interesting text features. We reread favorites over and over again. We start one text and then find ourselves attracted to something more relevant or appealing, sometimes coming back and sometimes abandoning the first altogether. Deciding not only to accept but to teach many different ways to read a text increases both opportunity and engagement levels for young readers.

Avoid using text levels as the primary means of student text selection.

Systems for "leveling texts" abound these days (Lexiles, guided reading, DRA, Accelerated Reader, etc.). With the good intentions of efficiently matching students to just-right texts, many well-meaning teachers have made choosing by level the primary means of directing students to find self-selected reading material. Although knowledge of text levels can have an important place in a teacher's tool kit, we agree with Backman (2016) that levels are intended to be a teacher's tool, not a child's label.

In moderation and through various coding systems (colored dots, different stickers, etc.), reading levels may have a limited place in the classroom library, especially in the primary grades, but we are extremely wary of an overreliance on them as the primary means of student text selection. Focusing on levels can limit readers' sense of possibility, give students a misguided message about why readers read and how readers choose books, and be harmful to children's self-esteem when a focus on higher and lower levels leads to them being defined as a level rather than as reader. Outside of school, our students will need skills and motivation for choosing books that go far beyond finding or getting through a level if they are to become lifelong readers.

Cocreate an anchor chart with students focused on book selection strategies.

Regardless of the grade you teach, we recommend teaching a number of whole-group book selection lessons beginning right away in the fall and continuing as needed throughout the school year. Each time you teach students an actionable strategy to help themselves find good-fit books, add it to a classroom anchor chart posted near the classroom library. This chart, cocreated with students, can become a powerful tool for students as they apply these strategies to their own book selection practices. Examples might include:

- Study the front and back covers.

- Explore the pictures or features.

- Try out a few pages.

- Use your interests as a guide.

- Get clues from books you have loved in the past.

- Read the blurb on the back cover or inside flap.

- Ask a friend for recommendations.

Curate the classroom library.

A well-stocked, well-organized classroom library is the heart and soul of a thriving reading classroom and is paramount to ensuring that students have access to high-interest texts for independent reading. Although your students will also find books in other places (school library, public library, or bookstore, etc.), the research about classroom libraries is compelling. Access to a robust collection of books in the classroom contributes to higher levels of engagement and reading success (Guthrie, Wigfield, and VonSecker 2000). We offer a few specific tips to leverage the classroom collection to support book choice:

- **Keep the collection growing.** A reading teacher can simply never have enough books. Thriving classroom libraries are organic, ever-evolving things. Each year, you'll want to add books to expand the variety of topics, authors, genres, and reading levels represented in your library. Appendix A of *Simple Starts: Making the Move to a Reader-Centered Classroom* (Yates 2015) is available free online and is packed with resources to help you grow a robust collection without breaking the bank.

- **Weed out the duds.** A smaller collection of high-quality books outshines a bigger collection that includes beat-up, outdated, or unappealing titles. Every time a reader leaves the library with a dud, you increase the likelihood of disengagement during reading time.

- **Organize in a way that students understand.** Once you've organized your classroom library into categories that your students understand and care about, you can make book browsing even easier with clear and inviting labels on book bins that allow books to stand up facing forward for easy viewing. As soon as you find that you have multiple bins within a single category, it may be time to consider how you might subdivide the category, providing even more specificity within this wonderful sea of books you're accumulating. Also, enlisting students to help in this process will not only liven up the library organization but also give them more ownership and pride in the classroom library.

Keep growing your own awareness of great children's books.

If you're lucky, you've probably inherited or collected books faster than you could read them all. Don't worry. If you are keeping up with every single book your students read, they likely are not reading enough. You can confer successfully even when you haven't read the book. However, when it comes to conferring with students who are having trouble finding books they can and want to read, you will want to be able to recommend some surefire options that you are familiar with. Here are some suggestions to get you started in learning more about great children's books:

- **Read, read, read**. Read broadly within texts written for the age group, including picture books, chapter books, poetry, and informational texts. While striving to expose yourself to variety, consider reading the first in a series, a variety of genres, and a few from each beloved author.

- **Study book lists and recommendations**. One way to keep yourself current on the best books available in various categories and age groups is to study book lists, read recommendations, and watch video trailers about books. Here is a list of some of our favorites:

  ○ The Nerdy Book Club (https://nerdybookclub.wordpress. com/)

  ○ Betsy Bird, School Library Journal (http://blogs.slj.com/ afuse8production/#_)

  ○ We Need Diverse Books (http://weneeddiversebooks.org/)

  In addition to consulting these sources, ask your students what they'd like to see more of in the library. No one knows what your students want to read better than they do.

- **Become an expert on your own collection**. The simple care and keeping of your classroom collection is a chance to get to know more about the books within it. Time spent organizing, tidying up, and paying attention to what's popular and what doesn't ever seem to make it out of the library provides invaluable information. Learn from your students' choices. Ask them. Listen to their answers.

View imperfect book choices as formative data.

When you confer with students who are having trouble finding their way to worthy and engaging books, you'll want to be careful that you don't swoop in and protect them from the messiness and missteps of their own decision making. The trick is to learn to embrace these imperfect choices as information to inform your teaching. Giving students room to make decisions means giving them room to make mistakes and then learn from those mistakes. So don't be startled or surprised when students make some less-than-stellar book choices. The messiness of choice is a predictable part of the process and is a perfect focus for our conferring conversations.

Imperfect choices are not evidence that students are incapable of choosing their texts for themselves; they simply mean the reader has not yet had enough practice or support learning to choose texts. Every book choice (successful or not) is a chance to learn. In the short run, it might be quicker and easier to simply hand kids the books you think they should read. But, in the long run, it is your patient efforts to help students reflect on and adjust their choices that will largely determine whether they are able to maintain their reading lives when we are not there beside them pointing them to the next book.

By helping our students build their capacity for this messy work of book choice, we send them out into the world a little more courageous, a little more resilient, and a maybe a whole lot more equipped to make thoughtful decisions, not only about books but also about other matters because learning to navigate choice isn't just a reading skill, it's a life skill. What could be a more powerful use of our time as educators than helping students make their own choices, reflect, and adjust accordingly?

The Book Choice Conferring Reference

Before we end this chapter, we want to offer a reference tool to help you on the move while you're conferring. The Book Choice Conferring Reference (Figure 5.6) will help you systematically both know and nurture readers in the direction of book choice. We want to be clear that this is not a conferring to-do list. Rather, we offer it simply as a starting point to guide you as you set out to use wonder, affirm, extend, and remind to support the book choice strategies of your readers.

Figure 5.6
Book Choice Conferring Reference

ESSENTIAL QUESTION:
Is the reader consistently finding texts that lead to high levels of engagement?

Does the reader regularly and purposefully choose . . .

- Books that are of high **interest**.
- A **variety** of text types including a range of types, genres, authors, topics.
- A balance of **stretch** reading and **relaxed** reading.
- Texts for different purposes, i.e. to learn more, to be entertained, to learn how to, etc.

Does the reader use a range of strategies to consistently find good-fit texts?

- Easily navigate the classroom library and other collections.
- Know how to "sample" texts before selecting them.
- Follow personal interests and preferences.
- Use the recommendations of others to find new possibilities.
- Read more than one book from a favorite author, series, genre, or topic.

Recognize when and why a text is not a good-fit?

- Realize when a book choice is not working.
- Make the decision to abandon the book or save it for later.
- Name why a book is not a good choice.
- Use factors from past book choice mismatches when selecting new reads.

If it seems right for you, we invite you to print this tool for quick reference. To make it even more accessible, the information from Figure 5.6 has also been included as one of four quadrants in the Four Square Conferring Reference in Appendix C. This tool is designed as a quick on-the-go support and includes a quadrant for each of the possible directions for conferring; book choice, healthy habits, strategic process, and authentic response.

6

confer to develop
healthy habits

An intentional focus on healthy habits is a commitment to empower students to take charge of their own reading lives, learning to make choices, design plans, and set goals that will help them develop and sustain a habit of joyful and purposeful reading throughout their lifetimes. We offer the following essential question to inform your work in the direction of healthy habits:

Is the reader making intentional decisions that result in
lots of time spent reading both in and out of school?

Healthy reading habits are the routines that students intentionally build and the decisions they make to nurture vibrant, high-volume reading lives for themselves. Establishing healthy habits requires students to learn to make thoughtful choices and take responsibility for their own engagement, volume, and planning as readers. This, of course, is enormous work for young readers. So, it is important to keep in mind that these habits are not something that readers establish all at once. They are established bit by bit across time and often need to be nurtured in new ways at each stage of development, from the most emergent stages of reading in the kindergarten classroom to the fluent reading of much more complex texts in the intermediate classroom. As conferring teachers, our goal is to help readers learn to reflect on their own

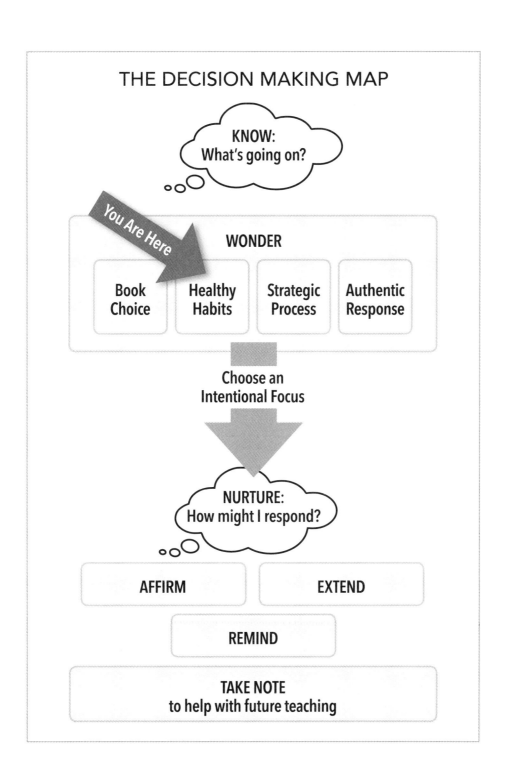

habits so that they are able to make intentional adjustments to both the quantity and the quality of their time spent reading.

Why Do Healthy Habits Matter?

If you mention healthy habits in the teachers' lounge, the conversation will probably turn to workout routines, gym memberships, special diets, or getting more sleep. You'll likely also hear some moans, groans, and lamenting. We all seem to have a clear idea of what constitute the habits of a healthy lifestyle. We just aren't always sure how to maintain them. When it comes to building a healthy lifestyle, thoughtful commitments, smart decisions, and practical action steps are key. The same is true of healthy reading habits. They aren't something we establish once and for all and then move on. Developing healthy habits in any area requires commitment and intentionality. Without a plan for action, consistency, and reflection, our best intentions easily fall by the wayside.

Kari wants to be committed to an exercise routine. She knows that when she is in the routine of getting a run in first thing in the morning, everything in her life works better. Her stress level is lower and her energy level is higher. Christina sets goals around athletic races such as triathlons and cycling events. She knows that if she doesn't train most days of the week, she will not reach her goals of finishing these events. Despite the benefits of lower stress levels and achieving a big goal, getting out the door is often the hard part for both of us. Without a plan, some effort, and a great deal of intentionality, the day's workout can quickly be derailed by excuses: it's a busy week, there are no clean workout clothes, the bed is so much more comfortable than the frigid morning temperatures, an inbox full of email is waiting, and so on.

The same can be true for students. So, if we want them to become avid readers, accumulating lots of minutes with books in a variety of genres for a range of purposes, we will need to help them recognize and create the right conditions for themselves to carry on with agency, independence, and determination.

At the heart of our emphasis on conferring toward healthy reading habits is research that proves high volume matters (Allington 1977, 2009a). To grow as readers, students need to do lots and lots of reading. They become better readers, not by completing worksheets or packets or stations (Krashen 2004) but by spending time doing the books-in-hand, eyes-on-print, minds-engaged kind of reading. And when that kind of reading is paired with books they love, because they've chosen them for themselves, the likelihood is much higher that they'll develop more stamina, think more deeply, and set in motion a series of plans and goals for themselves as readers.

When we see healthy reading habits in action in the elementary classroom, we'll see students who are aware of personal preferences and are intentional about nurturing their own reading lives. Students with healthy reading habits consistently.

- Choose a good-fit reading spot.

    ○ Zoe knows she is best able to focus in a quiet classroom nook, away from her best friend Rosa, who might distract her from her reading.

    ○ Although many of his classmates prefer the floor or soft seating around the classroom, Liam finds it easier to read, write, and stay organized right at his table.

- Make time for reading in their busy lives.

    ○ Because she has a busy gymnastics schedule, Abby knows that it's important for her to have a book tucked in her gymnastics bag. This way, she can make use of the car rides to and from practices each night for some of her reading time.

    ○ Every day before leaving school, Elijah double checks that he has his current book in his backpack so he can continue his reading that evening. When he's done reading at home, he makes a point to put it back in his backpack right away. He knows that the morning rush at his house can be loud and hectic, and he doesn't want to be without his book at school the next day.

- Make daily plans for their reading.

    ○ Amid the buzz of reading workshop in the kindergarten classroom, Tegan makes a plan for the day by taking the books out of her book box and ordering them in a neat stack to the left of her reading spot. As she finishes each book, she places it in a separate stack on the right, creating a "done" pile. If she reads through all of her emergent texts before independent reading time ends, she reorders the books and begins again.

- ○ In his fourth-grade classroom, Riley begins each day by reading a few poems from his beloved Shel Silverstein book before moving on to *Harry Potter and the Sorcerer's Stone*. He knows that Harry Potter is more of a challenge for him, but he really wants to keep making progress in this text. So, he usually sets a goal of ten pages before he takes a break to explore his National Geographic football book.

- Make future reading plans.

  - ○ When a classmate gives a book talk that intrigues her, Elizabeth is careful to take time to jot the title in the Possible Future Reads section she created in her reading journal. Plus, she always keeps two nonfiction titles and two chapter books in her book box, one she's reading now and one that is in the wings.

  - ○ Zander captures digital images of books he wants to read in the future and keeps them organized on a Padlet. He and his classmates also have Books I'd Recommend pages, and he frequently visits those of his classmates, looking for suggestions.

- Set goals.

  - ○ Because he sometimes takes a couple weeks to get through a single novel, Roberto is trying to shift the balance of his reading time, working to spend at least thirty minutes on that same text each day. This time allows him to focus more deeply and to jot notes and ideas while he is in his dedicated reading time.

  - ○ Before reading time each day, Daniella reminds herself of her current reading goal by rereading the sticky note she and her teacher created at their last conference.

Choosing good reading spots, making time and plans for reading, and setting goals are all important habits of healthy readers. When one of these habits is not in place, reading lives often suffer.

Signs a Reader Might Benefit from a Conference Focused on Healthy Reading Habits

---

Essential question:

Is the reader making intentional decisions that result in
lots of time spent reading both in and out of school?

Ultimately, healthy reading habits are high-volume reading habits; they are the sum of everything readers do to ensure that they spend lots of time every day reading texts that matter to them and responding to what they read by thinking, talking, writing, and taking action.

So, using conferring time to affirm effort or success toward a healthy habit is a sure way to nurture more of the same. But how else will you know to focus on healthy habits in a conference? We suggest that anytime there's evidence a student isn't making the most of independent reading time, either in or out of school, they'll likely benefit from your helping them to reflect on the choices they are making and consider adjustments. Common examples include:

- When readers are choosing reading spots that don't work

- When readers don't seem to have a plan

- When readers aren't making time for reading

- When readers show signs of disengagement

In the sections that follow, we'll again share classroom scenarios that illustrate each of the signs, suggestions and consideration for each scenario, and an invitation for you to think about how you might respond as a conferring teacher, drawing on the interactive moves paired with your experiences and instincts.

When readers are choosing reading spots that don't work.

Alexei has switched spots multiple times during
independent reading time the past few days. His

teacher, Ms. O'Brien, has noticed him sit down
with his book, read a few pages, look around the
room, and then move to another spot twice within
the first few minutes today. Because of this pattern,
Ms. O'Brien worries that Alexei hasn't been able
to settle into a sustained period of reading much at
all this week. She decides its time for a conference
to learn more about what's getting in the way of
Alexei settling into a good-fit spot.

Some conferences might simply focus on helping students reflect on and choose a more suitable spot for independent reading. If you reflect on your own habits, you probably have some very specific conditions that help you settle in and make the most of reading. Kari has a hard time reading when there's a lot of conversational background noise or catchy music with lyrics that make her want to sing along. Christina prefers to read in spaces with some sort of background noise: a bustling coffee shop, a beach with crashing waves, or a city train with people all around. She has a hard time focusing in complete silence.

As one of Christina's fifth graders, Vivian, puts it, "Where I read matters. It makes a difference in how I read." Vivian knows that for her it's really hard, if not impossible, to think about her reading if she is distracted, uncomfortable, or unfocused.

Yet what makes a spot a good fit is different for different readers. Some students work best at a table or a desk, while others might focus best in a quiet nook or on a comfortable beanbag. Many students even do well lying with their stomachs and legs stretched on the floor. Some students thrive while sitting near their best buddy, while others choose to have their back to the room, facing a wall or a window in order to have some privacy or to avoid the temptation of focusing more on others than on their own reading.

If your students have only been offered their own desks or tables as reading spots, you might consider branching out to allow students more choice about reading spots in the classroom. Chances are very few of us would be able to sustain reading for long periods of time in a traditional school-issued chair and desk. So, invite students to try a few different spaces on for size, emphasizing that the point of choice is to find the sort of spot that helps you do your best reading. Much like the coaching you do to support book choice, when you offer to confer with a student to reflect on a reading spot, you'll want to avoid simply telling students where to go. After all, learning to reflect on decisions and adjust is something they'll have to do their whole lives, without you there to direct things. The conversation might start with open-ended questions aimed to guide student reflection and the problem-solving process.

- What are you noticing about this reading spot? How is it working?

- What have you noticed about yourself as a reader? What makes it easy or difficult for you to stay focused?

- How might you help yourself find a spot that will help you make the most of independent reading?

- If you think back on a time when you were really focused as a reader, what do you remember about the type of reading spot you had selected?

Now, let's think back to Alexei: What are some ways you may choose to support him in this moment? Do you need to gather more information? How might you offer your partnership through conferring in collaborative problem solving rather than jumping in to solve Alexei's problem for him? Maybe you're ready to offer a next step to help him learn how to settle in to a good reading spot each time he sets out to read. How might you respond?

When readers don't seem to have a plan.

Ling's book box is stuffed so full of books that there's little wiggle room at all. Getting them in and out sometimes causes the covers and pages to bend and rip. When it comes time for independent reading, Ling often struggles with making a plan and getting started. She pulls out a handful of books and spreads them on the floor in front of her and then pulls out another handful and does the same. Next, she flips through the books left in her box. Although she is in a suitable spot and surrounded by books she wants to spend time with, she seems unable to get started.

Independent reading works best when readers have a variety of appealing, preselected, and stored texts in a personalized bag, basket, box, or stack. This customized collection of reading material is ready to go and is an important support to readers as they engage in long stretches of daily reading time. Because their books are shorter, beginning readers require many texts to stay engaged for fifteen to twenty minutes of independent reading. Most of the kindergarten to second-grade teachers we know want their earliest readers to have about ten to fifteen short books in their reading box or bag at any given time. And even though some older readers may be able to sustain attention with a single book for the entire independent reading time, it's still important that they have three to six options, containing a variety of types and genres. This will help them avoid a total interruption to reading if they finish a book or find they need a change of pace.

But for some students, like Ling, managing these collections of books can become a bit of a distraction that keeps them from actually digging in to read. These students may benefit from conferring support with things like weeding out a few books from their collections, learning to organize and care for their books more carefully, and making a daily plan by systematically selecting an

Figure 6.1
Ling's Plan

order for the books they will read each day. Figure 6.1 shows the visual that Ling's teacher created to help her apply her new planning strategies. Ling is able to keep the visual in her book box and pull it out at the beginning of independent reading each day until she is able to carry out the sequence without the scaffold of the visual.

We again invite you to think about Ling. What are some ways you might choose to support her? Do you need to gather more information? Perhaps you can affirm something she's already doing well. Or you might be ready to offer a next step to help her learn how to manage her books during independent reading time. How might you respond to Ling as a reader?

When readers aren't making time for reading.

Greyson is an engaged reader in class. He has no trouble finding books he is excited to read and talk about with his classmates. However, outside of school, it's a different story. Greyson is part of an active soccer family; when he's not playing or practicing soccer himself, he's often attending a sibling's soccer match or practice. This has made it particularly challenging for him to settle in to a reading routine at home. Greyson's teacher, Mr. Tanaka, decides to confer with him, zooming in on healthy reading habits. Together, they'll look for solutions to his "not really at home very much" challenge.

Finding time and space to read beyond the school day is a very real challenge for many of our students. Some of them have intensely scheduled lives, moving from gymnastics to soccer practice to rehearsal for the church play. Others live in crowded and chaotic households where quiet spaces are hard to find. Reading logs, points, and prizes usually fall miserably short when it comes to helping readers who haven't yet figured out how to make reading part of their life away from school. A one-to-one conference, in which we honestly and respectfully help students problem-solve and make concrete plans can be the difference between developing a regular reading routine at home and leaving reading for school time only. When we help students get creative and concrete about where, when, and how they might make time and space for reading in the hours outside of school, we can become a lifeline of support rather just one more source of stress in their already full lives. To do so, we can help students:

- Envision themselves with books in hand in a specific space (in the backseat of the car, nestled under their baby sister's crib, on a beach towel in the backyard, etc.). Some students benefit from actually drawing a picture and writing a caption to post in an obvious place at home as a reminder.

- Make a specific plan of action customized to their unique situation (offer to read aloud to a sibling in need of attention, ask the family to join in a half hour of TV-off time each night, clear a space in the corner of a messy room where they can snuggle up with a blanket and pillow).

- By checking in on a regular basis to reflect, offer encouragement, and modify the plan as needed.

Now, let's take a moment to think back to Greyson's struggle. What are some ways you may choose to support Greyson in developing a reading routine away from school? Do you need more information? Perhaps you can affirm something he's already doing well at school to help him transfer that habit to his time away from school. Or you might be ready to offer a next step to help him get an away-from-school reading routine up and running.

When readers show signs of disengagement.

Every week or so Ms. Patel takes about five minutes to quietly step away from her readers to observe and wonder during independent reading. During this focused observation, she's on the lookout for one thing: signs of disengaged readers. Sometimes she sees obvious evidence: a student who is lying on his back looking at the ceiling, a student who is obviously flipping pages of a chapter book faster than she could possibly read them, or a student who is at the drinking fountain and then immediately after at the pencil

> *sharpener. Sometimes the signs are not as obvious.*
> *But whenever she sees disengaged readers, she*
> *becomes curious about the root causes. To be able*
> *to use her observations to inform her conferences,*
> *she takes note of what she sees by jotting on her*
> *conferring clipboard. She can then refer to these*
> *notes when it's time for her to make a conferring*
> *plan for the week.*

If you take a few minutes to step back and observe what's happening during independent reading, you're likely to spot a few students who aren't making the most of these precious reading minutes; they may struggle to get started, keep going, or both. They simply aren't looking like deeply engaged readers. These readers are prime candidates for conferring, but even though on the surface distraction or disengagement may look similar from one student to another, the root causes can be very different. To help you sort things out in a somewhat systematic way, we've provided the Flowchart for Trouble-shooting Disengagement in Figure 6.2.

When you notice students having a hard time getting started or seeming unable to sustain their reading stamina beyond a couple of minutes, it's easy to blame habits. But before jumping in this direction, don't forget to consider book choice as well. Does the student have books that he can and wants to read? For disengaged readers, quite often the answer is no. When the answer is no, you will want to confer to support book choice before choosing to focus on reading habits, keeping in mind that self-selected, high-interest books are the magic fairy dust of engagement.

However, if a student appears to have engaging, good-fit texts, take a moment to consider whether the physical space is a good fit for the child. For some students, external distractions bar getting started or keeping going. If we suspect this is the case, we might confer to help the child reflect on their selection of a reading spot, considering other possibilities (as in the previous example).

If it seems that both book selection and the reading spot are relatively sound, then you might often find that lost minutes are a result of the student struggling with organization and therefore not having a plan or a system for how to proceed. If so, we dig in here, helping to teach strategies for planning and organization.

Figure 6.2
Flowchart for Troubleshooting Disengagement

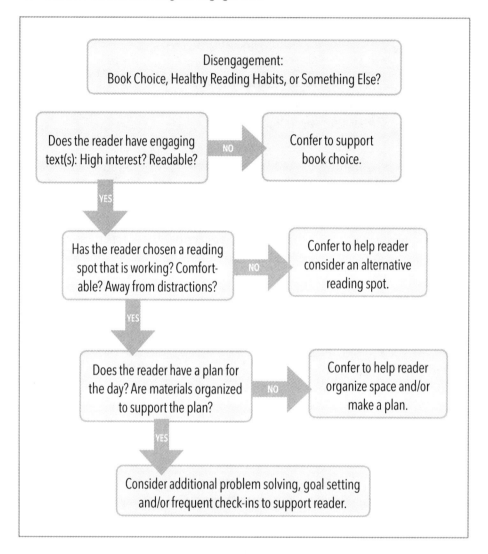

If the student already seems to have a clear and reasonable plan, we may decide to help the reader develop a goal focused on making better use of every precious minute of reading time in the classroom, for example, getting settled in and started within three minutes of the start of independent reading time. We share more information about supporting students with goal setting in the next section.

By starting with book choice, moving on to reading spot, and then thinking about planning and goals, you will be able to systematically work through a predictable set of the probable causes of disengagement for each student. When exploring reasons for disengagement with students, you might start with a question to get them thinking about their own disengagement. Here are a few to try:

- How is your reading time going today?

- Is there something you think you may be able to try to make the most out of your reading time?

- How is this book working out for you? How is this particular spot working out for you?

Take a moment to think about a few of your readers. You may want to close your eyes and visualize independent reading time in your classroom. As you do, look for disengaged readers just like Ms. Patel did in the earlier example. What are a few possibilities for conferring with these readers?

What Are Some Important Tools and Tips to Support Healthy Habits?

To add to the strength of your conferences focused on healthy reading habits, we offer these tools and tips:

- Set goals *with* students, not *for* them.

- Teach habits efficiently with whole-group and small-group instruction.

- Create anchor charts to help turn actions into habits.

- Study your own reading habits and the habits of those around you.

Set goals *with* students, not *for* them.

To make the most of goal setting, you'll want to let students do more of the work than you do. Yet, many elementary-aged readers do not arrive at our classroom doors ready to set compelling goals for themselves. So, you may need to develop your own skills for guiding students through the process. If you simply tell the student, "Here's what you need to work on; I'm setting this goal for you," you'll miss an important opportunity to foster the ownership and motivation that comes when students have a voice in selecting and reflecting on their own reading goals.

Helping students set reasonable and worthwhile goals can feel like a tap dance at times. But we promise you, it is a challenge worth the effort. Here, we offer some tips to guide you:

1. **Start with reflection.** Even if you already have an idea of what might be getting in a reader's way (very little at-home reading or not choosing a good spot for reading, for instance) and what the solution might be (set a daily goal for at-home reading minutes or trying out a couple of good spots before settling on one), try starting with a question likely to lead the student to reflection:

    *   So, what are you noticing about your at-home reading habits?

    *   As you reflect on _____, what are you thinking?

2. **Present the possibility of setting a goal as an optional strategy.** Rather than telling a student that she needs to set a goal for herself, empower the student by offering goal setting as one possibility to help her stretch and grow.

    *   Do you think that setting a goal for yourself might be helpful?

    *   Some other readers have set goals to help themselves focus this very thing. Is that something you'd be interested in thinking about?

3. **Support the student in naming a goal that is within reach.** Sometimes, especially when goal setting is new, students go a bit wild. ("I'm going to read four hours every night!") But setting unattainable goals only leads to frustration and goal abandonment. So, when guiding students toward their goals, help them to keep it logical and attainable. One way to do this, especially with goals about reading volume, is to set a short-term goal. For instance, set a goal for this week rather than for this month. This sets the child up for a quick win as well as a natural opportunity to reflect and adjust if needed.

    *   If you were to set a goal to help yourself focus on this, what would it be?

    *   What do you think might be a reasonable goal in the coming week?

4. **Make it visual**. To increase the likelihood that a goal results in action, you'll want to consider a visual reminder. Our two favorite ways to make goals visual are bookmarks and sticky notes. Consider carrying a collection of precut blank bookmarks with you when you confer. You'll be amazed at how many uses you'll find for them.

- Here's a bookmark. How might you use it to remind yourself of the goal?

- Is there any kind of symbol or picture that would be helpful to add?

5. **Check back**. Once you've supported a student in setting a goal, be sure to make a note to yourself to check back. Usually, with new goals, it's good to check back within a few days to a week. Doing so lets the student know you take the goal seriously, too, and you're there to confer with them toward success.

- I've been thinking about you and your goal. How's it going?

- I'm interested to know how it's been going with the goal you set for yourself.

As we observe and interact with readers, inevitably we will discover lots of situations in which goal setting might increase intentionality and stretch our readers in new ways. A goal is simply a commitment to be more intentional about something you've decided will make your life a little better. Learning to set and work toward goals is a healthy habit with far-reaching value both in and beyond the classroom.

Teach habits efficiently with whole-group and small-group instruction.

As is true of so many things in the literacy classroom, the most efficient way to help all students identify and develop healthy reading habits is to use whole-group mini-lessons. In the beginning, many of the lessons you'll likely want to teach will focus on healthy reading habits. Then, again, throughout the school year, you'll want to revisit, to expand, and to check in on habits with the whole group. As you confer, you can look for patterns, taking note of students who have a common area of need in order to form flexible small groups focused on developing specific reading habits. For example, you might find you have a number of students who are not developing a habit of at-home reading. Setting goals for at-home reading might be the focus of this group. To help you plan for whole- or small-group instruction, we offer some language ideas for instruction with students.

- Let's define healthy habits and make a list.

  - What does it mean to be a reader with healthy habits?

  - What do readers with healthy habits actually do?

  - How are readers with healthy habits different from other readers?

- Let's make a list of things to consider when choosing a good-fit reading spot.

  - What defines a good-fit reading spot?

  - What is important to you personally in a just-right spot?

  - What might make a spot a not-so-good choice?

- Let's make plans for reading away from school.

  - What will we read when we're away from school?

  - Where will we read?

  - How will we make the time for reading?

- Let's learn to set goals for ourselves that will help us keep growing as readers.

  - What kind of goals do readers set for themselves?

  - What is a reasonable goal?

  - How can you check up on yourself as a reader?

The Building Healthy Reading Habits sheet is a simple T-chart to help students reflect on habits and set goals. A full-sized blank copy is provided in Appendix B. In the first column, students can identify and list current reading habits. In the second column, they record goals they've set in order to become more intentional in some area of their reading lives. Having students use sticky notes in the goal column draws more attention to the goal while it is current and makes it possible to retire the goal once it is met, moving it to the reading habits side of the tool and inserting a new goal. Figure 6.3 shows a picture of one student's healthy habits T-chart.

Figure 6.3

Example of a Student's Healthy Reading Habits Goal Setting Sheet

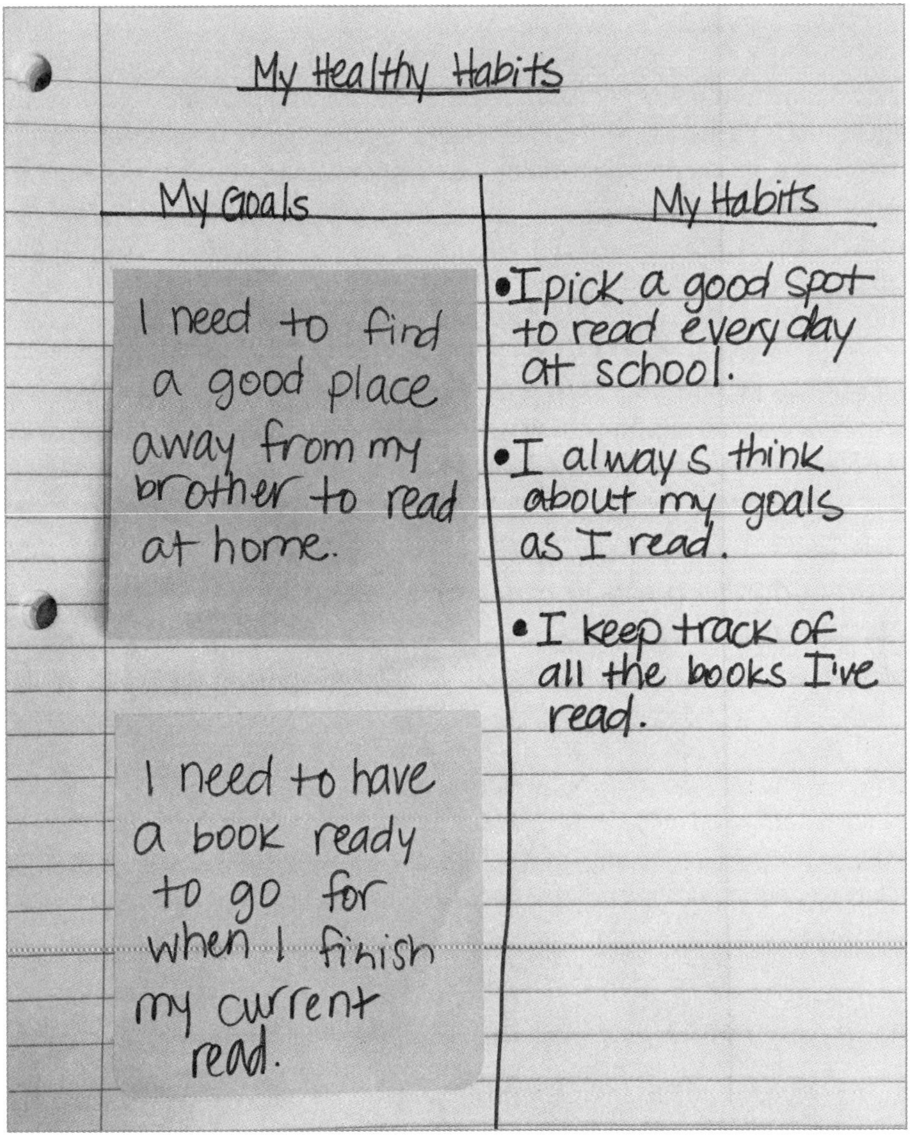

Create anchor charts to help turn actions into habits.

Anchor charts are footprints we leave to remind students of our teaching. They are created together with students in the moment that the teaching is taking place. Figure 6.4 shows a chart that Christina cocreated with her students.

Anchor charts are not just posters with information meant to teach on their own. Anchor charts are developed with our students present and involved as cocreators. For instance, as you conduct a conversation about what healthy reading habits are, you can take the words of your students, shaping them into key points to become a reference for future teaching and application. Please keep in mind, charts don't have to be cute or decorative. That's not the point or the purpose. Cute clip art and fancy borders do not help readers grow. Useful information and strategic, actionable steps do. Usually, less is more. So, keep it simple. Anchor charts should focus on one central idea listed as a title, with no more than a handful of supporting points. Most important, make the chart available to your students for as long as it is useful to them as a point of reference. Anchor charts are meant to be scaffolds for students as they work to transfer and internalize each chart's contents. To learn more about creating charts with students, we recommend two books: (1) *Smarter Charts* by Kristine Mraz and Marjorie Martinelli (2012) and (2) Kari's book, *Simple Starts* (2015).

Study your own reading habits and the habits of those around you.

Being a great reading teacher would be impossible if you weren't a reader yourself. So, go on, set some goals to strengthen your own reading habits. Find great books. Make more time for reading in your own life outside of school—and be sure to do some spying on yourself as you do. Pay attention to what conditions make reading work for you and which work against you. Watch other readers read. And finally, ask a few questions of the most voracious readers you know:

- How are their habits different from yours?

- Everyone has busy lives, so how do they make time for reading?

- Where and how do they read?

- How do they find their steady stream of great books?

- Do they read one book at a time or more than one? How many?

Figure 6.4
Example of Healthy Habits Anchor Chart

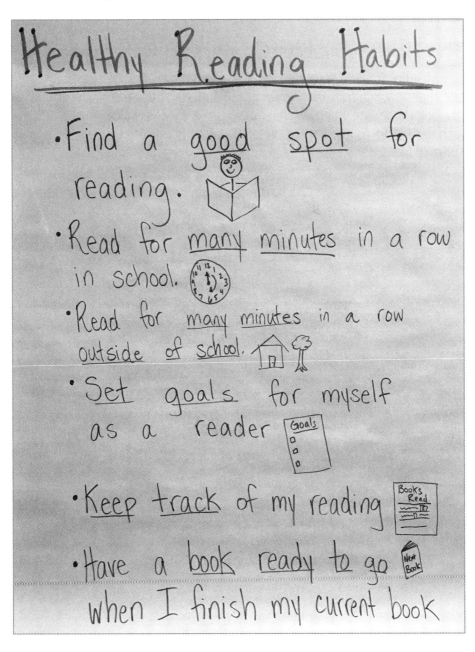

By reflecting on adult reading habits you'll be better prepared to support your students in developing healthy habits for a lifetime of reading.

The Healthy Habits Conferring Reference

The Healthy Habits Conferring Reference (Figure 6.5) will help you systematically know and nurture readers in the direction of healthy habits. As with the Book Choice Conferring Reference, we want to be clear that this is not a conferring to-do list. Rather, we offer it simply as a starting point to guide you as you set out to use wonder, affirm, extend, and remind to support the healthy habits of your readers.

Figure 6.5
A Healthy Habits Conferring Reference

ESSENTIAL QUESTION:

Is the reader making intentional decisions that result in lots of time spent reading both in and out of school?

Does the reader make choices that result in high levels of engagement?

- Choose reading spots that are comfortable.
- Choose reading spots that are away from distractions.
- Consistently choose engaging texts.

Does the reader take responsibility for high-volume reading?

- Read for longer and longer stretches of time.
- Read for many minutes at school every day.
- Read for many minutes outside of school every day.
- Read on weekends, holidays, and during summer vacation.
- Reflect on reading volume and recognize why things are or aren't going well.

Does the reader make intentional choices and plans?

- Keep reading materials organized for easy access.
- Make a daily plan to maximize available time.
- Keep a selection of next-reads ready to go or written down for future reading.
- Set meaningful goals to keep growing as a reader.
- Reflect on how things are going and make meaningful adjustments.

If it seems right for you, we invite you to print this list for quick reference. To make it even more accessible, the information from Figure 6.5 has been included as one of the quadrants in the Four Square Conferring Reference in Appendix C. This tool is designed as a quick on-the-go support for each of the four directions for conferring: book choice, healthy habits, strategic process, and authentic response.

7

confer to strengthen
strategic process

*An intentional focus on strategic process is a commitment to equip readers
with the skills and strategies to confidently problem solve and make meaning
of increasingly diverse and complex texts, therefore opening up more and more
possibilities for them as readers. We offer the following essential question to
inform you in the direction of strategic process:*

What strategic actions is the reader taking to solve problems
and make meaning of the text?

To help readers develop strategic process is to help them learn to strategically take in all that is on and across the pages of a text. Strategic process
is not only learning to decode letters, turning them to sounds and words,
but it is also about weaving together words, visual features, and thinking in
an attempt to understand clearly what it is the author has put on the page.
Developing a deep understanding of how to best support readers at each of
the incremental stages of reading development is critically important work
for every educator and, of course, stretches way beyond the boundaries of
this chapter. We offer this chapter, however, as a simple starting point to help
you support reading process within individual reading conferences.

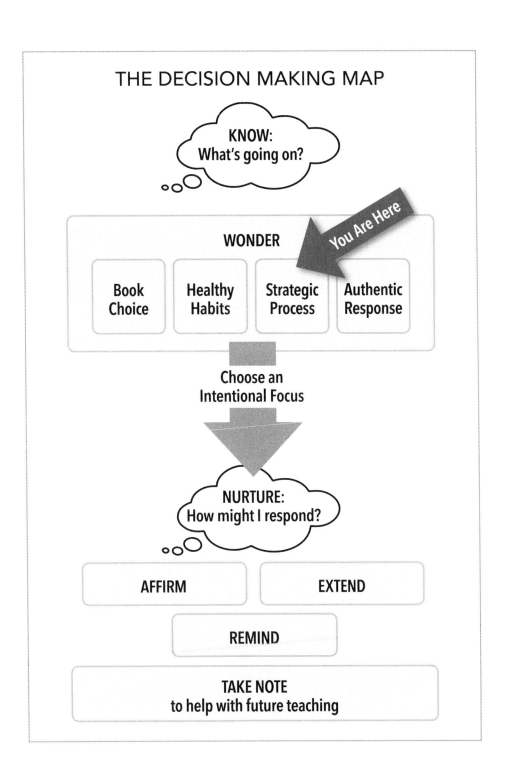

Why Does Strategic Reading Process Matter?

Strategic reading process includes all the things that go on in a reader's head as they navigate texts, such as solving problems and making meaning. When readers develop strategic reading process, they become what Marie Clay (1993, 2015) calls "self-extending" readers, using a full range of strategies to help themselves seamlessly monitor, problem-solve, and make deep meaning of the different types of texts. Self-extending readers proceed with awareness, accuracy, fluency, and comprehension, noticing and solving problems along the way. And, by doing so, they actually strengthen and extend themselves with each new reading experience.

Learning to make sense of all those little black marks on the page is no easy task. It is complex, in-the-head work that requires the orchestration of a sophisticated set of cognitive operations. To become truly strategic, not only must readers develop skills and strategies, but they must also learn to use them on the run (Fountas and Pinnell 2007) in different combinations at different times or, as Johnson and Keier (2010) put it, in overlapping and concurrent ways, all in the name of meaning-making.

Because our time with each student is limited, it would be impossible to carry out the heavy lifting of teaching reading process primarily through conferring. Instead, much of this crucial work is woven across the other instructional formats as well, including read-aloud, shared reading, and guided reading. Miller and Moss (2013) refer to conferring as an opportunity to personalize instruction:

> *Conferring is differentiation at its finest! When we confer with children one-to-one, we're working hard to personalize our instruction and support children as they apply what we've taught them in large and small group settings. (60)*

This personalization in the area of strategic process often comes in bite-sized teaching, gentle nudges, and reminders of how what has already been taught can be transferred to the reading of self-selected texts. Whether we decide to respond to what we see with personalized instruction in the moment or use our observations to plan more effectively for whole-group, small-group, or individual teaching points down the road, time spent up close with readers has the potential to enrich and strengthen our planning across the entire literacy framework.

Signs a Reader Might Benefit from a Conference Focused on Process

---

Essential question:
What strategic actions is the reader taking to solve problems
and make meaning of the text?

Every reader, regardless of age, will at one time or another benefit from conferring with an intentional focus on strategic problem-solving and meaning-making strategies. From the earliest stages of reading in the preschool and kindergarten years to the upper elementary grades, all readers pass through several predictable stages of development: preemergent, emergent, early, transitional, and fluent. And, although the descriptors may vary slightly from one researcher to the next, five distinctive stages have been consistently identified (Chall 1983; Dorn and Soffos 2001; Fountas and Pinnell 1996; Snow, Burns, and Griffin 1998). In today's diverse classrooms, teachers at every grade level can potentially encounter readers at any or all of these stages at once. Figure 7.1 provides overview information about each stage.

No matter what the stage of development, the overarching goal with regard to strategic reading process is virtually the same with all readers— bolster self-initiated problem-solving and meaning-making strategies—but the differences in development require some specialization stage by stage. Because of this, we've used the developmental stages to organize our examples and suggestions in this section. We hope this helps you see how conferring might be leveraged to support strategic process with a reader in any of these stages of development. At the beginning of each stage, we again introduce a reader, provide some insight into the specifics of the stage, and then invite you to consider how you might support readers at this stage in your classroom.

When readers are at the preemergent stage: Conferring to support use of oral language for storytelling and/or teaching about the pictures in their books.

Rowan is deeply engaged with Paul Galdone's The Three Bears *(1985), a book that his teacher, Ms. Park has read aloud to the class many times. If you weren't up close, it would be difficult to tell that*

Figure 7.1
Overview of Stages of Reading Development

Stage of Reading Development	Guided Reading Levels (Fountas and Pinnell)	Ways to Learn About Reading Process in a Conference	Strategic Actions to Develop at This Stage
Preemergent stage	Pre–A	Listen in as the student uses oral language to tell the story or teach the content of the text by reading the pictures. How does the reader use pictures, illustrations, and language to make meaning of the text?	Study the pictures in familiar and unfamiliar texts in order to make meaning (Sulzby 1985). Use oral language in ways that sound increasingly like "book talk" for both storytelling (fiction) and teaching (information; Collins and Glover 2015). Start to notice familiar or distinctive letters, words, or other features of texts.
Emergent stage	A–C	Listen in on oral reading already in progress at the beginning of the conference. What does the reader do to independently solve problems along the way? Is the student reading left to right with one-to-one matching? Does the student use more than one source of information at the point of difficulty? Engage in conversation that provides insight into the child's understanding of the text.	Begin to process simple text conventionally. Move left-to-right across a line of print. Use finger to match one spoken word to one written word. Begin to check one source of information against another to monitor (words and picture).

Early stage	D–I	Listen in on oral reading already in progress at the beginning of the conference. What does the student do to solve problems along the way? Does the reader draw information from the visual features of the text? From meaning? From the language patterns? Engage in conversation that provides insight into the child's understanding of the text.	Consistently use meaning, structure, and visual information as sources of information. Self-monitor, problem-solve, and make self-corrections. Develop a growing repertoire of strategies for word solving. Read with more expression and in longer phrases.
Transitional stage	J–N	Engage in conversation that provides insight into the reader's understanding of the text. Ask the reader to choose a selection to read aloud. What does the reader do to help solve problems related to meaning? Related to unknown and multisyllabic words?	Strengthen skills for reading with meaning, accuracy, and fluency. Develop skills for decoding multisyllabic words and making sense of new words in context. Notice when meaning breaks down and reread strategically. Connect ideas across chapters.
Fluent stage	O and above	Engage in conversation that provides insight into the reader's understanding of the text. What are the self-initiated problem-solving strategies that the reader draws on at the point of confusion or difficulty? Ask the student to use evidence or examples from the text to support or clarify points of conversation.	Develop and fine-tune skills for deep comprehension of more complex and varied text types. Utilize a range of strategies for determining meaning of complex vocabulary.

Rowan is composing the text of his own words
rather than those on the page. He's engaged,
animated, and a convincing storyteller as he does
the meaning-making work of pairing pictures and
language to construct this rich narrative. Suddenly,
Rowan stops, "Wait a minute!" and flips back to the
previous page. "Oh, yeah. I missed this page," he
confirms, before jumping back into his storytelling.
Although this simple action of discovering a missed
page might seem inconsequential on the surface,
Ms. Park sees an opportunity to affirm the roots
of a powerful problem-solving behavior. "Rowan,
you just did something so powerful to help yourself
as a reader," she says. "You noticed something
didn't make sense to you, and you took the time
to go back and try to figure it out. You're not just
making up a story, you're working to tell the story
the author and illustrator put on these pages.
Keep doing this to help yourself with every book
you read."

When conferring with readers in the preemergent stage, interactions will often center on the essential work of helping readers learn to appreciate books as powerful tools for storytelling and learning about the world. Conferring supports the newest readers in developing skills for interacting with books and elaborating on what they see by using their texts for storytelling (fiction) or teaching (informational). And although preemergent readers may not yet be processing print conventionally, the work they are doing to combine, to observe, to infer, and to use oral language builds a strong foundation for all later reading. Figure 7.2 provides sample language to support preemergent readers.

Even when your conferring moves in the direction of strategic reading process, you'll likely find yourself noticing the inseparable relationship between book choice and reading process. One critical way to support the work of preemergent readers is to make sure that they have access to a rich array of high-quality storybooks and informational texts, including texts they are already familiar through read aloud, as well as some that are new to

Figure 7.2
Examples of Language to Support Preemergent Readers

WONDER You may look for evidence to indicate the reader . . .	AFFIRM Language for noticing evidence of strategic action.	EXTEND Language for moving a reader toward strategic action.
Handles books conventionally and turns pages one at a time.	"When you finished one page, you knew to turn to the next page."	"When we read, we turn one page at a time. Try it."
Takes time to study each page, working to draw meaning from the pictures.	"You are taking your time reading the pictures. This helps you understand the story."	"To understand the story, readers take time looking at the pictures."
Elaborates with story language, including description and dialogue.	"You told what the characters in the book might be saying."	"When you read a story, you can think about what the characters might be saying."
Uses teaching voice and language for information texts.	"You told what you know about the picture using a teaching voice."	"When you read books that teach, you can read with a teaching voice."
Works to connect the content of one page to the next (i.e.. "And then. . ." "The next day. . .").	"You're showing how all the parts of the story fit together by using phrases like, 'At first. . .' or 'After that. . .'"	"You can hook all the parts of the story together with special words like, 'The next day . . .' and 'Then. .'"

readers but of high interest and visual appeal. Figure 7.3 provides some characteristics of high-quality preemergent texts.

The advantages of narrative picture books with illustrations that carry the story line in a highly supportive way (Sulzby 1985), as well as high-quality informational texts that make content visually accessible through rich photos and drawings, will become more apparent each time you sit next to a preemergent reader in a conference. For instance, when Rowan pauses for a moment in his reading of *The Three Bears*, Ms. Park points to the dialogue and says, "Oh, look. I'm noticing that some of the words on the page have different size letters. Did you see that? I wonder why the author would do that?"

Although you won't want to let a focus on print become heavy-handed when conferring with preemergent readers, you're likely to find many opportunities to naturally weave the noticing of print features into your conversations, like Ms. Park does with the baby-sized, mama-sized, and papa-sized letters on the page. Preemergent readers are delighted to begin to interact with familiar letters or words, speech bubbles, repeating phrases, or words that stand out using different fonts or sizes. As you gradually draw attention to bits of interesting and important print, you prepare students for their transition to the emergent stage.

Figure 7.3
Characteristics of High-Quality Preemergent Texts

Familiar texts that have been read aloud several times

Visually engaging informational text

Storybooks with pictures that easily carry the story line

Engaging story line and characters in familiar or relatable situations

Repeating lines, including dialogue

Take a moment to think about readers you've known who are in the preemergent stage of reading. They are working to make their own meaning of the picture books and informational texts they hold in their hands. How might you shape your interactions with these students to support the development of oral language and early print concepts? In what ways might you support deep thinking and meaning-making even prior to students reading the words on the page? What types of texts will you advocate for students to access? How might you deepen your own understanding of how to best know and nurture readers in the preemergent stage of reading development?

When readers are at the emergent stage: Conferring to integrate early print work with meaning-making.

Lea is nestled into a corner nook during independent reading. Her teacher, Ms. Shirani, approaches as she opens her A-level text and starts to read the first page. She works to carefully touch each word as she reads. "I see a pig." Immediately, she shakes her head, showing that she's noticed

a mismatch between her spoken words and the number of words on the page. Lea goes back to the beginning of the line and tries again. "I see . . ." again she stops. "No," she says aloud, and moves her finger to the beginning of the line once more. "I . . . can see a pig." She goes back one more time for good measure, "I can see a pig." She nods confidently and moves on to the next page. Ms. Shirani simply smiles and says, "You helped yourself by going back to make it match. You can do this anytime something doesn't seem quite right."

When we welcome readers to the emergent stage, we invite them more formally into the world of print. By the time they leave this stage they will have mastered many critical early reading behaviors.

On a single first line of print, Lea demonstrated many of these early behaviors, including self-monitoring for voice-print match, self-correction of one-to-one matching, and even rereading to confirm. Again, much of the teaching and learning of these behaviors happens prior to conferring, through shared and guided reading. However, because emergent readers like Lea read and think aloud in observable ways (self-talk, head shaking, and using a finger for voice-print match), it's easy to spend the first few moments of each conference observing for these strategic early reading behaviors, reinforcing those that are becoming more consistent, and noticing which ones might need more coaching . Figure 7.4 provides suggestions for how you might support these emergent oral reading behaviors during a conference.

To tackle this delicate new print work, readers need access to lots of high-quality, emergent-level texts (Fountas and Pinnell 2016c, guided reading levels A–C) designed specifically for this stage. Part of what makes these little texts so mighty is the fact that emergent readers don't just read their books one or two times; rather, they read them over and over again, potentially noticing something new with each subsequent reading. Figure 7.5 shows some of the distinctive characteristics that are hallmarks of texts designed with precision and care to support reading behaviors of the emergent stage. As you confer, you can check to be sure that emergent readers have access to about eight to ten texts of this type.

Figure 7.4
Examples of Language to Support Emergent Readers

WONDER You may look for evidence to indicate the reader . . .	AFFIRM Language for noticing evidence of strategic action.	EXTEND Language for moving a reader toward strategic action.
Moves left to right with crisp one-to-one matching.	"You used your finger and made it match."	"You can use your finger to touch each word as you say it."
Rereads in an attempt to repair a mismatch	"You went back and worked it out. You made it match."	"You can read it again to make it match."
Uses picture clues to determine what would make sense (meaning).	"You used the picture to think what would make sense."	"Look at the picture. Think what would make sense in the story."
Uses oral language structures to predict what would sound right.	"You made it sound like talking."	"Think how you would say it if you were talking."
Cross-checks meaning (use of picture) and visual information (use of initial consonant sound).	"You checked the picture and the word. It makes sense and looks right."	"Check the picture and think about the first sound."
Uses the text itself as a tool for retelling and answering questions.	"You helped yourself by going back to the page about _____."	"You can look back at the pages of the book to help you think about what you learned".
Makes connections between the text and personal experiences.	"You helped yourself by using what you know about _____ to understand what is happening."	"You can help yourself by thinking what you already know before you start to read."
Uses pictures to make basic inferences about characters feelings and situations.	"You helped yourself understand what's happening by studying the picture."	"You can study the pictures/ characters' faces to learn more about what's happening."

Figure 7.5
Some Characteristics of High-Quality Emergent Texts (Levels A–C)

A few simple and predictable lines of print on each page

Explicit match between the pictures and the words

Predictable patterns with natural language structures

Repeated use of several high-frequency words

Crisp black font on a white background

With joyful reading at the top of our wish list for every reader, it's critical that introduction of leveled texts happens alongside the storybooks and self-selected informational trade books that children were already reading in the preemergent stage, not as a replacement for these other rich and wonderful texts. With both leveled texts (read the words) and a handful of trade books (retell or read the pictures) in their book boxes or bags, emergent readers will be able to extend their time spent engaged with text far beyond what would be possible with leveled texts alone. This is good news for everyone in the class because if students can read for longer periods, you get more time to confer, and these self-selected storybooks and informational texts provide you with many possibilities for supporting deep meaning-making work alongside the new focus on print.

As you confer with emergent readers, you set the stage for problem solving down the road, patiently and expectantly allowing students to notice problems and work things out for themselves as much as possible. Also, you affirm and extend the problem-solving tools in their bag of tricks to prepare them for the early stage of reading development.

Imagine yourself pulling alongside an emergent reader to confer. Which of the earliest print behaviors will you notice and affirm? What language might you use to help them start thinking about the pictures, the print, and the language patterns of their books? How might you ensure that every reader at this stage has access to lots of high-quality emergent texts to support the critical work of this stage of development? How might you deepen your own understanding of how to best know and nurture readers in the emergent stage of reading development?

When readers are at the early stage: Conferring to support problem solving and resilience.

> *Tuan is an early reader who loves to learn about animals. He is tackling a new text about the animals of Africa. "The hippo baby and its mother have be-bell-bellies that are shaped like bar-reals … barreals. I don't know that word." Tuan looks up at his teacher, Mr. Bagali. He nods toward the text and says, "What could you try?" Tuan looks at the word* barrel *one more time and then goes back to the beginning of the sentence. "The baby hippo and its mother have bellies that are shaped like bar—shaped like barrels." Mr. Bagali makes a quick note in his conferring notebook. He's excited to see Tuan help himself at the point of difficulty by rereading the entire sentence, returning to the challenging word with the context of the sentence rebuilt in his memory. "Tuan, going back to reread helped you think about what would make sense and look right."*

If you work with early readers, you already know that problem solving and resilience are the name of the game. If ever there was a place for a growth mind-set (Dweck 2007), it is while students are reading texts in the early stage of reading development where success depends on learning to expect and even welcome challenges in these increasingly challenging books. Readers in the early stage of development need to learn to spot trouble and persistently work to sort things out. So, much of our conferring at this stage will center around exactly that. Figure 7.6 provides suggestions for how you might support these early oral reading behaviors during a conference.

Because early stage texts are much less patterned and predictable than texts in the emergent stage, they naturally provide many opportunities for fluent, flexible problem solving on the run. When early readers encounter tricky words, they must dig deep into their tool kits, becoming persistent enough to try multiple strategies when needed. When you confer with early readers, it's important to notice effort and process, even before accuracy.

Figure 7.6
Examples of Language to Support Early Readers

WONDER You may look for evidence to indicate the reader . . .	AFFIRM Language for noticing evidence of strategic action.	EXTEND Language for moving a reader toward strategic action.
Self-monitors noticing when something doesn't look right, sound right, or make sense.	"You noticed in your reading when something sounded not right."	"You can listen to your own reading, noticing when something doesn't sound quite right. Watch while I show an example . . ."
Routinely cross-checks one source of information against another.	"You helped yourself by checking to see that it made sense and looked right."	"You can help yourself by checking more than one way. It has to make sense, look right, and sound right. Let me show you."
Rereads to monitor, to get more information, or to confirm.	"You went back and reread to check one more time."	"You can reread to help yourself find more information. Let's try it out here."
Uses a variety of word-solving strategies flexibly and without prompting.	"You tried it more than one way."	"When you come to a tricky word, you can try more than one thing to help yourself. Listen while I do it here."
Uses expression, especially for dialogue.	"You made it sound just like the character would have sounded."	"When you see quotation marks, you can think about how the character would say it."
Tells about characters, setting, and plot.	"You're getting to know each of the characters in your story in ways that help you predict what they might do next."	"One thing you can do as a reader is to think and then talk about what the characters in your book are doing."
Refers to the text to show evidence of thinking.	"When you were telling about the _____, you found that part in your book and used it to help you."	"You can help yourself talk about the book by paging through it to find important pictures to support what you are saying. Watch while I show you . . ."

You've likely worked hard in other settings to help early stage readers move away from letter-by-letter and sound-by-sound decoding, instead starting to look across whole words, using pieces and parts with growing efficiency. Conferring is your chance to see these skills in action and to provide additional coaching when needed.

Fluency becomes an important path to comprehension during the early stage. As you listen to short segments of oral reading, you can nudge early readers toward longer phrasing, attention to punctuation, and reading with more expression. Character dialogue can also add a layer of interest and richness for early readers as they learn to match their own voice to the intonation they infer the characters in their stories might use.

As you confer with early readers, you'll want to be particularly vigilant and intentional with your language, keeping your desire to "help by pointing out" or "help by suggesting solutions" at bay. Being patient at the point of difficulty or point of error is a critical way to support the development of independent problem solving versus teacher dependence. If we jump in too quickly, readers won't be able to build their own capacity for recognizing when there's trouble, let alone choosing a strategic action to work things out. In *Who's Doing the Work?*, Jan Burkins and Kim Yaris (2016) recommend rather than immediately offering a solution, teachers can explore and encourage independence by asking, "What can you try?" In the critical work of learning how to read, it is vital that we do not do the heavy thinking work for our students. After all, when readers are doing the thinking, they are the ones doing the learning.

Readers will find an array of even more delightful and engaging text possibilities when they're reading in the early range (D–I). Often these texts, with their more entertaining story lines and compelling informational content, give readers more to think, talk, and write about than emergent texts did.

Readers at this stage can grow leaps and bounds by mastering the orchestration of meaning, structure, and visual information. With increased skills for problem solving, word solving, fluency, dialogue, and navigation of text features, early readers are not only positioned to read more complex texts but more importantly to joyfully engage in deeper levels of meaning-making as they do.

Take a minute to picture yourself pulling alongside a student like Tuan at the early stage of reading development. What thoughtful language choices will you make to help the reader build ever-increasing resilience and flexible problem-solving skills? What might you do to keep meaning-making as a central focus, even while helping the reader develop a growing repertoire of skills for tackling tricky words? How might you deepen your own understanding of how to best know and nurture readers in the early stage of reading development?

When readers are at the transitional stage: Conferring to integrate and strengthen strategies for comprehension and fluency.

When Ms. Frenkel sits down with Jeremy for a conference, it becomes clear through the conversation that he has confusions about what's really going on with the characters in his text. Whenever his teacher suspects a reader's meaning-making is suffering, she knows it is a call to look more deeply at reading process. Asking the student to read a bit of the text aloud is one way she can help herself do this. Jeremy chooses a page toward the beginning of his chapter and begins to read aloud. He reads accurately, problem solving a few tricky spots with relative ease. But, when Jeremy comes to a stretch of dialogue, Ms. Frenkel immediately notices something important. Here, his phrasing does not match either the punctuation or the line returns. He often runs the dialogue of one character into the next, not seeming to understand how to tell that someone new is talking. Ms. Frenkel realizes she has not shared any strategies for navigating dialogue with the whole class, and suddenly wonders how many other transitional readers might also be confused by these more complex passages in their texts.

The transitional stage is just as the name suggests, a bridge between early and truly fluent reading. It represents a time to firm up strategies for self-monitoring, strategic problem solving, fluency, and comprehension. Beginning chapter books are exciting new territory for many transitional readers, and early chapter series (Henry and Mudge, Houndsley and Catina, Amelia Bedelia, etc.) can serve as an ideal transition tool in this stage, keeping readers moving smoothly from one text to the next with the familiarity of favorite characters, settings, traits and situations, and structures.

But one size definitely does not fit all when it comes to conferring with transitional readers. They are extremely diverse in their development, and so each conference offers a prime opportunity to provide them with the personalized support they need. Without one-to-one conferring in this stage, teachable moments, like the one presented by Jeremy earlier, might go unnoticed. Figure 7.7 lists key considerations and some sample language that might help guide your reading process work with transitional readers.

Many transitional readers need support building skills for decoding and understanding multisyllabic words that they now encounter with greater frequency in their texts. Their self-selected texts provide many authentic opportunities to apply what they've learned in word study, working to efficiently recognize word parts and chunks, make analogies on the run, and use context clues to predict word meaning, to name a few. As you confer, you'll be able to both spot evidence of successful application and notice when students need more strategic word-solving support.

Because transitional readers are now doing much of their reading silently, it's not as easy to eavesdrop on reading process as it was in the earlier stages. So, exploring reading process with a transitional reader often starts with conversation intended to help gain insight into how well the reader understands what they're reading. If comprehension is strong, it's usually safe to assume that reading process is strong. But when you sense that something seems off with comprehension, you might decide to invite the student to read aloud from the current text to provide insights into what's possibly getting in the way of understanding.

As you listen to transitional readers read, watch to see that they use a balance of meaning, structure, and visual information; that they notice miscues affecting meaning; and that they start to problem-solve and make corrections closer to the point of error. Taking quick running records is a great way to do this. Also, we recommend listening for the kind of phrasing and intonation that contribute to understanding rather than detract from it, as with Jeremy in the previous example. With transitional readers, it is also important to pay attention to how readers help themselves when they encounter unknown multisyllabic words in print, as many of them might need support in extending their bag of tricks.

Figure 7.7
A Few Examples of Language to Support Transitional Readers

WONDER You may look for evidence to indicate the reader …	AFFIRM Language for noticing evidence of strategic action.	EXTEND Language for moving a reader toward strategic action.
Notices when meaning breaks down and works to repair.	"When something didn't sound quite right, you knew to stop and try out a couple strategies to figure it out."	"When something doesn't sound quite right, you can stop and try to work it out, using all that you know. Watch and listen as I show you how …"
Rereads the word, phrase, sentence, or passage to look to check, search, or confirm.	"You went back to the beginning of the paragraph to try to figure this out."	"When you lose your way, it's important to back up a bit and try to get back on track."
Flexibly uses a variety of strategies for solving multisyllabic words.	"Wow! You looked across that big word for chunks that could help you figure it out."	"When you come to a big, long word, you can help yourself by looking for chunks that look familiar. For instance, on this word …"
Retells narrative text, including characters, setting, problem, events, and resolution.	"When you talked about your book, you focused on the most important events that led up to the big problem your character has encountered."	"Once you've read one book in a series, you'll have already learned some important traits about the main character(s) that can help you predict how things might go in the next book."
Works to determine the meaning of unknown words through context.	"You helped yourself think what that word could mean by thinking about the words in the sentence around it."	"One way you can try to figure out what a word means is to think about words you already know that would also seem to make sense within the sentence. Listen while I do that in this sentence."
Regularly makes inferences to support comprehension.	"You've helped yourself understand things the author isn't telling you by paying careful attention to the sneaky actions of the character and by forming your own ideas about what he might be trying to do."	"The dialogue can help you make inferences about characters if you think about what they say to others and how they say it."

Because the needs of transitional readers can be so varied, teachers with lots of readers at this stage will want to be particularly attuned for patterns of need in order to inform both whole-group instruction and short-term strategy groups. For instance, as Ms. Frenkel from our previous example begins considering the challenges readers might encounter when they read extended dialogue passages, she becomes curious about who else would benefit from the same coaching Jeremy needs. Her wondering causes her to tune into dialogue more purposefully during her conferences with other transitional readers. This will help her decide whether Jeremy's needs are unique or whether she should offer a mini-lesson, a set of shared-reading lessons, or short-term small groups with strategies for reading dialogue as the focus.

The transitional stage is a time of helping readers become whole and confident in their ability to strategically tackle longer and more complex texts. Conferring offers the perfect chance to understand and address their unique differences.

Which readers in your classroom are in the transitional stage? What are some ways you might prepare yourself to meet their wide range of needs? How might you help yourself learn to balance listening to reading with engaging in comprehension conversations to get the information about both fluency and comprehension? How can you deepen your own understanding of how to best know and nurture readers in the transitional stage of reading development?

When readers are at the fluent stage: Conferring to support access to increasingly complex texts.

Coral reads fluently and accurately in O–P level texts (Clementine or Time Warp Trio series for example). But holding onto important ideas across longer chapters, and weaving them together as a whole, has proved challenging for her. As her teacher, Mr. Curry, sits down to confer with her, he notices Coral using a sticky note strategy he offered in a previous conference. "Coral, you're making a strategic choice to use a sticky note as a reminder to stop at the end of each chapter and jot down important thinking. I'm curious to know, what has seemed really important about this chapter so far?" Coral shakes her head slowly and says, "Well I'm not really sure. I feel like I was understanding it at first, but then toward the end I just got really confused."

"Noticing you've lost your way in your reading is an important step toward figuring things out," he says. Coral nods again. "So, what ideas do you have about how you could help yourself?" Coral begins to page back through the chapter.

"I could read it over again, I guess," she says, looking deflated by the idea.

"You could," her teacher agrees. "Rereading is one possible strategy, but you might not have to reread the whole chapter. May I show you a way to help yourself without rereading the entire chapter?"

Coral nods, looking a bit hopeful again. Mr. Curry begins to demonstrate as he talks. "If you can find the place where things were still making sense and where they started to get confusing, you may be able to help yourself by digging in there to take a closer look. I'll show how you can do that by sampling a part of a page and deciding if you were still understanding or not . . ."

Fluent readers have mastered the mechanics of reading at the earlier stages. They have internalized strategies for monitoring, self-correction, accuracy, and fluency, which free them up to focus on the deeper levels of comprehension that the content of their more complex texts requires. Fluent readers are often able to retell and identify key ideas, but they might still need support establishing new strategies for texts that include complex language, sentence structures, and text structures. For example, navigating a story line told from multiple points of view, following a complex passage of time (flashbacks/ flash-forwards), and synthesizing ideas from across an entire text are examples of possible focus for strategic reading process work with fluent readers.

Figure 7.8 provides several examples of content and language you might use to support fluent readers.

With readers at this stage of development, the primary signal that might direct you to focus more deeply on reading process is suspicion that something is off with comprehension.

As long as fluent readers seem to be doing lots of reading and readily understanding what the author has to say, it's likely safe to turn more of your attention to authentic response, which is the focus of the next chapter. Here, we work to help readers consider ways to insert more of themselves into the text through reflection, conversation, writing, or action. Much of this deeper meaning work encourages fluent readers to tackle straddling the two worlds of strategic process and authentic response.

As you think back to Coral, or other readers in the fluent stage with similar needs, what sort of plan might you make to support her reading development? What follow-up ideas would ensure that Coral becomes more strategic in her reading process? In what ways might you deepen your own understanding of the fluent stage of reading development in order to better know and nurture your readers?

What Are Some Tools and Tips to Support Strategic Process?

To add to the strength of your conferences focused on strategic reading process, we offer the following tools and tips:

- Listen to students read and learn to utilize a running record.

- Don't be too eager to assist or correct.

- Learn to initiate a comprehension conversation.

- Don't assume every confusion a reader encounters is a sign of trouble.

- Continue to build your own understanding of strategic reading process.

Figure 7.8
A Few Examples of Language to Support Fluent Readers

WONDER You may look for evidence to indicate the reader …	AFFIRM Language for noticing evidence of strategic action.	EXTEND Language for moving a reader toward strategic action.
Reads for meaning, noticing confusions and taking time to work them out.	"You noticed your own confusion, going back for clarification and reading forward to get more information."	"Whenever you notice yourself starting to feel confused, you can try both backing up to reread and moving forward, on the hunt for information to clear things up. Let me show you what I mean."
Uses a variety of vocabulary strategies to determine meanings of unknown words.	"When you weren't sure of that word, you went back to read and think about the sentences around it to give you more context for figuring it out."	"One thing you can do when you come to an unfamiliar word is to think about it in the context of the sentence or sentences around it. Give that a try to see whether it helps."
Thinks about the arc of the story in fiction or the big ideas and supports in nonfiction.	"You just mentioned one way the author resolved the big issue of the story."	"When readers come to the end of a story, one thing they do is think about one or more of the big issues and how the author chose to resolve those issues. For example …"
Demonstrates understanding of text through summarization, determining importance, identifying main idea and key details.	"You're using the section heading to help you figure out what's the most important point of each part."	"You can help yourself remember key ideas from each chapter by browsing through the headings and pictures again."
Adds thinking to the text through envisioning, predicting, inferring, and synthesis.	"You're thinking of the actions a character took as a result of something another character said, and by doing that you're able to help yourself make some important inferences that would have been easy to miss."	"When you're trying to more deeply understand a character, sometimes it can be helpful to think about why that character took action. Continuing to think about why a character is doing or saying certain things will help you understand their motivations in a deeper way."
Shows evidence of changed thinking from beginning to end of a text.	"You have been noticing how your own thinking about animals in captivity has changed from the beginning of this text until now."	"To tell about how your thinking has changed from the beginning of text until the end, you might try the sentence frame, 'At first I thought … but now … '"

Listen to students read and learn to utilize a running record.

Listening to even a minute or so of oral reading during a conference has the potential to provide a wealth of information about strategic reading process. While listening in, you can see for yourself what learning is being applied as a reader navigates a self-selected text.

The value of the time spent listening to oral reading can be multiplied by incorporating the use of a running record (Clay 1985), as well. A running record is a standardized form of notation that allows teachers to record observed behaviors while listening to oral reading. Much like a slow-motion replay, the running record allows us to come back for further analysis of the reading, to formulate theories about what strategic work is happening "on the run." A running record allows us to consider:

- How accurate is the child when reading the text?

- Does the child self-monitor, noticing and attempting to repair when things don't seem right?

- Does the child use a balance of cues from meaning, structure, and visual information?

- What does the child do at the point of error or difficulty? Do they ask for help, or do they work to solve the problem on their own?

Don't be too eager to assist or correct.

Every reader inevitably encounters challenges. And as Clay (1993, 2000, 2015) has highlighted, the point of difficulty is a rich source of information for the curious teacher. Thoughtful reading teachers heed this moment as a call to perk up and pay attention. What the reader does when they encounter a challenge tells us about strategic reading process, or what's going on inside that reader's head.

If we are patient, here is where we'll learn, *When things get hard, what does the reader do?* Rather than jumping in immediately to bail the reader out with directive strategies (check the picture, sound it out, look for chunks, go back to the beginning), our inquisitive thinking leads us to wait. Sitting on the edge of our seats, we're poised and eager to learn what the child will do.

Burkins and Yaris (2016) remind us of the power of asking process-focused questions (*What can you try? How can you help yourself? How did you do that?*) rather than jumping right in with more directive, problem-fixing focused prompts. When a child stops, appeals, or seems to need some kind of nudge, a prompt like, "What can you try?" is powerful in its simplicity, calling on the child to reach into their own store of strategies to reveal what previous teaching has (or has not) stuck—which, in turn, helps us to know what future teaching we might consider. For instance, if, when asked "What could you try?" a child consistently responds by saying, "Sound it out?" You might infer that "sound it out" is the child's go-to strategy at the point of difficulty and that they will likely benefit from being introduced to other, more efficient strategies, as well.

Learn to initiate a comprehension conversation.

Some teachers who are new to conferring worry they won't know how to carry on a productive conversation with students about texts that they themselves have not read. But conversations in conferences aren't intended as quizzes about literal facts or details, requiring you to judge responses as correct or incorrect. Nor do you want them to become long, laborious retellings of every detail of the text. Instead, the goal of these reader-focused conversations is to get readers talking in ways that reveal their thinking process. In the end, we want to discover not only what specific meaning they are making but also how they are making meaning of the text. A student's thinking is neither right nor wrong. As Barnhouse and Vinton remind us, "Our goal, after all, is to teach the process of meaning making, not to direct students to a particular meaning" (2012, 65). So, some of our open-ended questions will be aimed at understanding what meaning the child is deriving from the text and some will be aimed more at understanding how the child is helping himself to make this meaning. Figure 7.9 provides some examples of both types of questions, so you can see the important differences.

Don't assume every confusion a reader encounters is a sign of trouble.

When it comes to active meaning-making, there are two very different types of confusion that readers experience. The first is the disorientation that comes with losing your way in understanding the text. This can happen when readers let their minds wander, because there were words or phrases they didn't understand, because they skipped important information, or because they simply misread something. Confusion caused by disorientation requires readers to recognize that the comprehension train is veering off the tracks, to

Figure 7.9

Examples of Questions that Reveal the What and How of Meaning-Making

Examples of Questions to Reveal What Meaning the Reader Is Making of the Text	Examples of Questions to Reveal How the Reader Is Making Meaning
How would you explain what you just read? What's important to know about the characters in this book? What seems like the big idea of this section? What have you been thinking about as you read this part? What predictions are you making? What questions do you have?	How did you figure that out? What did you read that made you say that? How did you help yourself decide what was most important here? How did you come to that thinking? How did you help yourself make that prediction? How are you helping yourself look for answers?

put on the brakes, and take time to go back and work until they understand their reading.

The second type of confusion is puzzlement. Puzzlement is a healthy awareness readers have of their own wondering and uncertainty about certain things as they read. Authors often plant the seeds of curiosity or puzzlement in intentional ways—sometimes even in the first line or two of a text or chapter to grab the reader's attention—as a mechanism to hook them in and move them forward. In this case, readers may start to become curious about decisions an author made. They may start to ponder things such as, *What will happen? Who is that strange man in the window? Where did the girl get the locket in the first place?* Puzzlement can often lead to high levels of engagement.

Understanding the difference between confusion caused by disorientation and confusion related to puzzlement is essential. Working out disorientation usually requires going back, while working out puzzlement often requires moving forward. Figure 7.10 offers a few examples of what disorientation and puzzlement may look like in a conference.

Figure 7.10
Examples of Disorientation Versus Puzzlement

Examples of Disorientation	Examples of Puzzlement
When a reader retells a certain part of a story and clearly misunderstands the author's writing. When a reader's mind wanders away from the story while reading. When a reader recognizes that they do not know or understand what they just read.	When a reader is unsure of why a character did or said something but knows she needs to read on to learn more information. When the author writes a twist in the story and the reader is not sure of what to make of it yet. When the author intentionally leaves some information out of the story so the reader needs to ponder further.

Continue to build your own understanding of strategic reading process.

We end the chapter where we began, with humility and caution. This chapter is just a toe dip in the ocean of strategic reading process. Deep understanding of strategic reading process is far beyond the scope of this text. This type of expertise evolves over the whole career of a reading teacher, through professional development, professional reading, coaching, and experience working with students. Building these skills not only enhances our work with individual readers in the conference but strengthens our instruction in small group and whole group as well. Committing to confer to learn involves continually deepening your knowledge of how our kids learn to read. Figure 7.11 lists helpful texts that have stretched our thinking and informed our practice with regard to strategic reading process.

Strategic Process Conferring Reference

We've provided the Strategic Process Conferring Reference (Figure 7.12) to help you systematically know and nurture readers in the direction of strategic process. Again, remember, this is not a conferring to-do list. Rather, we offer it simply as a starting point to support you as you set out to use Wonder, Affirm, Extend, and Remind to strengthen the strategic process of your readers.

Figure 7.11
Texts to Help You Grow Your Understanding of Strategic Reading Process

Becoming Literate: The Construction of Inner Control (Updated ed.)	Marie M. Clay Heinemann (2015)
The Fountas and Pinnell Literacy Continuum: A Tool for Assessment, Planning, and Teaching, PreK–8 (Expanded ed.)	Irene C. Fountas and Gay Su Pinnell Heinemann (2016)
Teaching for Comprehending and Fluency: Thinking, Talking, and Writing About Reading, K–8	Irene C. Fountas and Gay Su Pinnell Heinemann (2006)
Strategies That Work: Teaching for Comprehension and Engagement (3rd ed.)	Stephanie Harvey and Anne Goudvis Stenhouse (2017)
The Literacy Teacher's Playbook, Grades K–2: Four Steps for Turning Assessment Data into Goal-Directed Instruction	Jennifer Serravallo Heinemann (2014)
The Literacy Teacher's Playbook, Grades 3–6: Four Steps for Turning Assessment Data into Goal-Directed Instruction	Jennifer Serravallo Heinemann (2013)
Catching Readers Before They Fall: Supporting Readers Who Struggle, K–4	Pat Johnson and Katie Keier Stenhouse (2010)
Preventing Misguided Reading: New Strategies for Guided Reading Teachers	Jan M. Burkins and Melody M. Croft International Reading Association and Corwin (2010)
Who's Doing the Work? How to Say Less So Readers Can Do More	Jan M. Burkins and Kim Yaris Stenhouse (2016)
Still Learning to Read: Teaching Students in Grades 3–6 (2nd ed.)	Franki Sibberson and Karen Szymusiak Stenhouse (2016)

Figure 7.12
Strategic Process Conferring Reference

ESSENTIAL QUESTION:
What strategic actions is the reader taking to solve problems and make meaning of the text?

Does the reader rely on themself as a problem-solver while reading?

- Pay attention, noticing when something's not right.
- When something doesn't seem right, spend time trying to work it out.
- Use a variety of strategies learned to make the most of the text.
- Flexibly try more than one strategy at the point of difficulty or confusion.

Does the reader utilize information from a range of sources?

- Use the picture and the context to think what would make sense.
- Consider the sound of the sentence to decide what would sound right.
- Look carefully within the word for clues about what would look right.
- Reread to clear up confusions, to get more information, and to confirm.

Does the reader demonstrate fluency in ways that indicate a focus on understanding?

- Read at a comfortable speed, not too fast and not too slow.
- Use expression to make reading sound like talking.
- Read in smooth phrases, pausing appropriately for punctuation.

Does the reader draw on a variety of strategies to maximize meaning-making in the text?

- Notice when he or she starts to lose track of meaning and work to get back on track.
- Use the text to retell and/or summarize, capturing big ideas and key details.
- Connect actions, events, and dialogue in the text to make meaning.
- Synthesize information and ideas from across the text (actions, events, and dialogue) to understand the big ideas?
- Use what they know about how texts are constructed to better understand and evaluate the text.

Just as before, if it seems right for you, we invite you to print this list for quick reference. To make it even more accessible, the information from Figure 7.12 has also been included as one of four quadrants in the Four Square Conferring Reference in Appendix C. This tool is designed as a quick, on-the-go support and includes a quadrant for each of the possible

8

confer to support
authentic response

To know and nurture readers in the direction of authentic response is to help them do the things that readers in the world outside of school naturally do in response to reading: think, feel, question, wonder, talk, and take action as growing readers and deep-thinking, contributing citizens of the world. To inform your work in the direction of authentic response we offer the following essential question:

How is the reader using reflection, connection,
or action in authentic ways?

Take a moment to reflect on your own reading life. As adults with thriving reading lives, we find ourselves responding to reading in countless ways. We laugh. We cry. We are affirmed by recognizing our own human struggles in a story. We are inspired by the courage of others, and therefore become a bit braver as we respond to our own circumstances. We may experience a renewed sense of optimism about the good in the world or we may experience the opposite. We become more well-informed about steps we might take to make the world a better place. We are called to action; now that we *know something,* we must *do something.* We feel compelled to share with a colleague, a friend, a neighbor. We feel the urge to write to someone or about something. We might go online and write a review. We organize what

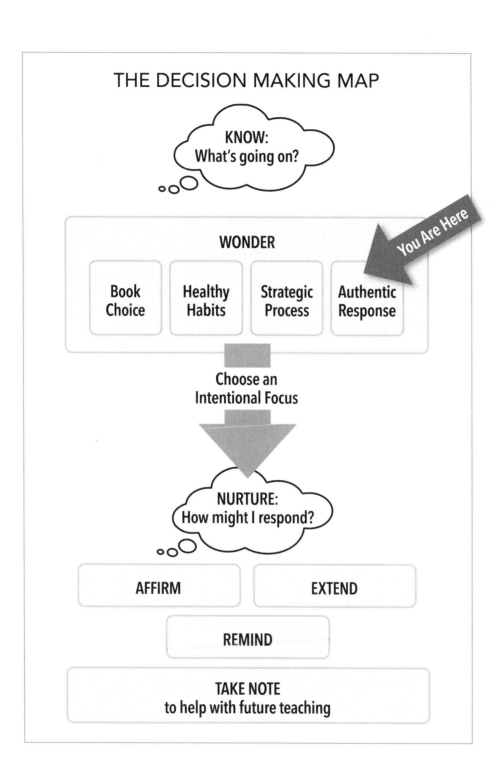

we've read into summary notes for ourselves or for others, synthesizing a longer text into its most important ideas. We feel a new sense of empathy and understanding for those whose lives we've not previously understood. We fall in love with an author or become engrossed with a new topic. We start a new series and feel the frantic compulsion to find the next book and the next. Sometimes we even decide to go right back to the beginning of a book and start again. Each reading experience influences the next.

Texts affect readers—triggering thinking, stirring up emotion, creating the desire for connection or further exploration, or calling us to action. So, when you confer to support authentic reading response, you partner with your readers toward finding deeper, more meaningful ways of recognizing and exploring the thoughts and feelings they've had as a result of the texts they've chosen to read. Authentic response goes far beyond basic comprehension to a focus on how the text has changed us as readers and as people. We do this through:

- **Reflection**—Looking within to notice and name our own thinking and feeling:

    - "I felt like I was going to cry when the kids just kept being so mean to her. She was so sad and alone, and it really made me think a lot about all the kids at school that probably feel that way sometimes."

    - "I can't stop thinking about Thomas Edison and how persistent he was when things didn't work out. He tried like a thousand times before he figured out the light bulb. Just knowing that makes me feel like I could go on trying things even when they don't work out at first."

    - "I'm wondering a little bit more about why the animals in the forest are not accepting Roz the Robot. I'm thinking that Roz is different from them and that sometimes people are afraid of what's different than them, so it's kind of how the animals are responding. I think that's why Peter Brown wrote it that way."

- **Connection**—Reaching out to connect with other readers about what we've read, both within and beyond the classroom walls:

  - "I can't wait to tell Alicia about Owl Diaries. I think she's going to love them because she loves books about friend adventures. There's a whole series, so I'm going to see if she wants to read some at the same time."

  - "For sure I'm going to make a video recommendation for this book. If I make a QR code to put on the back cover, I think a whole bunch of kids will want to check it out and decide to read it."

  - "After reading about the main character and the struggles she had with her mom, it made me so grateful and even more connected to my own mom. I'm going to tell her that after school today."

- **Taking action**—Deciding to do something because of what we've read (more reading, research, advocacy, lifestyle changes, etc.):

  - "I've been reading this book about volcanoes, and it has a part about how you could make a volcano experiment of your own. I'm going ask my dad to help me do it at home, and if it works out, I might bring it to school so I can teach some other kids in the class about what I've learned and show them what I made."

  - "This book helped me learn a lot about frogs. I still have questions though. So, I'm going to check out a few more books about frogs at the library."

  - "Trent and I are thinking of making some signs for our lunchroom to remind kids to include everyone. We don't want kids in our school to feel like the lunchroom is the loneliest place on earth like Lucinda did in the book."

Although authentic response can take many forms, they all start with having a text that calls us to respond.

Why Does Authentic Response Matter?

Authentic response is so much more than simply wanting to hold students accountable for proving to us that they've read by assigning comprehension questions, book reports, or reading logs. As Kylene Beers and Robert Probst state so beautifully in *Disrupting Thinking*, "Skills are important. But if we aren't reading and writing so that we can grow, so that we can discover, so that we can change—change our thinking, change ourselves, perhaps change the world—then those skills will be for naught" (2017, 20). Authentic response is an outcome of the connection between the reader and the text. And although it starts with understanding what the text says, it goes further to include deeper layers of thinking about how its meaning affects us and what we might do as a result. And, of course, when it comes to authentic response, one size does not fit all. How each reader is affected determines how each reader might respond.

Our heartfelt wish for every reader is that the emphasis is on the reader's experience with the text rather than on their completion of assignments about the reading. Response to reading will not always require a pencil and paper and definitely won't come from completing packets and worksheets or creating a diorama of the setting. We also hope response is not narrowly considered as the writing students do in a composition book labeled *reader's response* or *reader's notebook*. The most heartfelt responses to reading happen *because we have been affected* by what we've read, not because we are assigned to prove that we have read. We advocate for reading responses that mirror responses to reading that happen in the world outside of school.

In his meta-analysis of research around free voluntary reading, or what we call independent choice reading, Stephen Krashen found that these compliance-based activities, such as vocabulary worksheets or comprehension quizzes, do not have a positive effect on students' comprehension, vocabulary development, or engagement in reading (Krashen 2004). In other words, the most meaningful responses are reader driven, not teacher assigned. Examples of reader-driven responses might include approaching a friend who has already read the book to discuss something one of the characters did or said, choosing to abandon the book because it is just not appealing or worthwhile for right now, or deciding to write to a local government representative after reading an editorial about something happening in the community. The quality of what a reader reads has everything to do with the quality of the reader's response and the options available within the classroom.

Once a text is chosen, a reader's first response is often to decide whether the text is worthy of their time and effort. When a reader can't wait to turn the page or doesn't want to put the book down, an authentic response to reading is taking place. This response is the hook all readers seek. A worthy text keeps the experience grounded in every author's ultimate purpose—to somehow affect the reader.

Choosing to focus our conferring in the direction of authentic response, working to nudge the reader toward more awareness, connection or action, is crucial at every age and stage of development. But, for fluent readers, who are regularly finding worthy books and accumulating lots of reading minutes, we'll likely find ourselves focusing on response in many if not most of our conferences. Because of the complexity of the texts that fluent readers choose and their ever-evolving repertoire of skills for conversation and writing, the depth and complexity of their responses will be qualitatively different from readers in the beginning stages of reading.

That said, we want to emphasize that reading response is not something we reserve for once the skills are in place. It is not an outcome to be pursued only after the last page has been read. Rather, it is at the heart of every meaningful reading experience, woven throughout, and serving as a motivation that keeps us moving forward.

Signs a Reader Might Benefit from a Conference Focused on Authentic Response

---

Essential question:
How is the reader using reflection, connection,
or action in authentic ways?

Even when readers need continued support with book choice, healthy habits, and strategic process, a focus on authentic response will play a critical role in strengthening the experience of every reader. Response, after all, is the reason for reading. We don't just read to make meaning of the text, we read to make meaning of ourselves and the world around us. Examples of when we might choose authentic response as the intentional focus of the conference include:

- To help readers show visible excitement about their reading.

- To help readers when they've developed misconceptions about the purpose of reading.

- To help readers pay closer attention to their own responses to the text.

- To help readers make meaningful connections with other readers.

- To help readers consider or plan for next steps.

When readers are showing visible excitement about their reading.

Imani is obviously loving Funny Girl. Funniest. Stories. Ever. *by Betsy Bird (2017). She quietly giggles as she turns the pages and sometimes even laughs out loud! Now is the perfect time for Imani's teacher, Ms. Norris, to offer a conference focused on authentic response. Imani will definitely have a lot to say about this book, and Ms. Norris sees an opportunity to build on her excitement, helping her to name ways to extend and build on it in future reading. She sits down with Imani to learn more about her experience with this text that is so obviously delighting her.*

Think about a time you saw a student laugh out loud while reading. How about a time when you asked the class to put their books away, but some students just couldn't pry themselves away from their reading? Or, when a student was bursting at the seams to talk about their book because it sparked something inside of them? These are moments to notice, affirm, and capitalize on as conferring teachers. Remember, conferring doesn't have to be focused on fixing something. Some conferences directed toward response will simply focus on pointing out to readers that the way they are responding to their reading in that moment is authentic and important, possibly nudging them to dig deeper and perhaps push their thinking a little about what the author has done to make this text work this way for them. In *Mindsets and Moves*, Gravity Goldberg (2016) encourages us to show students what they are doing well as readers so that they continue to do it. She calls this being a mirror. We want to be a mirror especially when students are excited about their reading and giving authentic responses, affirming what we see in ways that help students build on it. How might you support Imani by mirroring back what she is doing in order to help her recognize and build on it?

When readers have developed misconceptions about the purpose of reading.

Jacques is new to his classroom. On his first day, his teacher, Ms. Gupta, sits down with him to learn more about his past reading experiences. Jacques quickly reveals that points earned through computerized comprehension quizzes have been the driving factor behind his past book choices. He tells her that he usually looks for shorter books worth one or two points because they are easier, and he can get points more quickly that way. Ms. Gupta immediately realizes she has an opportunity to help him see a more authentic purpose for reading, one bigger than simply earning points or passing quizzes.

In this age of efficiency and competition, some of our students have developed misguided ideas about reading. Some believe that reading is about finishing the book as fast as they can, reading the most pages, getting the most points, or getting through as many books as possible in the time allotted. In many cases, readers who race through their texts have had their ideas about reading heavily influenced by external rewards or competitions of some kind.

It's our job to help students like Jacques revise their ideas about why we read: shifting from a sole focus on quantity (how many pages, words, books, levels, minutes) to quality (What's going on inside of me as I read this book? What does it mean? Why does it matter? How am I stretching myself to grow as a reader?). The conferring we do with competition-focused readers will often begin with simple encouragement or permission to slow down and take time to really process and enjoy what's being read. They'll also likely benefit from being helped to discover the ways readers reach out and connect with other readers as a result of what they've experienced in a book, as opposed to a focus on "passing the test" or "getting the points." We need to promise these kids (and make sure our words, actions, and environment support the idea) that reading is not a race or competition. It is not something we do to earn rewards, points, or a prize. Instead, reading is a gift we give ourselves to make our lives better.

As you think about Jacques, what next steps might you consider? What previous experiences might have contributed to his misguided ideas, and how might you safeguard against reinforcing these? In what ways might you support him in redefining these ideas about what it means to be a reader?

To help readers pay closer attention to their own responses to the text.

Michelle easily finds books and is happy to take recommendations from other readers, often choosing to read what her friends have read before her. In the past, Michelle has shown a basic understanding of her books; yet, her conversations have typically focused around a simple retell of the events unfolding. After a recent mini-lesson demonstrating how to use sticky notes as a tool to capture important thinking in texts, Michelle's teacher, Mr. Washington, notices Michelle has been filling her latest book with so many notes it seems unlikely she'd be able to prioritize or make sense of all of them.

As he sits down to confer, Mr. Washington reads some of these notes and notices a familiar pattern. Much like her conversations about text, the writing Michelle is spending so much precious reading time doing is mostly a direct retell of the story line, without much evidence of her own thinking at all. Both her conversation and her notes seem to indicate that Michelle is skimming along on the surface, unsure how to dig into the deeper layers of her thinking as she reads. Mr. Washington realizes that it's time to confer with Michelle in the direction of authentic response. Helping Michelle become a reader who slows down to insert and examine her own thinking in response to a text isn't likely to happen in one quick conference, but Mr. Washington is excited to make a plan. He jots a few notes for himself and decides to connect with a respected colleague next door to do some brainstorming about this big work he wants to help Michelle tackle.

Our classrooms are full of readers at different levels and experiences who can benefit from our support in learning to discover deeper layers of the texts they are reading and what those deeper layers mean for them and our larger world as a whole. From the youngest readers, who might benefit from learning to more thoughtfully study illustrations and photographs, to older readers, whose reading lives can be transformed by learning strategies for reading texts more closely and critically, working to uncover the deeper layers of a text is a cornerstone of authentic response. Often this work includes helping readers to slow down in some way so they can be more aware and reflective, not only about what the author wrote but also about the deeper thinking behind the author's words and why the author may have chosen this course in their writing. Even more importantly, how has the writing affected the reader's thoughts and feelings? Here are just a few examples of questions that might support readers to dig deeper into their thinking about a text:

- How did what you just read make you think or feel?

- Are there any words (phrases, sentences, ideas, lessons) that you want to carry with you after the book is done?

- What is changing about your thinking as you read?

- Think a little more about what you just read. What is some of your thinking that might be worth talking about with others?

- Why do you think the author decided to include this? Why else? Is there a deeper reason?

- What do you find yourself wondering about as you read? What do you suppose you might keep thinking about even after you've finished reading?

This list is just a sampling of possibilities, of course. If you feel unsure about how to help readers go deeper into their thoughts and feelings around a text, you're not alone. We both know this is an area in which we need to continually push ourselves to grow. Luckily, there has been much written on this topic, and if you're ready to learn more, you might check out some of the titles provided at the end of this chapter.

Some students will also benefit from encouragement to tune in more closely to their own responses, to really notice what's going on inside of them as they read. Some language you might use to extend or remind readers of this include:

- Readers notice when they are confused and take the time to go back and try to sort things out.

- Reading isn't about racing through or getting to the end. It's about noticing as much as you can along the way and noticing how it makes you feel.

- It's okay to linger, laugh, and feel big feelings.

- Sometimes we completely disagree with the author and decide to keep reading a text anyway. Taking time to consider ideas different from our own is important.

- The places in a text in which we have big thoughts and feelings can give us clues about what's worth coming back to think, talk, or write about.

Take a moment to think back to Michelle. Imagine you are the trusted colleague Mr. Washington comes to for a collaborative conversation about Michelle's responses. What are some ideas you may suggest for him? How might you support him in his thinking of how to best support Michelle?

To help readers make meaningful connections with other readers.

During a conference with Carmine, his teacher, Ms. Nguyen, notices his high level of engagement with his current book, and smiles at the insightful thinking Carmine shares. In addition to naming what Carmine is doing well in this moment, Ms. Nguyen encourages Carmine to think about ways he might share his excitement about this book with other readers. Carmine is leery of doing a traditional book talk in front of the whole class, but luckily for him, he's in a classroom that offers many meaningful opportunities for readers to connect with one another—both within and beyond the classroom walls. After giving it some thought, Carmine decides he'd like to create and post a video trailer for his book on the class blog. His teacher offers a few suggestions to extend this thinking, including making a QR code of the trailer to attach to the inside cover of the book after he creates the trailer, or, writing a short recommendation to tape to the inside back cover of the book.

In thriving reading communities, readers are committed to both sharing and seeking the recommendations of other readers. And the more authentic opportunities our classrooms offer for readers to reflect, connect, and respond, the more likely it is that they will thrive not only as individuals but also as a true community of readers. Figure 8.1 provides a list of ideas to help you create and extend possibilities for meaningful interaction around books in your classroom.

Opportunities such as those in Figure 8.1 are just a few examples of the many ways we can nurture a true community of readers in our classrooms. By using drawings and a few simple words from their books, even beginning readers can begin to make meaningful recommendations to other readers. By creating opportunities like these, we let students do what readers in the world outside of the classroom authentically do: reach out and connect with others in order to extend and deepen the reading experience. Even once we have these structures embedded in our classrooms, some students will be more comfortable or adept at making use of them than others will be. Some may need more scaffolding or support. The conference is the perfect place to give that extra coaching or preparation that some students might need to expand their own sense of what is possible in connecting with other readers. Figure 8.2 shows examples of how we might support a reader in a conference in this way.

Figure 8.1
Some Ways Readers Might Respond to Their Texts

Seek recommendations within and beyond the classroom

Draw a picture to tell or teach about the text

Participate in book talks: whole class, small group, partner, digital

Participate in partner or book club discussions

Talk informally about books and other texts read throughout the entire school day

Write reviews to be displayed on the walls or in the library

Write reviews to be shared digitally on a blog, a shared document, or other digital tools

Leave thoughts and recommendations on sticky notes inside book covers or on baskets or shelves for other readers

Tape QR codes inside book covers that lead to video trailers, audio reviews, or written recommendations

Use designated shelves or baskets for showcasing favorite reads

Use writing, conversation, video, or audio to teach about something being studied

Use writing, conversation, video, or audio aimed at persuading others to make a change

Use research, writing, or conversation to continue exploration of the topic

Take a moment to think about the readers in your classroom. What options have you highlighted as invitations for response? How do your readers give and get support from each other in finding one great read after another? We bet you have a few students similar to Carmine: engagement is high while reading, but shyness or a slight fear of speaking in front of others may discourage them from sharing books with others. What are some methods that may work to encourage those students to share their reading experiences with others? What might you try?

To help readers consider or plan for next steps.

*Rashad has just finished a book on the Civil War,
a topic that fascinates him. As he talks about
the book with his teacher, Ms. Duncan, in a*

Figure 8.2
Examples of How We Might Support Authentic Response in a Conference

If you observe the student . . .	You might confer to support . . .
Is struggling to make effective use of partner time	Planning for what is important to share with a reading buddy and how
Tends to retell the whole story in a book talk without adding additional thoughts or feelings	Prioritizing what seems most important to share about a text and writing a few simple notes to prepare
Can't decide what to say in a reading partnership, club, or book talk	Sorting through sticky note jots to select those most worthy of conversation or writing
Doesn't seem to be interested or motivated by a particular format for connection	A new option for providing review or recommendation
Is very shy and hesitant to participate in a book club conversation	Encouraging the student to initiate a book partnership instead
Has trouble getting started with writing a recommendation or review	Talking it out first, using the conversation of the conference as oral rehearsal for writing

conference, he says he's really bummed that it's finished. Although he's read other books on the same topic, this particular text was by far his favorite, both because of what he learned and because of how it made him feel like he was right there experiencing the conflict firsthand. Rather than encouraging Rashad to rush on to find a new book, his teacher decides to use the conference to share some ways readers can linger in a beloved book, extending the experience after they've reached the last page.

Whenever we finish or are deeply moved by a book, we are faced with a decision: What now? What will I do as a result of having read this book? Think more about it? Read it again? Tell someone about it? Write about it? The more powerful our experience with the text, the more thoughtful and important the response is likely to be. So, as we confer with readers, we note those texts that have been especially meaningful to our students and confer with them to plan for next steps. The support we provide here might fall on a continuum from simple suggestions to more specific guidance as students makes concrete plans for their response. You might help students consider any of the following options:

- Spend more time with the text itself.

  ○ Reread parts or all of the text, taking notes about strong thinking or feelings.

  ○ Spend time analyzing text features, such as charts, diagrams, and photos.

  ○ Look more closely at the craft moves and structures within the book. Determine what the author did to stir up strong feelings.

- Make a plan to connect with others.

  ○ Who else might like to know about this book?

  ○ How could you share your thinking about this book: verbally, in writing, or digitally?

  ○ Is there someone to talk to who has also read it?

- Write.

  ○ Review sticky notes or notebook entries to select those that might be worthy of writing more about.

  ○ Use a combination of words and sketches to capture big ideas and thinking from the book.

  ○ Write a review or a book talk.

- Recognize a call to action and plan manageable steps.

  ○ Read more on the topic.

  ○ Persuade others to do something.

- ○ Write or do something that can deepen the experience.

- ○ Become involved to help or create change inspired by the text.

Many times, in the busy reading classroom, our students may feel limited or uncertain when it comes to choosing next steps. Of course, ultimately, we want students to spend most of their time reading. Response should add to the reading experience, not replace it. Occasionally, the next step a child considers takes them too far away from reading or for too long. For instance, if Rashad had decided he wanted to recreate a three-dimensional battle scene, his teacher might have helped him think about how to carry out that response outside of the reading classroom.

As you reflect on your current practice, take time to consider whether there is room for students to linger a bit at the end of a particularly meaningful text. What are some ways you may approach a conference with Rashad? You know you want to help him find a way to deepen his experience with this beloved book but not replace valuable reading time with an activity that should be completed outside of the reading classroom.

What Are Some Important Tools and Tips to Support Authentic Response?

Conferring with an intentional focus on response is rich and rewarding work, but work that can sometimes feel more unfamiliar or challenging than conferring in some of the other areas. So, to help you strengthen your conferences aimed in this direction we offer the tools and tips below.

- Rely on read-aloud as an opportunity to model authentic responses to reading.

- Value and support internal responses as well as external responses.

- Leverage reading, thinking, speaking, and writing as connected processes.

- Provide a menu of options for response.

- Be a reader yourself.

- Continue to build your understanding of authentic response.

Rely on read-aloud as an opportunity to model authentic responses to reading.

Whether our students were lucky enough to be read to at home before starting school or whether their first read-aloud experiences happened inside the school walls, authentic response begins when students are able to experience the full wonder of a text read by a more capable other. A toddler shrieks with delight at her mother's reading of the farm animal book, responding to every single sound with an attempt to imitate, begging immediately, "More! More!" when the mother reaches the last page of the book. A preschooler holds their breath in fearful anticipation when the mother in *Owl Babies* is gone too long; the connection to the emotion of separation and longing are so relevant and raw. The kindergarten teacher reads *The Very Hungry Caterpillar*, which leads to a barrage of questions about the life cycle of a butterfly, which leads to a hunt for informational texts at the library, which leads to more reading, more conversation, and some students deciding to write about the topic. The first-grade teacher reads *Our Class Is Going Green*, which leads students to initiate a recycling effort in their school. These first experiences with books read by others are the birthplace of authentic response for young readers.

The read-aloud is such a powerful platform for teaching reading response because all students, regardless of reading stage, have the opportunity to observe (as you model) and engage in thinking and conversation around a rich and worthy text. Read-alouds provide a platform for modeling and scaffolding a full range of reader response options from simple reflection to taking action in some way.

During the read-aloud, we can model our internal responses by thinking and feeling aloud; we can demonstrate how readers reach out to other readers through conversation; we can demonstrate jotting important notes to ourselves about the things we want to come back to for more thinking, conversation, or writing; and we can even demonstrate step-by-step how we might construct a book talk about a favorite read-aloud. As we model authentic response during read-aloud, we actively work to draw attention to the fact that what we're doing is something students can replicate in their own reading, time and time again. Figure 8.3 provides sample language that you might use during read-aloud to support authentic response.

Figure 8.3
Sample Language to Support Authentic Response During Read-Aloud

When	Example Language to Support Authentic Response
Before read-aloud	"To help myself get ready to read, I'm going to _____" "Listen as I get myself thinking about _____."
During read-aloud	"What's worth talking about so far?" "Did you notice how this part changed my thinking? Listen as I keep going." "I'm realizing this is making me feel _____." "Wow! I just have to read this part again–the way the author has said this is helping me to think about _____."
After read-aloud	"This book has given me so much to think about. I'm going to take some time to take a picture-walk back through it, helping myself remember and deepen my thinking." "I just _____. As you read, this is something you might want to try." "I'm so excited about this book. I think I have to let others know about it. I'm going to start by thinking about my audience and choose the format I think would work best for a recommendation."

Value and support internal responses as well as external responses.

The first thing that comes to mind for many teachers when they hear reader response is the outward signs of response, the things readers say, write, and do as a result of having read. But, as you confer with readers focusing on response, we urge you to nurture internal responses as well. Internal responses include the silent and invisible thoughts, feelings, and wonderings that go on inside a reader's head and heart. Meaningful internal response forms the basis for more thoughtful external response, such as conversation, writing, or taking action. Without the external response, of course, we won't know what readers are thinking or feeling or how their texts are changing them. Yet, the quality of the external response depends on the internal response. But for many students, the external response is just the tip of the iceberg compared to the internal response. *Therefore*, we need to help students become increasingly metacognitive with regard to how the text affects them, even as they learn how to express these responses externally.

A few examples of conferring language to support this idea with students might include:

- *Take your time with your thinking. This is an important process that you should not rush.*

- *Please feel comfortable to say exactly what you're thinking. There is no wrong way to communicate your thoughts.*

- *Consider jotting a few words that are in your head. You can always cross them out or come back to them later.*

- *During your reading, periodically stop and take note of what you're thinking.*

Leverage reading, thinking, speaking, and writing as connected processes.

Reading strengthens thinking. Thinking strengthens our conversation with others. These conversations, in turn, strengthen and stretch our thinking some more. And, on one hand, conversation with others can help us prepare for writing; however, on the other hand, writing can prepare us for conversation with others as well. So, weaving deep and authentic reading response into the fabric of our classrooms requires a rich combination of opportunities for reading, writing, thinking, and speaking.

In some classrooms, conversation and informal talk between readers are not valued as much as other forms of response. But, when we stretch ourselves to make more time for purposeful student talk in the classroom, we are taking a critical step toward helping readers deepen understanding and potentially grow their thinking and improve their writing. Conversation supports our students in discovering, revising, and extending their thinking about texts in ways they might not be able to on their own. As they engage in dialogue with others, their ideas expand and evolve. Reading, thinking, talking, and writing are connected and inseparable processes. The connectedness of all four work together to enhance the quality of response.

Provide a menu of options for response.

Choice matters as much with response as it does with books and habits. Different students will want to connect with others about their reading experiences in different ways. So we provide a wide array of options that allow students to deepen their transactions with texts through reflection, connection, and action (Rosenblatt 1987). This can be accomplished by working with your students to gradually introduce options, creating a menu or an anchor chart as you go. This tool will remind students of the many available options for responding to reading in your classroom community, and when new possibilities surface, they can be easily added. Figure 8.4 shows an anchor chart Christina uses in her fifth-grade classroom. The chart was created over time with students as new options for response were introduced. While this particular chart was created with fifth graders, similar charts can be created with readers of any age as a classroom reference.

Be a reader yourself.

To recalibrate your thinking about reader response, you may want to start by reflecting on the ways you respond in your own reading life. As you do this, consider the differences in how you respond to fiction versus informational texts and how you respond to texts that you choose for yourself versus those that are assigned to you by others. You'll also want to think about ways in which you talk with others about books or news articles. Think about a time when reading something prompted you to action—maybe you just had to rush to the store to buy certain ingredients after reading an article in a cooking blog or you might have written a response to someone's viewpoint on a social media platform. Also, consider how you choose your next piece of reading material—sometimes you might intentionally seek out something similar to what you just read. Other times, you may choose something different. When you authentically respond as a reader, we bet you rarely, if ever, write a book report based on someone else's guidelines, make a diorama with found objects, or use clay to create a sculpture of the main character. Because these responses are not authentic and simply wouldn't happen in the world outside of school, why would we ever ask such things of our students? Being readers ourselves and paying close attention to how we authentically respond is an essential starting point as we work to bring the gift of authentic response to the readers in our classrooms.

Continue to build your understanding of authentic response.

To delve more deeply into supporting students with authentic response to reading, we suggest the texts in Figure 8.5. These are texts that have had a profound impact on our own thinking and practice with regard to supporting authentic response with independent choice reading and developing a true community of readers within the classroom.

Figure 8.4
Anchor Chart Showing Options for Authentic Response

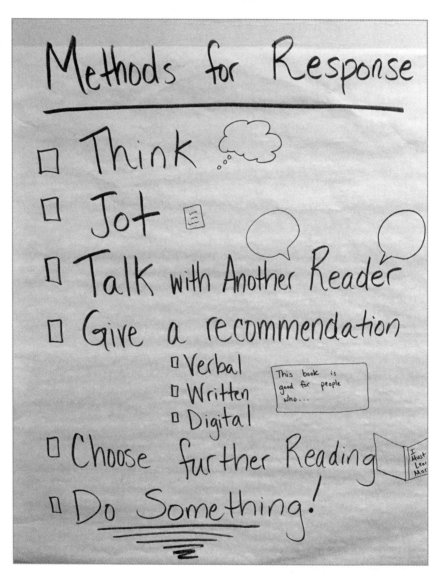

Figure 8.5
Texts to Help You Grow Your Understanding of Authentic Reader Response

What Readers Really Do: Teaching the Process of Meaning Making	Dorothy J. Barnhouse and Vicki Vinton Heinemann (2012)
Disrupting Thinking: Why How We Read Matters	Kylene Beers and Robert E. Probst Scholastic (2017)
Notice and Note: Strategies for Close Reading	Kylene Beers and Robert E. Probst Heinemann (2012)
Reading Nonfiction: Notice and Note Stances, Signposts, and Strategies	Kylene Beers and Robert E. Probst Heinemann (2015)
Reading for Real: Teaching Students to Read with Power, Intention and Joy in the K–3 Classroom	Kathy Collins Stenhouse (2007)
Strategies That Work: Teaching Comprehension for Understanding, Engagement, and Building Knowledge, Grades K–8 (3rd ed.)	Stephanie Harvey and Anne Goudvis Stenhouse (2017)
Comprehension and Collaboration: Inquiry Circles for Curiosity, Engagement, and Understanding (Revised ed.)	Stephanie Harvey and Harvey "Smokey" Daniels Heinemann (2015)
Amplify: Digital Teaching and Learning in the K–6 Classroom	Katie Muhtaris and Kristin Ziemke Heinemann (2015)

The Authentic Response Conferring Reference

We leave you with a tool that summarizes many of the key ideas for getting to know and nurture readers in the direction of Authentic Response. The Authentic Response Conferring Reference (Figure 8.6) is not intended as a comprehensive checklist. Rather, we offer it simply as a starting point to support you as you learn to systematically explore, affirm, teach, or reinforce authentic response.

Figure 8.6
Authentic Response Conferring Reference

ESSENTIAL QUESTION:
How is the reader using reflection, connection, or action in authentic ways?

Does the reader respond authentically during reading?

- Laugh out loud, cry tears of sadness or joy, smile, nod in agreement, or sigh with relief.
- Annotate directly on the text or on sticky notes, in order to come back to thinking.
- Engage others in a conversation about the ideas or wonderings from the text.
- Seek out additional reading or multimedia sources to learn more, extend, or clarify thinking.

Does the reader respond authentically at the end of a book?

- Write, talk, or draw to explore thinking from the text in greater depth.
- Use books to further reflect on preferences and interests as a reader.
- Reread the entire text or parts of the text.
- Look for more of the same (author, series, genre, topic).
- Write, draw, or talk about a text in order to encourage others to read (or not read) it.
- Teach others about the content of the text.
- Write to persuade others (blog post, letter to the editor, speech, etc.) to take action or make change.

Does the reader respond in authentic ways as a result of having read?

- Keep thinking/talking about the ideas in the text, even after the reading is done.
- Articulate deeper empathy or understanding of the lives of others.
- Take action or make a change as a result of what has been realized, or experienced.
- Develop a new interest, hobby, or inquiry.

Once more, we invite you to print this list for quick reference. The Four Square Conferring Reference is also included in Appendix C.

behind the scenes

There's something a bit mysterious and intriguing about getting a backstage pass to a concert or a behind-the-scenes tour of a favorite restaurant. Pulling back the curtain to reveal an insight into how people make things happen, the things that really matter to us, somehow always feels like a gift.

In Part 3, that's exactly what we set out to do—provide you, the hard-working teacher, with the gift of time and planning. Here, we want to show you what happens behind the scenes—the nitty-gritty, not-so-sexy details—to make conferring the dynamic practice it has the potential to be. In the chapters ahead, we share some tried and true resources and tips that we, and many conferring teachers we know, rely on each day in busy classrooms.

It's important to keep in mind that we don't plan for conferring in the same way we plan for other instructional formats. With conferring, we're there to discover what's going on with a reader and follow their lead, right? So, the planning and organization for conferring isn't necessarily as complicated or time consuming as planning for other instructional formats. But if you're serious about growing your practice, you will need to figure out some basic systems to make your practice manageable.

Of course, any teacher can sit down next to readers, chat about reading and books from time to time, and call it conferring. However, if you're serious about this practice, it will be so much more than that. It will be an ongoing commitment to students. One that helps you get to know and nurture them across time in intentional and connected ways.

The chapters in Part 3 are short but practical. They focus on three behind-the-scenes moves for getting and staying organized in your conferring practice—before, during, and after conferences with readers.

You can't plan for exactly what will unfold in a conference. You don't know what students will do or say as they lead you. But you do know that time is short, that there are more of them than you, and that they're going to say and do things worth remembering. So, to make the very most of every minute when you're conferring with readers, you'll want to be prepared with the stuff you need, with a plan to guide you, and with pen in hand to jot whatever notes might be relevant to guide your next steps. To that end, we offer three organizational moves of conferring:

- Gather materials

- Make a plan

- Take note

So grab a pen and a notepad—let's take a look behind the scenes.

9

gather materials: getting ready for teaching and learning on the go

GATHER MATERIALS MOVE AT A GLANCE	
Why choose this move?	To gather what you'll need for teaching and learning on the go.
Guiding questions	What will I carry with me for teaching on the go?
Possible supplies	Clipboard (or binder, portfolio, tablet, digital tool, etc.) Writing utensils Sticky notes Paper Four Square Conferring Reference Four Square Conferring Questions

Conferring is fast-paced, fluid, on-the-go teaching. To make the most of every minute, you'll want all your tools and supplies at your fingertips and ready to go. This behind-the-scenes move is another place where your individual personality and organizational preferences will shine through as you set yourself up with materials that are both functional and fun to carry around. After all, what teacher doesn't love a fresh new pack of brightly colored sticky notes, slick new pens, or a brightly colored clipboard?

Making It Happen

If you're like us, you'll most likely end up trying out a few different tools and systems before you find what works best for you. Over the years, Christina has tried many different systems, from binders to digital note-taking tools, but has now comfortably settled in with a basic notepad and four square grid (see Appendix) for record keeping in addition to using sticky notes with students. Kari still prefers using a trusty clipboard, blank paper, colored pens, and of course, a collection of sticky notes. (How did anyone teach before sticky notes, anyway?) Whatever it is you choose, you're going to spend a lot of time with these tools, so take your time to play with a few different options and be prepared for your tools to evolve along with your skills. To get you started, here are some basic suggestions for taking your teaching on the move.

- **Clipboard**—No matter what else you decide to take with you, you'll definitely want to start with a tool that can serve two purposes: (1) a hard surface to write on and (2) a way to stay organized as you move around the room. Although a clipboard is probably the most common tool used, some teachers discover they prefer a binder, an electronic tablet, a notebook, or a portfolio system. You get the idea, right? A clipboard is a functional, versatile, and economical way to get started; some are even designed with supply storage on the inside.

- **Writing utensils**—Everyone seems to have a different preference for their ideal writing tool: pen or pencil, fine point or medium, black or blue. Again, it doesn't matter what you write with. What matters is that you outfit yourself with something that makes you feel like writing. In the beginning, you may simply need something to jot a few notes. But, eventually, you'll start to teach in interactive ways, such as leaving behind visual reminders on sticky notes. Christina carries a pencil case that contains two pencils (an extra in case one breaks) and a couple of pens or felt-tip markers. Kari keeps a pen attached to her clipboard with a long piece of yarn. This way, no matter how many other pens or pencils she somehow leaves behind, she is assured of having at least one at the ready.

- **Four Square Conferring Reference**—This tool synthesizes the Conferring Reference information from each of the four directions on one page. It can be carried with you on the go. You may use it to jog your memory about some of the more critical behaviors to wonder about, affirm, extend, and remind within the conference. You can find a full-page master of this tool in Appendix C.

- **Four Square Questions for Conferring**—This tool is a collection of some of our favorite go-to questions in each of the four directions for conferring. You can find a full-page master of this tool in Appendix D. Print a copy and attach it to your clipboard so you have it right at your fingertips in every conference.

- **Sticky notes**—We admit, we have a bit of a love affair with sticky notes. They are our go-to for all types of quick-writing tasks. In conferences, we use them to jot notes to ourselves, and we leave them behind with students to use as bookmarks or visual reminders of our teaching (see Chapter 4, "Remind"). Because we never know for sure the next way a sticky note might enhance our teaching, we like to keep a variety of colors and sizes at hand for easy access.

- **Paper**—Figuring out what is most important to write down in a conference takes time and experimentation and is the focus of the Take Note move in Chapter 11. But to get started you can simply grab a stack of blank paper, clip it to your board, and give yourself permission to use it in whatever way makes sense as you discover important bits of information about your students to hold onto for further consideration. In Chapter 11, we'll share with you some templates and specialized papers that we find useful for sorting our thinking across the four directions for conferring.

- **Digital tools**—Whether it's a cell phone for snagging photos or audio recordings, or a tablet used for note taking, when it comes to staying organized on the move, digital tools definitely offer some advantages. When, or if, to go digital and how is something you'll discover for yourself. The options seem to expand and improve almost by the day.

Functional Tools Are Key

We offer two questions to help you reflect on the functionality of your tools for conferring:

- Do the tools allow you to conveniently and effectively take notes on the go?

- Do the tools support meaningful interaction with students?

When your answer to each of these questions is yes, you've likely found the right tools to get you started. Until then, keep experimenting or check in with a conferring colleague for ideas. We encourage you to keep it simple, especially in the beginning. Cumbersome systems can detract from rather than support your interactions with students. When in doubt, start with a clipboard, blank paper, and a favorite writing tool. You'll naturally discover additional things you may need as you go.

10

make a plan:
creating time to confer
with all students

📅 MAKE A PLAN MOVE AT A GLANCE	
Why choose this move?	To make intentional plans to maximize your time spent conferring with students
Guiding questions	Who will I decide to confer with? How often will I return?
Possible supplies	Conference Record Sheet Planning calendar Conference Planning Tool

To build a vibrant conferring practice, you'll want to confer every day, as much as you are able. After all, you can't get better at conferring by staying on the sidelines. You learn to swim by spending time in the water. You learn to cook by spending time in the kitchen. And you learn to confer by spending time next to readers.

By setting manageable goals, celebrating early successes, and keeping a simple daily record of conferring progress, you can build your conferring muscles reader by reader, day by day, conference by conference. Practice feeds success and success feeds confidence.

It's time to make a plan. When you commit to confer with tenacity, you commit to partner with every student in your class on a consistent and predictable basis. That doesn't mean you meet with every student the same amount of time. It simply means you are aware and intentional about the ways you use your time as a conferring teacher. In this section, we provide tools and suggestions to help you do just that.

Making It Happen

Whether you are new to conferring or have tried to get going but are still grappling with consistency or timing, the planning stage can provide the simple but critical boost you need to confer with more tenacity. After all, the things we plan for are more likely to happen than things we leave to chance.

To help yourself to make a plan, we suggest you:

- Keep track of the big picture.

- Set ambitious yet reasonable goals.

- Adjust based on student needs.

Sound like a lot of work? It doesn't have to be. The following pages will introduce you to a few simple tools that can help you plan efficiently and effectively.

Keep track of the big picture.

Whenever you begin to build or to refine your conferring practice, you'll want to create a Conference Record Sheet (see Figure 10.1 and Appendix E for template). The Conference Record Sheet is an effortless way to track the big picture of your conferring practice. At a glance, it shows who you've met with and when, from the first day you conferred until today. It allows you to track your own patterns of conferring, to see progress, to adjust, and to celebrate along the way.

To use the Conference Record Sheet, just fill in the names of your students in the first column, and then (and here's the magic), at the conclusion of each conference, take a second to add the date you met with each student in the next box to the right of their name. That's it!

Figure 10.1
Example of Conference Record Sheet

Conference Record Sheet

Student Name	Date of Conference									
Caren	9/7	9/14	9/23	9/27	9/29					
Vishali	9/8	9/15	9/26							
Andre	9/12	9/19	9/28							
Carson	9/7	9/13	9/21	9/22	9/26	9/30				
Amad	9/9	9/16	9/26							
Soong	9/6	9/13	9/21	9/29						
Clayton	9/2	9/12	9/19	9/28						
Helen	9/8	9/15	9/19	9/21	9/22	9/27	9/29			
Jason	9/2	9/9	9/16	9/23	9/27					
Raj	9/6	9/14	9/22	9/23	9/28	9/30				
Omar	9/2	9/12	9/19	9/29						
Clara	9/2	9/8	9/15	9/23	9/28	9/30				
Lee	9/7	9/13	9/20	9/27						
Megan	9/2	9/13	9/20	9/30						
Ernesto	9/6	9/14	9/17	9/22	9/29					
Shaun	9/2	9/9	9/14	9/19	9/20	9/21	9/26	9/28	9/30	
Reva	9/5	9/9	9/20	9/30						
Yasuki	9/7	9/15	9/27							
Layla	9/7	9/14	9/22	9/28						
Enid	9/5	9/12	9/20	9/29						
Philip	9/6	9/14	9/22	9/23	9/27	9/30				
Van	9/5	9/8	9/16	9/23						
Anna	9/5	9/8	9/16	9/27	9/30					

Yates & Nosek 2018

This sensible, uncomplicated tool can influence your practice in powerful ways. The ultimate goal of conferring, of course, is not to see all students the same frequency or amount of time. Rather, it is to meet with students according to their unique needs. However, without a conferring tool like this one, you can inadvertently develop patterns that don't match your intentions. Used with regularity, the Conference Record Sheet starts to look like a bar graph of dates, providing the data you need to consider:

- How many students have you conferred with overall?

- How many times have you conferred with each individual student?

- When was the most recent time you conferred with each child?

- Which students have had more or less conferring time? Was that intentional?

- What adjustments might be important to make in your conferring practice?

By building a habit of consistently jotting the date in one of those little boxes after each conference, you will see your new practice blossom and grow before your eyes, celebrating progress one dated box at a time.

Set ambitious yet reasonable goals.

Setting ambitious yet reasonable goals for yourself will provide a jump-start as you get rolling with a conferring practice. A common question teachers ask when they try to set conferring goals for themselves is, *How often should I confer with each reader?* Many teachers set a goal of conferring with every reader about once a week, but every teacher's situation varies based on student needs, class size, and time available to confer. Teachers with larger classes may decide they need to stretch the conferring cycle over a slightly longer period, while kindergarten and first-grade teachers often strive to see students in shorter more frequent conferences.

Even though conference frequency may vary, we recommend anchoring your conferring practice with a weekly goal in mind. This end goal provides both a clear starting point and a sense of urgency for daily planning. For instance, if you decide you want to confer with each of your twenty-four students roughly once per week, a quick calculation will indicate that you'd want to confer with about five students per day. With that number in mind as a starting point, you can plan for which five readers to prioritize each day. Of course, the quality of conferences will always be more important than the quantity, but without setting a weekly target, many teachers are surprised to find how easily two or three days can slip away with only a handful of conferences taking place.

Figure 10.2 will help you to consider the specifics of your situation to determine how many conferences you might try to do each day and about how much time you'll realistically have to spend in each of them. On average, we suggest you allow yourself about three to six minutes per conference. Some, of course, will go longer, while others will be much shorter. But, as a rule, this range seems to be about right for most readers.

Figure 10.2
Setting a Conferring Cycle Target for Yourself

Number of daily conferences = Number of students / Number of days

Minutes per conference = Number of independent reading minutes / Number of conferences

    A. Number of students. What is the total number of students in your class? (Example: 28 students)

    B. Number of days. What is the estimated length of the conferring cycle? How often do you hope to return to most readers for subsequent conferences? Every week? Every two weeks? Somewhere in between? Name a number of instructional days. This is the estimated length of the conferring cycle. (Example: 5 days, or about once per week)

    C. Number of daily conferences. Divide the number of students (A) by the number of days in the cycle (B). This will give you an idea of how many students you would need to confer with each day to meet your conferring cycle goal. (Example: 28 students divided by 5 days = 5.5 students per day)

    D. Number of minutes available. How long is your reading workshop or independent reading time? How many of those minutes will you consistently commit to conferring with students? This is the available number of minutes. (Example: 40 minutes of independent reading time)

    E. Average number of minutes available for each conference. Divide the number of minutes available by the average number of conferences each day. This will give you an idea of the average number of minutes you can spend in each conference. The target would be for this to be at least three to six minutes. (Example: 40 minutes / 5.5 conferences = 7 minutes per conference)

Once you have an idea of how many conferences you'll try to conduct each day, you'll be ready to make a plan. To help you get started, we offer a few simple planning tools. Some teachers favor a simple calendar page as a planning tool. Dozens of options can be found for free with an online search. You can print one for each month of the school year, showing which days your particular school is in session (see example in Figure 10.3). Other teachers use a more basic weekly planning tool, with room to write the names of

Figure 10.3
Example of Calendar Showing Available Conferring Days

NOVEMBER

M	T	W	T	F
2 Jack (3) Santiago (EO) Joseph Amber Konner	3 Caylin (2) Brooklyn Jacob Reina Ryan	4 Jack (3) Brady (EO) Landon Ellie Jasper	5 Caylin (2) Doronda Natalie Abshiro Chantelle	6 Jack (3) Mara Serenity Cole Amina
9 Jack (3) Penny (EO) Joseph Amber Konner	10 Caylin (2) Brooklyn Jacob Reina Ryan	11 Jack (3) Isabella Landon Ellie Jasper	12 Caylin (2) Doronda Natalie Abshiro Chantelle	13 Jack (3) Mara Serenity Cole Amina
16 Jack (3) Penny (EO) Joseph Amber Konner	17 Caylin (2) Brooklyn Jacob Reina Ryan	18 Jack (3) Brady (EO) Landon Ellie Jasper	19 Caylin (2) Doronda Natalie Abshiro Chantelle	20 Jack (3) Mara Serenity Cole Amina
23 Jack (3) Caylin (2) Joseph Ellie Reina, Ryan	24 Doronda Abshiro Chantelle Serenity Cole	25 NO SCHOOL	26 NO SCHOOL	27 NO SCHOOL
30 Jack (3) Penny (EO) Joseph Amber Konner	1 Caylin (2) Brooklyn Jacob Reina Ryan	2 Jack (3) Brady (EO) Landon Ellie Jasper	3 Caylin (2) Doronda Natalie Abshiro Chantelle	4 Jack (3) Mara Serenity Cole Amina

3 = Three times per week   2 = Two times per week   EO = Every Other Week
Week of Nov 2: 16 are Pattern A • Weeks of Nov 9, 30: Pattern B • Week of Nov 23: High Priority Students

Figure 10.4
Example of Horizontal Planning Tool

This Week's Conferring Plan

Monday Date	
Tuesday Date	
Wednesday Date	
Thursday Date	
Friday Date	

students they plan to meet with each day of the week. Examples are provided in Figures 10.4 and 10.5, and you'll find templates in the appendix.

These tools can be used to plan a day at a time or a whole week at once. Either way, you'll want to place the most essential conferences at the top of each day's list, so that they don't get cut short. If a student is absent on their scheduled day or you run out of time, simply cross the name out and move it to another day. This way you'll be able to use the tool as a record to help you honestly reflect on how much conferring you've been able to do and adjust for future planning.

Adjust based on student needs.

Once you've completed a few rounds of conferring with every reader, it's likely that you'll naturally start to adjust both frequency and length based on individual student needs. Many teachers discover that, even though a once-per-week conferring cycle might be right for most of the students in their

Figure 10.5
Example of Vertical Planning Tool

This Week's Conferring Plan

Monday	Tuesday	Wednesday	Thursday	Friday
Date	Date	Date	Date	Date

class, some students can soar with more in-depth but less frequent conferences, some need shorter more frequent conferences to thrive, and still others
require almost daily quick check-in-type conferences to keep them engaged
and growing as readers. But how do you prioritize to meet the most urgent
needs in the available time? In Figure 10.6, we present some questions that
can help you spot readers most urgently in need of some extra time.

By making the questions in Figure 10.6 a regular part of your practice,
you'll be able to identify those students who need you to confer with them
more frequently. Then, when you're ready, planning tools such as those
shown Figures 10.7 and 10.8 can help you take another step forward in allo-
cating your conferring time more intentionally based on the diverse needs of
your students.

In Figure 10.7, the teacher has used three columns to systematically
consider which students need various levels of frequency. The totals in the

Figure 10.6
Questions to Help You Prioritize Conferring Plans

Who is not consistently engaged during independent reading?	Without engagement, it will be impossible for students to reap the benefits of having long stretches of time for independent reading, so step back and look around. Disengaged readers are usually easy to spot and should become our first priority when it comes to conferring. Although their disengagement might stem from any of the four directions for conferring–book choice, healthy habits, strategic process, or authentic response–an important starting point with any disengaged reader is to consider the types of books they are choosing.
Who has recently joined the class?	Whenever you have new students, you'll want to dedicate frequent conferring time to them during their first few weeks in the classroom. Conferring will allow you to build relationships, clarify routines and expectations, and start to gather formative data.
Who simply needs more individualized support and attention to grow as a reader?	Whether it's a student you're concerned about, a student you've struggled to build a strong connection with, or one with very specialized learning needs, a few extra moments of attention sprinkled on certain readers will go a long way.
Who have I not met with in the last two weeks?	Pull out that Conference Record Sheet and take a look. Are there students who've been a bit neglected? Even if it's just for quick check-in, striving to see every student a minimum of every two weeks will keep you connected with and informed about the strengths and needs of every student.

bottom row show the number of conferences required for the column for the week. The total number of conferences for this weekly plan is thirty-five

In Figure 10.8, the same teacher has used the information from Figure 10.7 to map out a daily plan and to verify that it is reasonable given the time she has. The class has thirty daily minutes of independent reading time, which means she'd need to confer with about seven students every day: two check-in conferences, one every-other-day conference, and four weekly conferences. This would allow roughly four minutes per conference on average, which falls on the lower range of the target of having three to six minutes per conference. However, given that two of these conferences each day are meant to be quick check-in-type conferences, this appears as though it might be a reasonable goal.

Figure 10.7
Weekly Planning by Desired Frequency of Conference

Daily Check In	2–3 times per week	Weekly
		Boden
		Carsten
		Claire
		Roberto
		Faduma
		Reese
		Julia
		Dean
		Ahmed
Joey	Anna (2)	Juan
Marcia	Solau (3)	Melissa
		Matthew
		Opal
		Serena
		Forrest
		Chetra
		Annika
		Johnny
		Sovanna
		Tony
10	5	20

Protect your plan by saying no to distractions.

Carrying out your plan for conferring will hinge on showing up and learning to be completely present in the moment during each conference. Conferring with tenacity means you don't allow yourself to be interrupted by the ringing telephone (students can learn to answer this for you) or student interruptions, such as "I need help" (students can learn to help themselves and each other), "May I use the restroom" (there's a system for that), or "Candice isn't working" (students are responsible for themselves).

We recommend teaching yourself and your students to honor the sanctity of the one-on-one conference. You may choose to model and demonstrate for your students that nothing (except blood, vomit, or fire) will distract us from this important work. You can arm your students with many strategies for relying on themselves and their peers to get their needs met during this time. When you hold firm to a no-interruptions policy, your students will begin to partner with you and with one another in unexpected ways to eliminate distractions. After all, they'll undoubtedly want your complete and undivided attention when you confer with them.

Figure 10.8
Daily Planning by Desired Frequency of Conference

	Monday	Tuesday	Wednesday	Thursday	Friday
Check-ins 1–2 minutes	Joey Marcia	Joey Marcia	Joey Marcia	Joey Marcia	Joey Marcia
Frequent	Solau	Anna	Solau	Anna	Solau
Weekly	Boden Carsten Claire Roberto	Faduma Reese Julia Annika	Dean Ahmed Juan Sovanna	Melissa Matthew Opal Tony	Serena Forrest Chetra Johnny

Remain Flexible

Of course these plans are written in sand, not in stone. Planning is a tool to help you best leverage your time. Yet, some of your most meaningful conferring will take place, not because a child's name is on the schedule for the day but because you observe a need and respond to it in the moment. A balance between thoughtful, proactive planning and the flexibility to respond to what unfolds in real time is an essential key to conferring. The best-laid plans can often be changed. And that's not a problem. Rather, that's called responsive teaching.

A Challenge to Get You Started

To get off to a strong start, we'd like to challenge you to commit to a two- or three-week period of conferring with four to six readers every day until you have conferred with everyone in your class at least twice. At this pace, it should only take you five to seven days for a class of twenty to thirty students. As long as your students have at least twenty-five minutes of independent reading time, this should be a manageable target, even for beginners.

Just choose a tool and map out a plan. By the end of your second round, you'll have forty to sixty conferences under your belt. You'll be able to watch your practice grow by developing the habit of marking each conference on your Conference Record Sheet as you go.

It's time. Grab a Conference Record Sheet and one of the planning tools offered in this chapter, set a goal, and start to scratch out a rough plan for yourself and your students.

11

take note: holding on to thinking to help pave the path ahead

☰ TAKE NOTE MOVE AT A GLANCE	
Why choose this move?	To keep track of important observations to inform future teaching
Guiding question	What would be important to remember to help with reflective planning, follow-up, problem solving, and tracking progress?
Possible supplies	Blank paper and sticky notes Four Square Conferring Reference Four Square Questions for Conferring Four Square Conferring Notes template Know and Nurture T-chart Digital record-keeping tools (Examples of these tools can be found in the chapter and in the appendix.)

We confer because we believe it is the best way to both know and nurture readers. We take notes because it allows us to hold on to and to come back to the ongoing wonderings, insights, and inklings that pop up in our conversations

Figure 11.1
Decision Making Map: Take Note

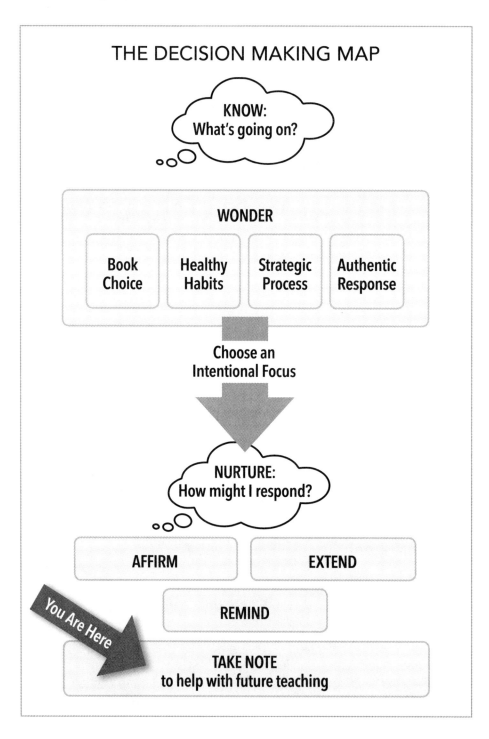

with readers, helping us better understand them and plan for the path ahead. Without our notes to help us, much of the investment in conferring would be lost to everything else we have on our schedules and in our minds—moving from one conference to the next and then on to a lunch meeting, a math lesson, and all of those unexpected interruptions that happen every day in our fast-paced classrooms.

Pushing yourself to take note of a few meaningful items during each conference can be the key to transforming your practice from a collection of isolated or disconnected check-ins to an ongoing series of interactions aimed at knowing and nurturing the reading lives of each of the children you serve. Although you enter each conference with a fresh sense of curiosity and wonder, you don't have to start completely from scratch each time. Rather, you can intensify your impact when you have notes to help connect one conference to the next, like links on a chain, past, present, and future.

Take Note sits patiently at the bottom of the Decision Making Map (Figure 11.1), ready to catch any worthy bits of information that shake out of the other moves. If you feel stressed and uncertain about the what and how of conference note-taking, you aren't alone. We've been there ourselves. And even as we write this chapter, our own ideas and systems continue to evolve. The same is true for even the most veteran conferring teachers we know. Yet taking note doesn't have to be complicated or overwhelming. These notes are for you, after all, a gift you give yourself to answer the following:

Essential question:
What would be important to remember to help with reflective planning, follow-up, problem solving, and tracking progress?

Making It Happen

Although there are an infinite number of possibilities for *how* to take note in a conference, the information most teachers find helpful and practical to record in a conference comes in response to one or more of the following questions:

- What strengths or successes is the student demonstrating?

- What teaching was offered today? (Affirm, Extend, or Remind?)

- What next steps might be considered?

- What am I still wondering about this reader?

In the pages that follow, we offer two of our favorite formats for organizing notes in a conference; the Four Square Conferring Notes template and the Know and Nurture T-Chart.

Four Square Conferring Notes template

The Four Square Conferring Notes template (Figure 11.2 and also in Appendix H) is designed to help you maximize the Four Directions for Conferring, systematically sorting and prioritizing information in each of the quadrants. It includes the essential question for each direction as well as room to keep a running log of your observations, actions, and next steps in each direction.

Figure 11.2
Four Square Conferring Notes Template

Student Name _____ Dates: _____ to _____

Book Choice *Is the reader consistently finding texts that lead to high levels of engagement?*	**Healthy Habits** *Is the reader making intentional decisions that result in lots of time spent reading both in and out of school?*
Strategic Process *What strategic actions is the reader taking to solve problems and make meaning of the text?*	**Authentic Response** *How is the reader using reflection, connection, or action in authentic ways?*

Alternatively, you may choose to create your own four square tool by simply dividing a blank sheet of paper into four quadrants and labeling the quadrants: (1) Book Choice, (2) Healthy Habits, (3) Strategic Process, and (4) Authentic Response. Either way, we suggest the following simple steps for jotting notes.

- Put one student's name at the top.

- Write today's date next to the information you record.

- As you Wonder, Affirm, or Extend, record your observations in the appropriate quadrant.

- Continue to add information in each quadrant over time, with subsequent conferences. We recommend adding the date at the start of each new, additional note.

- Before each conference, take a quick moment to review the previous notes.

- Use the tool to reflect, to collaborate, and to plan based on strengths and possible next steps in each of the quadrants.

You've probably recognized that the Four Square Conferring Notes tool, The Four Square Conferring Reference (Appendix C), and the Four Square Questions for Conferring (Appendix D) are all designed with the same format. Our hope is that will support you as you quickly learn to use the three tools in tandem, elevating the quality of both your conferring and your notes. The Four Square Conferring Notes tool can also be used to help you discover which of the four directions has been the focus of more or less of your conferring attention with each student. Even though equal time in each quadrant is not necessarily the goal, the data can be revealing and can help you to develop a more balanced approach, being sure to consider development in all four directions.

Know and Nurture T-Chart

The Know and Nurture T-Chart shown in Figure 11.3 is just as the name suggests: a two-column grid with one side labeled Know designated for notes about what you observe or affirm right here in this conference, and a second column labeled Nurture for jotting ideas about what the student might be ready for next, either in today's conference or into the future. T-charts have

Figure 11.3
Know and Nurture T-Chart

Know and Nurture T-Chart

KNOW Whats's going on? Book Choice? Habits? Process? Response?	NURTURE How did/will I respond? Affirm? Extend? Remind?

long been a mainstay of note-taking in the reading conference. We offer a template for you in Appendix I and suggestions for use here.

- Use a separate sheet for each student, putting the student's name at the top of a blank grid.

- Enter a fresh date on the far left side for each new entry.

- In the Know column, enter new information you learned from today's conference, including anything important you observed and what you chose to affirm.

- In the Nurture column, write notes about any teaching you offered to Extend or Remind. Use this column to also note anything you want to follow up on, or to consider teaching at a future time.

- At the conclusion of the conference, simply draw a horizontal line under today's entry to separate it from subsequent entries about the student.

Other tools

Of course, there are almost as many tools and styles for taking notes as there are conferring teachers. Some teachers we know use Google Forms as their tool of choice. Evernote is also a popular tool for keeping notes and digital artifacts together. By the time you're reading this, there will quite likely be an even more appealing digital option available.

The bottom line with note-taking tools is that the best tool is whatever makes note taking efficient for you on the go, allowing you to capture actionable information. Our own note-taking styles are constantly evolving. We feel confident that, with experience and a bit of playful experimentation, your preferences will become clearer and your notes themselves will become more focused and useful.

Reflecting on Your Notes Is Key

Ultimately, what matters is not how messy or neat, elaborated or brief your notes are. Instead, it is how they support you after the conference in making informed decisions. Your notes are meant to help you reflect on where a reader has already been in order to help you plan for the path ahead. We offer three valuable examples for how you might learn to use your notes to benefit students including at the beginning of a conference, when consulting with others, and when planning for future instruction.

At the beginning of a conference

Once you have even a few notes from your first round of conferring, no matter how much like chicken scratch they may appear, you now have a tool in your hands to help you become more focused and efficient in your next round of conferring. Now, before you pull up alongside a student to confer, you can take a quick look at your notes, jogging your own memory about the previous conference. You may then decide to focus on the Wonder move as a follow-up to past teaching or action steps that you and the student agreed to.

- Last time we were together you were working on _____. I'm curious about how that's been going.

- You set a goal for yourself last week to _____. How is that coming?

- How's it been going with _____ since the last time we visited?

When consulting with others

When it comes time to meet about a specific child with a parent, a special education teacher, a reading specialist, or another professional in your school, your conferring notes hold the power to be one of your most valuable assets. You don't need a fancy report to monitor the progress of students and do collaborative problem solving. Your conferring notes can serve as a rich source of information about strategies tried, what stuck, what didn't, and in which of the four directions you have attempted to know and nurture this reader. Notes can always be cleaned up later to share with others. Figure 11.4 offers a few examples of how your notes might translate into meaningful collaboration with colleagues.

When planning for future instruction

Of course, your notes can help you make plans for future conferences, but they can also help you plan for small- and whole-group instruction. Often similarities and patterns across multiple readers are not discovered on the spot. Instead, they often become clear when we step back to reflect on our notes. Using the Four Square Grid to collect and organize your notes will help you think categorically about each student and sort through their strengths and needs more efficiently.

Learning to write and use conference notes will help you make the most of your interactions as you pave the path forward. The best way to learn to take notes is to pick up a pen and paper (or electronic device) and begin, keeping your tools by your side whenever you confer. In the beginning, you might feel unsure about what to write. But keep that clipboard and pen close at hand because the moment when you start to recognize, more and more nuggets worth collecting will come sooner than you think. Initially, you may find yourself needing to take a few extra moments at the conclusion of each conference to jot those notes. Eventually, with consistency and practice you'll likely find valuable notes making their way effortlessly to the paper. In the final chapter, Putting It All Together, we offer several examples of the notes taken by teachers in each of the chapter's scenarios.

Figure 11.4
Examples of How Notes Might Support Collaboration with Colleagues.

Notes Taken During or Immediately After a Conference	Examples of Information You Might Share in Collaboration with Colleagues
Consistent in solving problems Makes multiple attempts	One strength that Brendan exhibits consistently is persistence in problem solving. When he encounters trouble, he consistently makes multiple attempts. Yet, I'm noticing the strategies are primarily decoding strategies, and he doesn't seem to use meaning to help himself problem-solve. How about we both focus on helping him consider, "What would make sense?" as a next step?
Growth shown in reading through entire word. Success in 3 of 4 attempts	Micaela has been really working at becoming more consistent with reading through entire multisyllabic words. I've noticed steady progress. My notes show that she was successful on the last 3 of 4 attempts I observed. Yet, I continue to grow concerned that she isn't taking time to think about what these long words mean in context. Using context to determine possible meaning might be a next step we could both focus on.
Accurate retelling Offered support in adding own thinking to reading.	As I review my notes, I notice that much of the time I've spent with Kegan in the past few weeks has focused on adding her own thinking to what she reads. She accurately retells but is still working on adding her own thoughts to her reading. Is that something you're focused on, as well? If so, perhaps it would benefit Kegan if we could agree on some common language.

putting it all together

the art of
decision making

Throughout this book, we've equipped you with a variety of tools to help you know and nurture readers through conferring: the Decision Making Map, the interactive moves, the directions for conferring, and the organizational moves. But now, it's time to focus on one critically important final ingredient for putting it all together—you, the teacher. Only you can bring the moves and directions we've offered to life in ways that affect the real readers in your classroom. Although the paints and brushes and canvases are important tools in an artist's workshop, it is how the artist learns to use them with both flexibility and intention that results in a work of art. And just like any successful creative venture, successful conferring requires more than having tools at your fingertips, it is born of the art of decision making, using those tools in thoughtful and purposeful ways.

To help you navigate this on-the-spot, in-the-moment thinking, we go back to the Decision Making Map (see Figure 12.1). The Decision Making Map helps you visualize possibilities, reminding you of the tools you might use to artfully answer the two driving questions for responsive teaching:

1. The Know question: What's going on?

2. The Nurture question: How might I respond?

Figure 12.1
Decision Making Map

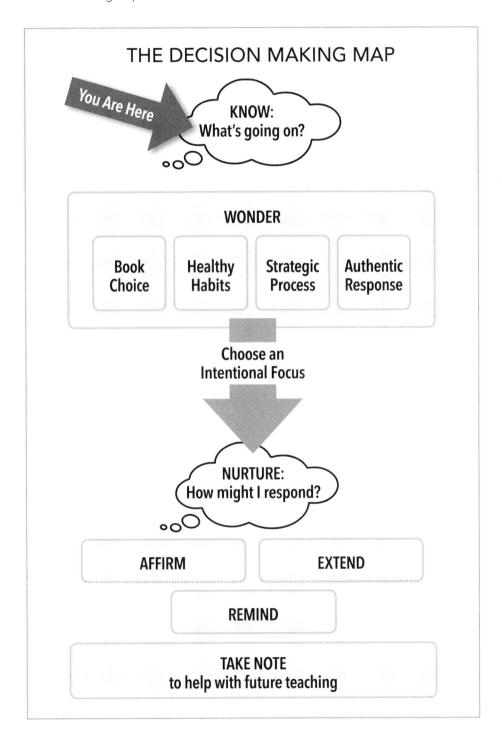

What's Going On? Every Conference Begins with Wonder

Take another minute to study the Decision Making Map (see Figure 12.1). Notice again that Wonder, champion of all conferring moves, sits proudly at the top. Although almost everything about the conference's structure can be flexible, the one imperative decision in every conference is the decision to begin with curiosity, or the Wonder move. To offer a truly responsive partnership, for each child's own reading pursuits and priorities, our conferences must be rooted in an honest desire to understand, "What's going on? What's really going on with this reader, right now?"

In all of its dynamic forms—observation, conversation, listening to reading, analyzing running records or written responses—Wonder will help you to keep an open mind when approaching every reader. Wonder helps you dance around in any of the directions, working to decide which of the four—(1) book choice, (2) healthy habits, (3) strategic process, or (4) authentic response—might provide the ripest or most urgent intentional focus for this reader right now.

The essential questions (Figure 12.2) for each of the directions for conferring provide powerful lenses to look through as you use Wonder to select an intentional focus with each reader.

Figure 12.2
Essential Questions for Each of the Directions of Conferring

As You Wonder About...	Intentionally Consider...
Book choice	Is the reader consistently finding texts that lead to high levels of engagement?
Healthy habits	Is the reader making intentional decisions that result in lots of time spent reading both in and out of school?
Strategic process	What strategic actions is the reader taking to solve problems and to make meaning of the text?
Authentic response	How is the reader using reflection, connection, or action in authentic ways?

Although you can explore these questions in any combination or order, we urge you once again to develop the habit of prioritizing engagement.

Sometimes, lack of engagement is about other things, but, in most cases, until readers have books in their hands that they consider worthy of their time and attention, work in the other directions for conferring can often turn out to be less than productive. (If you feel like we've overstated this point, you might be right. But if you only took one thing away from this whole book, we hope it might be this: book choice is crucial to engagement.)

Once you feel confident that a reader is choosing books they can and want to read, you'll be ready to turn your attention to any of the other three directions for conferring, trusting your students to lead the way. To make the most of the Wonder move in each of the directions for conferring, we remind you of the Four Square Questions for Conferring tool from Chapter 9 and also found in Appendix D. And remember, as long as you're conferring to support work that matters to the reader, there's not a right or a wrong way to go. The decision is yours.

However, as a quick reference to help you think about the reasons you might lean toward one direction over another, Figure 12.3 provides a summary of the Signs a Reader Might Benefit from a Conference, organized according to directions. You can refer to each individual chapter to refresh your memory or get specific recommendations about each of these signs.

To see this all put into action, let's look in on Ms. Demasi, a first-grade teacher, as she moves through the Decision Making Map, working to figure out, "What's going on with Diego?"

First grade conference—what's going on with Diego?

It's just a few weeks into the school year, and Ms. Demasi's first graders already have a well-established independent reading routine in place. Ms. Demasi is committed to trying to meet with every student in her first-grade classroom at least once per week and some students more often based on her observations. To do this, she has a weekly schedule that maps out four to five conferences per day while also leaving time for additional conferences with students who seem to need extra support.

Diego has caught her attention over the last couple of days. Today, as she passes between conferences, she notices him playing with his shoelaces and later rolling and unrolling a sticky note from his box, rather than reading his books. When she does catch Diego in a moment of deeper engagement, Ms. Demasi pays attention to the book he has in front of him and sees that it's an informational text titled *Kids Meet the Tractors and Trucks* (Abramson and Ross 2013). He hunches over the book as if carefully studying every detail. This is different from what she's noticed him doing with other books,

Figure 12.3
Signs a Reader Might Benefit from a Conference

You might focus on book choice when a reader …	Is new to you
	Isn't settling into engaged reading
	Requires extra care with book selections
	Seems frustrated with reading
	Is frequently abandoning books
	Seems to be in a rut
You might focus on healthy habits when a reader …	Is choosing spots that don't work
	Doesn't seem to have a plan
	Isn't making time for reading
	Shows signs of disengagement
You might focus on strategic process when a reader …	Needs support using oral language for storytelling and/or teaching about the pictures in the books in the Preemergent stage
	Could benefit from integrating early print work with meaning-making at the Emergent stage
	Needs support developing problem solving and resilience at the Early stage
	Could benefit from integrating and strengthening strategies for comprehension and fluency at the Transitional stage
	Needs strategies for accessing increasingly complex texts at the Fluent stage
You might focus on authentic response when a reader …	Is showing visible excitement about books
	Has developed misconceptions about the purpose of reading
	Needs help learning to pay closer attention to their own responses to the text
	Needs support making meaningful connections with other readers
	Could use support in considering or planning for next steps

half-heartedly flipping through pages and often putting books back in the box after just a few moments. Because engagement seems to be suffering, Ms. Demasi wonders what's going on with book choice for Diego. She wants to know more. Her first step is to review her notebook, refreshing her memory about notes she took last week, when something caught her eye during book shopping.

KNOW What's going on?	NURTURE How might I respond?
9/24 Book shopping • Rushed • Grabbing books without looking inside	9/24 Shopping supports to help with book choice???

Ms. Demasi's observations and instincts tell her it's time to move in for an up-close conversation about book choice, and even though today isn't Diego's typical conferring day, she does just that.

"Hi, Diego. May I sit down with you for a couple minutes?"

"Sure."

"I'm curious to know how it's going for you as a reader today."

"Sort of good," Diego says, shrugging his shoulders and looking uncertain.

She wants him to feel at ease so she can learn more about what's really going on. She moves to a focused question, "Can you tell me about your reading plans? Which of the books in your box will you spend time reading today?" Rather than scolding him about being off task, her words communicate a positive belief that he has a plan (even if he's not yet executing it) and that his intent is to spend time reading today (even if he's not right now).

Diego immediately grabs the truck book from the floor behind him and says, "Well, I think I'll read this book again. It's my favorite." He hugs it to his chest and then motions toward the box of other books. "And I might read some of these others, too. Maybe. After I'm done with this one."

Ms. Demasi smiles and nods, following up with a question to help her learn more about Diego's choices and motivations. "So, Diego, it seems like you're really excited about the truck and tractor book. Why do you think you love that one so much?"

Diego smiles, "Because I love trucks and tractors and stuff like that. And when I look at the book I can see lots of parts in the pictures. Sometimes I look for them on real trucks, too."

Next, Ms. Demasi asks Diego if there are other books in his box he's excited to read. He shakes his head and shrugs his shoulders. "Not really." He says, "This one is my favorite. The others seem sort of boring."

Ms. Demasi jots a few notes to help her remember the information Diego has just revealed. She has a hunch she'll be able to build on this to help with book choice down the road.

KNOW What's going on?	NURTURE How might I respond?
9/29 Book choice • Informational texts • Trucks/vehicles • Detailed visuals • Other books are "boring"	

If Diego is to become an engaged reader, it's clear to Ms. Demasi that he will need texts that actually draw him in and hold his attention, like this truck book. This quick conversation has confirmed for Ms. Demasi that Diego is in need of support with book choice.

How Will I Respond? Mixing and Matching Affirm, Extend, and Remind

Once you've identified an intentional focus for the conference, it's time to consider the second question on the Decision Making Map: "How might I respond?" Here the interactive moves can be used individually or in combination, mixing and matching just as you might mix and match pieces from your wardrobe. Some days the weather calls for a hat, gloves, and a jacket and other days just a light sweater will do. The same is true within the conference. Sometimes you may simply follow up your Wonder with Affirm to encourage repeated use of a reading skill, strategy, or practice. Other times you may decide you need to use all the moves together—Wonder, Affirm, Extend, and Remind—to move a reader forward. The choice is yours.

In some situations, you might arrive at the conference with a response already in mind; you want to follow up or build on what you've noticed over time or from a distance. When this is the case, we encourage you to also stay open to what the reader shows you in the moment. For instance, imagine you've made note in a previous conference that a reader could use support navigating certain types of features in an informational text. You arrive at the next conference ready to teach into that past observation but find the reader happily immersed in a picture book. Of course, you would want to adjust your plans rather than completely disrupt an engaged reader for feedback unrelated to what they're doing in the moment. Developing the confidence, flexibility, and creativity to notice and lean into what seems to matter in the right-now is one of the hallmarks of artful conferring.

So, how about Ms. Demasi and Diego? How will Ms. Demasi respond to what she's noticed? Let's check in as she chooses moves to support Diego with an intentional focus on book choice.

First grade conference continued—How will I respond?

Although she could jump right in with Extend and begin teaching, Ms. Demasi decides instead to take a moment to Affirm what Diego is already doing that works within the direction of book choice.

"Diego, as a reader you're doing something really strategic to help yourself. Would you like to hear what it is?" Diego smiles and nods eagerly. "As you made your plan for the day, you chose to start with a book you really love. You know that, as a reader, you'll be more engaged when you choose books you really care about, like you did today when you chose the truck book from your book box."

Diego sits up a little straighter and nods again. Ms. Demasi uses the Remind move to ensure that Diego will repeat this book-choice habit again and again. "You can help yourself as reader every day by spending lots of time with books that you feel really excited about or are interested in."

With a more engaged first-grade reader in the fall of the year, Ms. Demasi might have ended the conference right there, simply using the Affirm move to encourage the student to keep doing what's working. But Diego's disengagement is Ms. Demasi's clue that he needs more. He needs to see how he can take what he's already doing and Extend it.

"Diego, wouldn't it be great if there were lots of other books in your book box that you were just as excited about as the truck book?"

Again, Diego nods, "I wish I had more books about trucks and other cool stuff."

"So, last week when I saw you shopping for books in the classroom library, you looked like you were in a bit of a hurry. Did you feel like you were in a hurry?"

Diego shakes his head emphatically with wide eyes, "Yes, I was trying to go as fast as I could because remember you said we shouldn't fool around in the library."

This makes Ms. Demasi smile, remembering clearly the mini-lesson he was referring to. "I do remember that. But taking time to find books you love isn't fooling around. It's very serious work. So, when you go to shop for books you can take the time you need to find books about topics you really care about, like trucks and vehicles and other cool stuff."

Ms. Demasi picks up a book from Diego's book box to demonstrate.

"When you're there, you can open up each book, like this . . . As you look at the pages in the book, you can ask yourself, 'Does this look like a book I'd be excited to spend time with?' If it is, you can keep it. If it isn't, you can put it back and take your time to look for something you're more excited about. This is what readers do to keep their interest high when they read! Does this seem like something you could do?"

Diego nods his head. "Yes, I can do that! Could I go there and try it right now?"

Ms. Demasi artfully weaves the Remind move into her answer. "Yes! You can. When you're there, remember that readers take their time to look for books on topics they are interested in and want to spend time with. Go try it out, and I'll check in later to see what you've found."

As Diego heads to the classroom library, his teacher takes a moment to jot a few notes before moving on to her next conference.

KNOW What's going on?	NURTURE How might I respond?
9/24 Book shopping • Rushed • Grabbing books without looking inside	9/24 Shopping supports to help with book choice???

9/29 Book choice
 	
• Informational texts
 	
  ◦ Trucks/Vehicles
 	
  ◦ Detailed visuals
 	
  ◦ Other books are "boring"
	9/29 Affirm-Choosing books about a topic you love.
	
	Extend-Take your time to find books you really care about. Taking time in the library isn't "fooling around".
	
	Check back.

Tomorrow, she'll check back with Diego, hoping to spot an opportunity for a quick affirmation of the work he's tackling as a result of today's conference.

The Language of Conferring

Language matters.

As you navigate the Decision Making Map, remember that the success of the moves has a great deal to do with the language and tone you use to make those moves. The words we use with our readers affect not only the outcomes they achieve but also how they view themselves and their possibilities.

Throughout this text, we've woven ideas and suggestions about the language of conferring. The language we choose influences readers, building confidence and a sense of ownership over their own reading lives. For instance, you'll recall we emphasized the importance of working to use language that sounds less like "I really like what you've done" (after all, it's not really about us) and more like "As a reader, you've done something strategic . . ." Time and again we've promoted language that puts problem solving in the hands of our students, giving them the opportunity to solve things for themselves and communicating to them that we believe they are capable of finding their own solutions as readers. Language such as, "How might you help yourself?" or "What could you try?" is a staple for the work of nurturing self-reliance.

Yet, language shifts take awareness and intentional practice. We know this first hand, as both of us have some old habits we're continually working to reshape. But as our conferring practices evolve, we're always on the lookout for new ways to help our students depend less on us and more on themselves. Figure 12.4 summarizes many of the language suggestions we've offered throughout this book to foster independence and agency in readers (also see Appendix J).

Figure 12.4
Examples of Language to Foster Self-Reliance and Independence

Purpose	Because you want to . . .	It might sound like . . .
Be Respectful	Show respect for the child's reading time.	May I interrupt? Could we visit together for a moment? May I join you?
*Wonder	Learn what's going on. What is the reader doing, almost doing, or trying to do?	What are you working on as a reader today? I'm curious to know more about how things are going for you as a reader. What can you celebrate about your reading? What challenges have you had? What would you like to talk about today? Hmmm. I'm not sure I understand. Can you clarify that for me? Tell me more . . . I wonder why . . . I wonder if . . . What do you think about . . .? Why do you think . . .? What can you try? May I hear you read from where you left off? (Sometimes wonder is silent as we spend much of the time listening or observing.)

Figure 12.4 continued

Purpose	Because you want to . . .	It might sound like . . .
Affirm	Affirm a relevant behavior or strategy by verbally mirroring it back to the reader.	You are doing something strategic as a reader. Let me tell you what you did. Did you know that you are . . .? You're helping yourself in such an important way . . . As a reader, you . . . One thing you're doing well as a reader is . . .
Extend	Ask permission to teach something new. Teach. Or Ask the student to try a strategy they already know.	As a reader, you're ready for a next step. May I share it with you? May I show something that will be helpful? What can you try? Is there a strategy you can use? As a reader, you're ready to extend yourself . . . Let me show you how . . . You did something to help yourself right here. Do you know what it was? May I show you?
Remind	Remind the student that this strategy is transferable.	Keep doing this. It will help you with . . . This can help you anytime you're . . . Remember to do this every time you . . . Don't forget that this is something you can do as a reader every time you read. May I leave you this reminder on a sticky note?

*Refer to the Four Square Conferring Question tool in the Apppendix for a more elaborated list of questions to support Wonder in each of the four directions

Conferring with Flexibility and Intention: A Peek Inside the Classroom

In the following pages, we offer the chance to look in on several more teachers as they use the art of decision making to put it all together in a conference. You'll see each of them work to tease out what's going on and then decide how to respond, both in the moment and into the future.

We offer some questions to guide your thinking as you read about the conferences. You'll find these same questions on a reproducible sheet in Appendix K. They can be used any time you have the opportunity to watch a conference, in person, in a video, or otherwise:

Questions to Guide Conference Observations

- What do you notice about the language each teacher uses?

- How does the teacher establish and maintain a sense of respect, partnership, and/or student ownership?

- What do you notice about how the teacher navigates the Decision Making Map?

- What are you left wondering about this reader?

- What additional follow-up actions might be helpful?

Fourth grade conference—Healthy Habits with Karl

Karl is a fluent fourth-grade reader. His teacher, Ms. Shaman, has typically conferred with him only about once every week or two. However, in the last few days, Ms. Shaman has noticed that Karl is having difficulty with engagement during independent reading. From a distance, she's noticed that his usual long stretches of reading are much shorter this week, frequently interrupted by periods of looking around the room, peeking at his friends, and sometimes trying to get their attention. The book in front of him is *No Talking* by Andrew Clements (2007). Ms. Shaman remembers the conversation she had with Karl about this book at the end of last week, when he'd told her how excited he was to have found another great Andrew Clements book. During that conference, it had seemed obvious that Karl was attuned with what was happening within the story. Ms. Shaman peeks at her notes:

Book Choice	Healthy Habits
Is the reader consistently finding texts that lead to high levels of engagement?	**Healthy Habits** *Is the reader making intentional decisions that result in lots of time spent reading both in and out of school?*
10/15 Loves Andrew Clements books Current read: No Talking Affirm: Thinking about what you've loved in the past to help find more books you love.	
Strategic Process *What strategic actions is the reader taking to solve problems and make meaning of the text?*	**Authentic Response** *How is the reader using reflection, connection, or action in authentic ways?*

The previous conference had been quick, culminating in a simple affirmation. "Karl, after listening to you talk about your book, it's clear that you are a reader who chooses his books carefully. You think about what's worked for you in the past, and you use that to help you choose the next time. Keep doing this! It will help you find one good read after another."

Now, Ms. Shaman wonders many things. *Has Karl lost interest in this book? Has he somehow lost his way with understanding? What has changed?* She decides to check in with Karl to learn more about *What's really going on this week?*

When Ms. Shaman asks, "How is your reading coming along, Karl?" Karl responds with a smile.

"Good. I'm still reading this." He points to the cover of the Clements book. "It's a good book. I'm still liking it." He seems to be remembering their previous conversation about the book, as well. Ms. Shaman feels comfortable that she can rule out book choice as the root cause of Karl's recent engagement struggles and decides to invite Karl to join her in figuring out *What's really going on?* in the other three areas.

"Karl, I know this is a book you really care about, so I'd like to hear your ideas on something. The last couple of days I've been noticing that even with a book you really care about, you seem sort of distracted during reading time. Have you noticed this, too?" Karl nods slowly, in agreement. Ms. Shaman continues. "I'm wondering if you have any ideas about what might be going on? What are your thoughts?"

His teacher has not only invited Karl in as an active solver of his own problem, but she has done so in a way that is respectful, maintaining their partnership within the conference. Karl reflects for a moment and then says, "I don't know for sure, but sometimes it just seems hard to read when there is so much happening."

"Tell me a little more about that, Karl."

"Well, it's tough to read when I know my friends are so close by. I want to see what they're doing. It's hard to ignore them when they're just . . . right there." Karl points to a couple of his friends who are sitting at a table close by.

Because her students choose their own reading spots each week, Ms. Shaman wonders whether Karl may have been more affected by differences in this week's choice than he had been in the past. It seems as though the most basic of healthy reading habits, choosing a reading spot, might be tripping Karl up this week. Ms. Shaman confirms what she's heard Karl explain, "So one thing you're learning about yourself as a reader is that at times you can be easily distracted by having friends too nearby?" Karl nods. Now his teacher is ready to shift from Wonder into Extend. She decides to do so with a low level of scaffolding, empowering Karl to continue reflecting on his own situation, "So, I'm wondering how you might help yourself solve this. What could you try?"

Karl thinks for a moment, looking around at some of his friends close by. "Well . . . I guess I could sit in a spot over there." He points to an area in the classroom away from his friends. "Or maybe I could just face another direction, so I don't see them when I'm reading."

Ms. Shaman smiles and transitions into the Remind move.

"Karl, it sounds like you have just come up with your own possible solution for staying engaged during reading. By remembering that it can be hard to stay engaged near the distraction of your friends, you'll be able to protect yourself from that interference. When you do, you'll be more engaged in your current book and with your future books as well. Do you think this is something you can try right now and then again for the next few days?"

"Yeah. I'll try it."

"Okay. I'll check back with you in a couple of days to see how it's going for you, will that work?" Before she goes, Ms. Shaman jots a few notes about today's conference:

Book Choice	Healthy Habits
Is the reader consistently finding texts that lead to high levels of engagement?	*Is the reader making intentional decisions that result in lots of time spent reading both in and out of school?*
10/15 Loves Andrew Clements books Current read: No Talking Affirm: Thinking about what you've loved in the past to help find more books you love.	10/19 Distracted Asked what he thought was going on. "Hard to be so close to friends." Extend: Karl's idea: New spot or Face away from friends while reading
Strategic Process	**Authentic Response**
What strategic actions is the reader taking to solve problems and make meaning of the text?	*How is the reader using reflection, connection, or action in authentic ways?*

Third grade conference—Strategic Process with Lily

As third-grade teacher Mr. Graham looks up at the classroom clock, he notices he has only about three minutes left before it's time for the class to line up for lunch. A few conferences have taken longer than he'd anticipated today, and he hasn't yet gotten to Lily, whom he'd really hoped to spend time with. He quickly moves toward Lily, determined to make the most of the time he has. "Hi, Lily. How's it going?"

"Good," Lily replies, not taking her eyes from the page. This intense engagement is consistent with what Mr. Graham has noticed throughout the day with Lily. Her teacher wants to get a glimpse into what's happening with Lily's strategic reading process, so he asks, "Lily, would you mind reading aloud from where you left off, so I could listen in a bit?"

As Lily starts to read, Mr. Graham listens intently. Almost immediately he notices something about Lily's oral reading that seems to have changed since the last time he listened. Lily is using intonation in both subtle and more dramatic ways as she reads dialogue between the characters. Mr. Graham waits for a pause in the reading, before beginning.

"Lily, you're doing something really thoughtful as a reader. You are thinking about the words your characters are using. For example, here," Mr. Graham points to one particular section of dialogue, "when the characters are arguing, you changed your voice to match the tone of their voices in the argument. Did you realize that you were doing this as a reader?"

Lily nodded, "I've been working on that. I just try to think in my head what it would really sound like to hear them talking."

"As a reader, you pay attention to dialogue and how it may sound in real life outside the pages of a book. You're helping yourself bring the book to life through the dialogue. Keep doing this, Lily."

Mr. Graham jots a note on his tablet. And then he makes one final decision to use the Remind move before he goes. He says, "Lily, you've made such great strides with bringing your books to life through dialogue. I wonder if you'd be willing to share an example of this with a small group of classmates in the next few days?"

Lily beams and Mr. Graham thinks it likely that the opportunity borne out of this quick conference will stay with Lily far into the future. He jots a note so that he remembers to follow through on this agreement.

KNOW What's going on?	NURTURE How might I respond?
11/05 Bringing dialogue to life with inflection.	11/05 Lily could offer a student-led small group . . . Mention at morning meeting.

Fifth grade conference—Book Choice with Asad

Asad is new to Ms. Chang's fifth-grade classroom. Ms. Chang has paired Asad with Alex to help him learn to navigate the classroom library. Alex immediately showed Asad one of his favorite boxes filled with informational handbooks and how-to books. Alex's excitement and recommendations about these books was contagious. Asad quickly discovered a few high-interest books, including a Minecraft Handbook, and he has settled in for a longer period of reading today. As she passes by between conferences, Ms. Chang stops to Affirm what she sees Asad doing.

"Asad, you've done something really smart to help yourself as a reader. By considering the suggestions of other readers and following your interests, you've found the kind of book that can keep you reading for a long time. This is something you can continue to do anytime you're looking for a new book, learning from the experience of other readers with interests similar to yours."

Ms. Chang will confer with Asad in more depth later in the week. This quick check-in allows Asad's teacher to make a strong connection, affirming and encouraging the newest member of this community of readers in these early days. She doesn't feel new teaching is necessary at this moment. She knows that, sometimes, giving readers a small affirming boost and then allowing them to continue to read can go a long way. She jots a note before she moves on.

Book Choice	Healthy Habits
Is the reader consistently finding texts that lead to high levels of engagement?	*Is the reader making intentional decisions that result in lots of time spent reading both in and out of school?*
2/24 Found guidebook basket and Minecraft Handbook through recommendation from Alex. Affirmed book choice. Recommendation from friend Choosing based on interest	
Strategic Process	**Authentic Response**
What strategic actions is the reader taking to solve problems and make meaning of the text?	*How is the reader using reflection, connection, or action in authentic ways?*

Second grade conference—Authentic Response with Gina.

Mr. Skjaervo pulls up next to Gina in her favorite reading spot. Gina is a confident second-grade reader who has no trouble consistently choosing books she cares about and sustaining reading for twenty minutes or more. Gina has developed habits that lead to a high volume of reading both in and out of school. At the close of independent reading each day, Gina can often be heard giving a classmate a report of her numbers in minutes, in pages, or in books. Gina uses many strategies for navigating text and is capable of reading texts that many would consider to be well above grade level. In fact, she recently mentioned that she finished a Judy Moody book in just one day and that it had taken her older sister four days to finish the same book. Some of the notes Mr. Skjaervo has jotted about Gina in the past include:

KNOW What's going on?	NURTURE How might I respond?
12/10 Reading 40–50 pages or more per night	12/10 Affirm–High volume. Reading at home.
12/17 Reading aloud super fast without regard for punctuation or dialogue	12/17 Slow down. Put yourself in the story.
1/6 Finished Judy Moody in 1 day!	1/6 Reading is not a race. Take time to think about what you'll take away from a book.

Even though Gina is highly engaged, in fact almost competitive about her reading volume, Mr. Skjaervo has intentionally focused on authentic reader response in his past several conferences with Gina. Mr. Skjaervo wants to find ways to help Gina become more reflective about her reading, slowing down to make the reading experience about more than simply getting to the end of a book in order to start another. Today, Gina is reading *Clementine* by Sarah Pennypacker (2008).

"Hi, Gina, may I interrupt for a moment?" Gina nods. "How's your reading going today?"

"It's good. I'm reading the first book in the Clementine series. I think there are like five more books in the series, and I'll probably read them all.

This one is going pretty fast so far. So I'll probably be reading the next one by tomorrow or the day after, I think."

Mr. Skjaervo nods, mentally confirming his past observations about Gina's tenacious commitment to high-volume reading. "So what has drawn you into this series?"

"I just like it. It's sort of funny like Judy Moody." Gina responded.

Mr. Skjaervo waits to see if Gina volunteers more information. After a few silent seconds of wait time, he asks, "Tell me more about that: how is it like Judy Moody?"

"Well, they're both girls who sort of do funny things and get in trouble. They both make me laugh."

"Could you show me any parts that you particularly loved?" Mr. Skjaervo watches as Gina flips back through the pages and then shrugs her shoulders.

"Well, I can't find it right now, but there is this one part that made me laugh right out loud a few minutes ago."

Mr. Skjaervo can see that Gina is ready for a next step in her reading life. She is ready to slow down and pay more attention, finding places worth talking and writing about.

"Gina, may I tell you two things about your reading?" Mr. Skjaervo asks, smiling.

"Sure."

"Gina, you're a reader who notices what it is you like about a book. For example, you were able to tell that the current book you're reading draws you in because it is funny and it reminds you of another series you've read. This is one thing that readers often do, they reflect on their responses as readers, comparing one book to another."

In hearing this affirmation Gina nods and Mr. Skjaervo continues, "Now, it seems like you're ready for a next step as a reader." Gina continues to smile as she looks at her teacher.

Mr. Skjaervo transitions into the point he thinks will help Gina extend as a reader, "Gina, you're ready to learn to use specific examples to explain your thinking to others. Once you learn to do this, you can use it anytime you are talking or writing about a book."

Mr. Skjaervo opens the class book to a page he had read aloud earlier in the day. He rereads a familiar section aloud to Gina and then says, "Now, Gina, I'm about to tell you why I love this part so much. After I do, I'm going to show an example from the text. Then you can take a turn and do the same in your book." Mr. Skjaervo modeled, stating his opinion and then pointing to a specific example in the text. "Now you try the same thing," he says, nodding toward Gina's book.

Gina opens her book, reads a little bit, and again says, "I think this part is sort of funny." And stops.

Mr. Skjaervo says, "Keep going, Gina. Remember to tell why."

Gina thinks for another moment, studying the text, then says, I think this part is funny because of what Clementine says." Then Gina points to the dialogue in the text and adds, "Right here, listen to this . . ."

"Gina, you not only gave your opinion, but you went right into the text to find an example to back it up. This is something that readers often do when talking about their books. This is something you can do each time you talk about a book."

Mr. Skjaervo takes a moment to remind Gina of the strategy, quickly sketching on a sticky note to leave as a visual reminder of her next step.

"Here, let me leave a sticky with you to remind you of this important work you can do with any book. You can practice using specific examples to talk about your books with others. This is one way you let others know about what you're thinking while you read. I'll be eager to see how this is going when I come back next week." Before he goes, Mr. Skjaervo takes a moment to jot a few notes:

KNOW What's going on?	NURTURE How might I respond?
Recognizing Clementine is "funny like Judy Moody."	Affirm—Comparing this book to other books with humor. Extend—Using a specific example in the text to talk or write about a book.

As a reminder from the beginning of this book, with heart, tenacity, and a willingness to learn, when you take the time to know and nurture every reader in your classroom through conferring, you'll be able to put your practice all together in ways that will have a long lasting impact. You will honor and elevate every student not only as a reader, but also as a contributing member of the community who has so much to offer. With your readers always as your guide showing you what's really going on, you'll surely and continually find meaningful ways to respond.

A CLOSER LOOK: PUTTING IT ALL TOGETHER
VIDEO CLIP EXAMPLE(S)

Using the Questions to Guide Conference Observations (Appendix K), take a look at these two conferences. As you do, reflect on the questions introduced earlier in the chapter:

- What do you notice about the language the teacher uses?
- How does the teacher establish and maintain a sense of respect, partnership, and/or student ownership?
- What do you notice about how the teacher navigates the Decision Making Map?
- What are you left wondering about this reader?
- What additional follow-up actions might be helpful?

Sten.pub/
KnowNurtureTogether

Trust Yourself, Follow Your Students, and Choose Joy

One thing that can quickly zap the joy from conferring is the pressure we put on ourselves that conferences must follow a precisely prescribed path and that to deviate from that path is to do it wrong.

Throughout the book, we've offered a framework, moves, directions, and lots of tips and tools. But, in the end, every conferring practice is a unique mix of exploration and experience, heart and head, personality and pedagogy. No one else will confer precisely as you will. The conferring practice you build will be uniquely your own.

No one knows your students better than you. So, let go of the idea that someone else has the "right answers" for what to do or say. Conferring from the heart means you'll trust yourself to bring your own style, preferences, and experience to each conference. You're a professional, hired to make instructional decisions that respond to your students' needs. Your instincts are good and they'll only continue to get better as you go. Trust them.

Conferring with joy is a choice that we make when we initiate each conference from a place of love—love of children, love of books, and love of learning. The human brain is adept at finding what it looks for (Bastardi, Uhlmann, and Ross 2011). So, when we enter a conference anticipating joyful interaction, we are quite likely find it.

So go ahead. Be brave. Watch. Wonder. Relax. Smile. Have some fun. Lean in. Listen with your whole heart. Water seeds. Polish stones. Nurture. Affirm. Nudge. Persist. Offer hope. Shine light on possibilities. Show a fierce and unwavering belief in the capacity of every child. Trust yourself to know and nurture readers. Confer.

appendix

Appendix A

Book Choice Reflection Tool

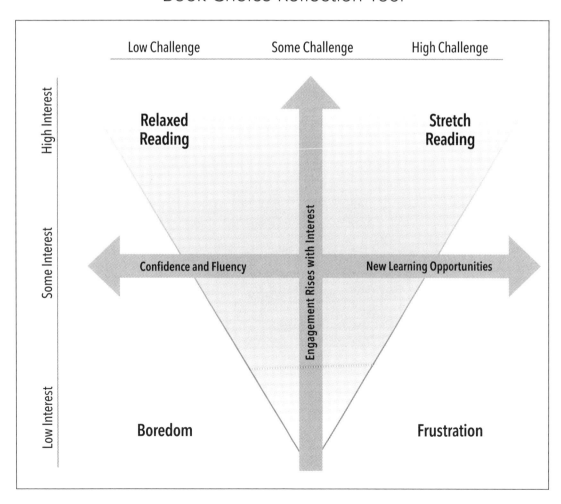

Appendix B
Building Healthy Reading Habits

Name _____

Current Reading Habits	My Goals

Appendix C
Four Square Conferring Reference

Book Choice	Healthy Habits
Is the reader consistently finding texts that lead to high levels of engagement?	*Is the reader making intentional decisions that result in lots of time spent reading both in and out of school?*

Does the reader regularly and purposefully choose . . .
- Books that are of high INTEREST
- A VARIETY of text types including a range of types, genres, authors, topics
- A balance of STRETCH reading and RELAXED reading
- Texts for different purposes i.e. to learn more, the be entertained, to learn how to, etc.

Use a range of strategies to consistently find good-fit texts?
- Easily navigate the classroom library and other collections
- Know how to "sample" texts before selecting them.
- Follow personal interests and preferences.
- Use the recommendations of others to find new possibilities.
- Read more than one book from a favorite author, series, genre, or topic.

Recognize when and why a text is NOT a good-fit?
- Realize when a book choice is not working
- Make the decision to abandon the book or save it for later.
- Name why a book is not a good choice.
- Use factors from past book choice mismatches when selecting new reads.

Make choices that result in high levels of ENGAGEMENT?
- Choose reading spots that are COMFORTABLE.
- Choose reading spots that are away from DISTRACTIONS.
- Consistently CHOOSE engaging texts.

Take responsibility for HIGH VOLUME reading.
- Read for LONGER and LONGER stretches of time.
- Read lots of minutes at SCHOOL every day.
- Read lots of minutes OUTSIDE of SCHOOL every day.
- Read on WEEKENDS, HOLIDAYS, and during SUMMER vacation.
- Reflect on reading volume, and recognize why things are or aren't going well.

Make intentional CHOICES and PLANS
- Keep reading materials ORGANIZED for easy access.
- Make a daily PLAN to maximize available time.
- Keep a selection of NEXT-READS ready to go or written down for future reading.
- Set meaningful GOALS to keep growing as a reader.
- Reflect on how things are going and make meaningful adjustments.

Strategic Process	Authentic Response
What strategic actions is the reader taking to solve problems and make meaning of the text?	*How is the reader using reflection, connection, or action in authentic ways?*

Rely on him or herself as a problem-solver while reading?
- Pay attention, noticing when something's not right.
- When something doesn't seem right, take time to work it out.
- Flexibly try more than one strategy at the point of difficulty or confusion?

information from a range of sources?
- Use the picture and context to think what would make sense.
- Consider what would sound right in the sentence.
- Look carefully at the word considering what would look right.
- Reread to clear up confusions, to get more information, and to confirm.

Demonstrate fluency in ways that indicate a focus on understanding?
- Read at a comfortable speed, not too fast and not too slow.
- Use expression to make my reading sound like talking.
- Read in smooth phrases, pausing appropriately for punctuation.

Draw on a variety of strategies to maximize meaning-making.
- Notice when he or she starts to lose track of meaning and work to get back on track.
- Use the text to retell and/or summarize capturing big ideas and key details.
- Connect actions, events, and dialogue in the text to make meaning.
- Synthesize information and ideas from across the text (actions, events, dialogue) to understand the big ideas?
- Use what he or she knows about how texts are constructed to better understand and evaluate the text.

Respond authentically during reading?
- Laugh out loud, cry tears of sadness or joy, smile, nod in agreement, or sigh with relief.
- Annotate directly on the text or on sticky notes, in order to come back to thinking.
- Engage others in a conversation about the ideas or wonderings from the text.
- Seek out additional reading or multimedia sources to learn more, extend, or clarify thinking.

Respond authentically at the end of a book?
- Write, talk, or draw to explore thinking from the text greater depth.
- Use books to further reflect on preferences and interests as a reader.
- Reread the entire text or parts of the text.
- Look for more of the same (author, series, genre, topic).
- Write, draw, or talk about a text in order to encourage others to read (or not read) it.
- Teach others about the content of the text.
- Write to persuade others (blog post, letter to the editor, speech, etc.) to take action or make change.

Respond in authentic ways as a result of having read?
- Keep thinking / talking about the ideas in the text, even after the reading is done.
- Articulate deeper empathy or understanding of the lives of others.
- Take action or make a change as a result of what has been realized, or experienced.
- Develop a new interest, hobby, or inquiry.

Appendix D
Four Square Questions for Conferring

Book Choice	Healthy Habits
Is the reader consistently finding texts that lead to high levels of engagement?	*Is the reader making intentional decisions that result in lots of time spent reading both in and out of school?*
• What are you reading right now? How is it working for you? • What kind of books do you most/least like to read? • Does this book feel like a good choice for you? Why or why not? • What makes you like (or dislike) this book so much? • I'm curious about what made you decide to choose this book? • Does this book seem more like relaxed reading, stretch reading, or somewhere in between ? What makes you say that? • What's the best book you've chosen recently? What made it such a good choice? • Have you recently chosen a book that didn't work for you? Why do you think that was? • What part of our library do you visit most often? Why? • What's the best book you're reading right now? How did you find it?	• What goals or plans do you have for yourself as a reader? • What else might you do to help yourself grow as a reader? • What habits are you most interested in developing as a reader? • When is reading the best for you? When is it most challenging? • How do you help yourself make the most of reading time? • How is this spot working for you? What else could you try? • How much reading are you doing each day? In school? Out of school? What do you think about that? • How might you help yourself get even more reading minutes? outside of school? • What can we celebrate about your life as a reader right now?

Strategic Process	Authentic Response
What strategic actions is the reader taking to solve problems and make meaning of the text?	*How is the reader using reflection, connection, or action in authentic ways?*
• May I listen in as you read aloud? You can choose a part you'd like to read aloud, or read aloud from where you left off. • How can you help yourself? What could you try? What else? • Are you right? How can you check? • What did you notice about your reading? • What are you thinking about (or learning) as you read? • What is the book mostly about? • What challenges do the characters face? What are you learning about the characters? • What questions do you have as you read this book (part, chapter, etc.)? • How might you summarize the part you just read? • What predictions are you making based on what you know so far?	• In your reading, what's worth thinking more about? Talking about? Writing about? • Does this text call you to action in any way? • What other reading does this book make you think about doing? • What questions do you have? How might you find answers • What big feelings has this book made you notice? • How has this book changed you? What will you take away from it? • How might you respond to a book like this? • Who might you like to tell about this book? Why? • How might you let others know about it? Talk? Draw? Write? • It seems like this book is really important to you. What next steps are you considering as a result of having read it?

Appendix E
Conference Record Sheet

Student Name	Date of Conference																					

Appendix F

This Week's Conferring Plan

Monday Date	Tuesday Date	Wednesday Date	Thursday Date	Friday Date

Appendix G

This Week's Conferring Plan

Monday Date	Tuesday Date	Wednesday Date	Thursday Date	Friday Date

Appendix H

Student Name _____   Dates: _____ to _____

Book Choice *Is the reader consistently finding texts that lead to high levels of engagement?*	**Healthy Habits** *Is the reader making intentional decisions that result in lots of time spent reading both in and out of school?*
Strategic Process *What strategic actions is the reader taking to solve problems and make meaning of the text?*	**Authentic Response** *How is the reader using reflection, connection, or action in authentic ways?*

Appendix I
Know and Nurture T-Chart

KNOW **Whats's going on?** Book Choice? Habits? Process? Response?	**NURTURE** **How did/will I respond?** Affirm? Extend? Remind?

Appendix J

Purpose	Because you want to . . .	It might sound like . . .
Be Respectful	Show respect for the child's reading time.	May I interrupt? Could we visit together for a moment? May I join you?
*Wonder	Learn what's going on. What is the reader doing, almost doing, or trying to do?	What are you working on as a reader today? I'm curious to know more about how things are going for you as a reader. What can you celebrate about your reading? What challenges have you had? What would you like to talk about today? Hmmm. I'm not sure I understand. Can you clarify that for me? Tell me more . . . I wonder why . . . I wonder if . . . What do you think about . . .? Why do you think . . .? What can you try? May I hear you read from where you left off? (Sometimes wonder is silent as we spend much of the time listening or observing.)

Affirm	Affirm a relevant behavior or strategy by verbally mirroring it back to the reader.	You are doing something strategic as a reader.
		Let me tell you what you did.
		Did you know that you are . . .?
		You're helping yourself in such an important way . . .
		As a reader, you . . .
		One thing you're doing well as a reader is . . .
Extend	Ask permission to teach something new. Teach. Or Ask the student to try a strategy they already know.	As a reader, you're ready for a next step. May I share it with you?
		May I show something that will be helpful?
		What can you try?
		Is there a strategy you can use?
		As a reader, you're ready to extend yourself. . .
		Let me show you how . . .
		You did something to help yourself right here. Do you know what it was? May I show you?
Remind	Remind the student that this strategy is transferable.	Keep doing this. It will help you with . . .
		This can help you anytime you're . . .
		Remember to do this every time you . . .
		Don't forget that this is something you can do as a reader every time you read.
		May I leave you this reminder on a sticky note?

Appendix K
Questions to Guide Conference Observations

1. What do you notice about the language the teacher uses?

2. How does the teacher establish and maintain a sense of respect, partnership, and/or student ownership?

3. What do you notice about how the teacher navigates the Decision Making Map?

4. What are you left wondering about this reader?

5. What additional follow-up actions might be helpful?

references

Allen, Patrick A. 2009. *Conferring: The Keystone of Reader's Workshop*. Portland, ME: Stenhouse.

Allington, Richard L. 1977. "If They Don't Read Much, How They Ever Gonna Get Good?" Journal of Reading 21 (1): 57–61.

———. 2009a. "If They Don't Read Much . . . 30 Years Later." http://textproject.org/assets/library/resources/IRA-2007-Allington-Additional.pdf.

———. 2009b. *What Really Matters in Response to Intervention: Research-Based Designs*. Boston: Pearson.

———. 2012. *What Really Matters for Struggling Readers: Designing Research-Based Programs*. Boston: Pearson.

Allington, Richard L., and Rachael E. Gabriel. 2012. "Every Child, Every Day." *Educational Leadership* 69:10–15.

Backman, Jill. 2016. "A Level Is a Teacher's Tool, NOT a Child's Label." *Fountas & Pinnell Literacy*. http://blog.fountasandpinnell.com/post/a-level-is-a-teacher-s-tool-not-a-child-s-label.

Barnhouse, Dorothy, J., and Vicki Vinton. 2012. *What Readers Really Do: Teaching the Process of Meaning Making*. Portsmouth, NH: Heinemann.

Bastardi, Anthony, Eric Luis Uhlmann, and Lee Ross. 2011. "Wishful Thinking: Belief, Desire, and the Motivated Evaluation of Scientific Evidence." *Psychological Science* 22 (6): 731–732.

Beers, Kylene, and Robert E. Probst. 2012. *Notice and Note: Strategies for Close Reading*. Portsmouth, NH: Heinemann.

———. 2015. *Reading Nonfiction: Notice and Note Stances, Signposts, and Strategies*. Portsmouth, NH: Heinemann.

———. 2017. *Disrupting Thinking: Why How We Read Matters.* New York: Scholastic.

Bomer, Katherine. 2010. *Hidden Gems: Naming and Teaching from the Brilliance in Every Student's Writing.* Portsmouth, NH: Heinemann.

Boushey, Gail, and Joan Moser. 2014. *The Daily 5: Fostering Literacy in the Elementary Grades.* 2nd ed. Portland, ME: Stenhouse.

Burkins, Jan M., and Melody M. Croft. 2010. *Preventing Misguided Reading: New Strategies for Guided Reading Teachers.* Newark, DE: International Reading Association.

Burkins, Jan M., and Kim Yaris. 2016. *Who's Doing the Work? How to Say Less So Readers Can Do More.* Portland, ME: Stenhouse.

Calkins, Lucy. 2001. *The Art of Teaching Reading.* New York: Longman.

———. 2015a. *A Guide to the Reading Workshop: Intermediate Grades.* Portsmouth, NH: Heinemann.

———. 2015b. *A Guide to the Reading Workshop: Primary Grades.* Portsmouth, NH: Heinemann.

Chall, Jeanne. 1983. *Stages of Reading Development.* New York: McGraw-Hill.

Child and Adolescent Health Measurement Initiative. 2012. *National Survey of Children's Health 2011/2012.* Data Resource Center for Child & Adolescent Health. Available at www.childhealthdata.org.

Clay, Marie M. 1985. *The Early Detection of Reading Difficulties.* Portsmouth, NH: Heinemann.

———. 1993. *Reading Recovery: A Guidebook for Teachers in Training.* Portsmouth, NH: Heinemann.

———. 2000. *Running Records for Classroom Teachers.* Portsmouth, NH: Heinemann.

———. 2015. *Becoming Literate*: The Construction of Inner Control.* Updated ed. Portsmouth, NH: Heinemann.

Cloud, Nancy, Fred Genesee, and Else Hamayan. 2009. *Literacy Instruction for English Language Learners: A Teacher's Guide to Research-Based Practices.* Portsmouth, NH: Heinemann.

Collins, Kathy. 2007. *Reading for Real: Teaching Students to Read with Power, Intention and Joy in the K–3 Classroom.* Portland, ME: Stenhouse.

Collins, Kathy, and Matt Glover. 2015. *I Am Reading: Nurturing Young Children's Meaning Making and Joyful Engagement with Any Book.* Portsmouth, NH: Heinemann.

Daniels, Harvey, and Sara K. Ahmed. 2015. *Upstanders: How to Engage Middle School Hearts and Minds with Inquiry.* Portsmouth, NH: Heinemann.

Dorn, Linda J., and Carla Soffos. 2001. *Shaping Literate Minds: Developing Self-Regulated Learners.* Portland, ME: Stenhouse.

Dweck, Carol S. 2007. *Mindset: The New Psychology of Success.* New York: Ballantine.

Fountas, Irene C., and Gay Su Pinnell. 1996. *Guided Reading: Good First Teaching for All Children.* Portsmouth, NH: Heinemann.

———. 2007. *Teaching for Comprehending and Fluency: Thinking, Talking, and Writing About Reading, K-8.* Portsmouth, NH: Heinemann.

———. 2016a. *The Fountas & Pinnell Literacy Continuum: A Tool for Assessment, Planning, and Teaching, PreK—8.* Expanded ed. Portsmouth, NH: Heinemann.

———. 2016b. *Fountas & Pinnell Prompting Guide: Part 1 for Oral Reading and Early Writing.* Portsmouth, NH: Heinemann.

———. 2016c. *Guided Reading: Responsive Teaching Across the Grades.* 2nd ed. Portsmouth, NH: Heinemann.

Goldberg, Gravity. 2016. *Mindsets and Moves: Strategies That Help Readers Take Charge.* Thousand Oaks, CA: Corwin.

Guthrie, John T., and Nicole M. Humenick. 2004. "Motivating Students to Read: Evidence for Classroom Practices That Increase Reading Motivation and Achievement." In *The Voice of Evidence in Reading Research*, ed. Peggy McCardle and Vinita Chhabra, 329–354. Baltimore: Brookes.

Guthrie, John T., Allan Wigfield, and Clare VonSecker. 2000. "Effects of Integrated Instruction on Motivation and Strategy Use in Reading." *Journal of Educational Psychology* 92:331–341.

Harvey, Stephanie, and Harvey Daniels. 2015. *Comprehension and Collaboration: Inquiry Circles for Curiosity, Engagement, and Understanding* (Revised ed.) Portsmouth, NH: Heinemann.

Harvey, Stephanie, and Anne Goudvis. 2017. *Strategies That Work: Teaching Comprehension for Understanding, Engagement, and Building Knowledge.* 3rd ed. Portland, ME: Stenhouse.

Harvey, Stephanie, and Annie Ward. 2017. *From Striving to Thriving: How to Grow Confident, Capable Readers.* New York, NY: Scholastic.

Hidi, Suzanne, and Judith M. Harackiewicz. 2000. "Motivating the Academically Unmotivated: A Critical Issue for the 21st Century." *Review of Educational Research* 70:151–179.

Johnson, Pat, and Katie Keier. 2010. *Catching Readers Before They Fall: Supporting Readers Who Struggle, K–4*. Portland, ME: Stenhouse.

Johnston, Peter H. 2004. *Choice Words: How Our Language Affects Children's Learning*. Portland, ME: Stenhouse.

————. 2012. *Opening Minds: Using Language to Change Lives*. Portland, ME: Stenhouse.

Krashen, Stephen. 2004. *The Power of Reading: Insights from the Research*. 2nd ed. Portsmouth, NH: Heinemann.

Krashen, Stephen, and Tracy D. Terrell. 1983. *The Natural Approach: Language Acquisition in the Classroom*. Hayward, CA: Alemany.

Martinelli, Marjorie, and Kristine Mraz. 2012. *Smarter Charts K2: Optimizing an Instructional Staple to Create Independent Readers and Writers*. Portsmouth, NH: Heinemann.

Miller, Debbie, and Barbara Moss. 2013. *No More Independent Reading Without Support*. Portsmouth, NH: Heinemann.

Miller, Donalyn. 2009. *The Book Whisperer: Awakening the Inner Reader in Every Child*. San Francisco: Jossey-Bass.

————. 2013. *Reading in the Wild: The Book Whisperer's Keys to Cultivating Lifelong Reading Habits*. San Francisco: Jossey-Bass.

Muhtaris, Katie and Kristin Ziemke. 2015. *Amplify: Digital Teaching and Learning in the K–6 Classroom*. Portsmouth, NH: Heinemann.

Owocki, Gretchen, and Yetta Goodman. 2002. *Kidwatching: Documenting Children's Literacy Development*. Portsmouth, NH: Heinemann.

Pearson, P. David, and Margaret Gallagher. 1983. "The Instruction of Reading Comprehension." *Contemporary Educational Psychology* 8 (3): 317-344.

Pressley, Michael. 2003. *Motivating Primary Grade Students*. New York: Guilford Press.

Probst, R. E. 1987. "Transactional Theory in the Teaching of Literature." *ERIC Digest*. https://www.ericdigests.org/pre-926/theory.htm.

Roberts, Kate, and Maggie Beattie Roberts. 2016. *DIY Literacy: Teaching Tools for Differentiation, Rigor, and Independence*. Portsmouth, NH: Heinemann.

Scholastic and YouGov. 2017. *Kids and Family Reading Report*. 6th ed. New York: Scholastic.

Serravallo, Jennifer. 2013. *The Literacy Teacher's Playbook, Grades 3–6: Four Steps for Turning Assessment Data into Goal-Directed Instruction*. Portsmouth, NH: Heinemann.

———. 2014. *The Literacy Teacher's Playbook, Grades K–2: Four Steps for Turning Assessment Data into Goal-Directed Instruction*. Portsmouth, NH: Heinemann.

———. 2015. *The Reading Strategies Book: Your Everything Guide to Developing Skilled Readers*. Portsmouth, NH: Heinemann.

Serravallo, Jennifer, and Gravity Goldberg. 2007. *Conferring with Readers: Supporting Each Student's Growth and Independence*. Portsmouth, NH: Heinemann.

Sibberson, Franki, and Karen Szymusiak. 2016. *Still Learning to Read: Teaching Students in Grades 3–6*. 2nd ed. Portland, ME: Stenhouse.

Snow, Catherine E., M. Susan Burns, and Peg Griffin, eds. 1998. *Preventing Reading Difficulties in Young Children*. Washington, DC: National Academies Press.

Sulzby, Elizabeth. 1985. "Children's Emergent Reading of Favorite Story Books: A Developmental Study." *Reading Research Quarterly* 20 (4): 458–481.

Vygotsky, Lev. 1962. *Thought and Language*. Cambridge, MA: MIT Press.

———. 1978. "Interaction Between Learning and Development." In *Mind in Society: The Development of Higher Psychological Processes*. Cambridge, MA: Harvard University Press.

Wiggins, Grant. 2012. "Transfer as the Point of Education." *Granted, and . . . Thoughts on Education by Grant Wiggins*. https://grantwiggins.wordpress.com/2012/01/11/transfer-as-the-point-of-education/

Yates, Kari. 2015. *Simple Starts: Making the Move to a Reader-Centered Classroom*. Portsmouth, NH: Heinemann.

children's books

Abramson, Andra Serlin, and Paula Kovacs Ross. 2013. *Kids Meet the Tractors and Trucks*. Kennebunkport, ME: Applesauce Press.

Bird, Betsy. 2017. *Funny Girl. Funniest. Stories. Ever.* New York: Penguin Random House.

Carle, Eric. 1987. *The Very Hungry Caterpillar*. New York: Philomel Books.

Clements, Andrew. 2007. *No Talking*. New York, Aladdin.

Galdone. Paul. 1985. *The Three Bears*. Reprint ed. New York: Houghton Mifflin Harcourt Books for Young Readers.

Oak Park Elementary Kindergarten Class. 1996. *Our Class Is Going Green*. New York: Scholastic.

Pennypacker, Sara. 2008. *Clementine*. New York: Disney/Hyperion.

Waddell, Martin. 2017. *Owl Babies*. Somerville, MA: Candlewick Press.

index

Page numbers followed by *f* indicate figures.

A

abandonment of books, 76, 84–85
Abramson, Andra Serlin, 197, 199
Affirm move, 5, 8, 10*f*, 26–37, 38
  action and, 36, 37*f*
  approximations and, 34–35
  book choice and, 79*f*
  building on with Extend, 42, 42*f*
  definition of, 28–29
  for early readers, 129*f*
  for effort, 33–34
  for emergent readers, 126*f*
  healthy habits and, 99
  language for, 29–31, 37*f*, 54, 205f, 227*f*
  making it happen, 29–36
  making it stick, 29, 31
  for preemergent readers, 123*f*
  public affirmation and, 53, 60–61
  reasons to choose, 26
  recognizing efforts and traits to affirm, 32–36
  responding with, 200–203
  specificity in, 29, 30–31
  with transferable strategies, 36
  for transitional readers, 133*f*
Allington, Richard L., 70, 73, 96
anchor charts, 56

on authentic response, 164*f*
  for book choice, 75*f*, 81, 82*f*, 87, 89
  for healthy habits, 107, 112, 113*f*
appreciation, 15
approximations, affirming, 34–35
artifacts, observing, 17, 17*f*
assessment
  Book Choice Tool in, 74, 75*f*
  formative, 14
Authentic Response Conferring Reference, 165, 166*f*
authentic responses, 5, 64, 144–166
  affirmation of, 37*f*
  connections with other readers, 149, 154–156
  continued learning about, 163–165
  definition of, 146–147, 148
  essential questions for, 196*f*
  helping readers consider next steps, 149, 156–159
  helping readers pay attention to their, 149, 152–154
  importance of, 148–149
  internal vs. external, 159, 161–162
  language for extending, 48f, 49*f*
  leveraging connected processes in, 159, 162
  menu of options for, 159, 162–163
  misconceptions about the purpose of reading and, 149, 151–152
  modeling, 159, 160–161
  note taking on, 188–189, 188*f*

overview of, 66*f*
Remind and, 54*f*
sample conference on, 212–215
signs a reader might benefit from
conferring on, 149–159
signs a student might benefit from a
conference focused on, 198*f*
supporting in conferences, 155, 157*f*
of teachers, 159, 163
texts on understanding, 165*f*
tools and tips to support, 159–163
using conferring observations in future
teaching on, 58, 59*f*
visible excitement, 149, 150–151
Wonder questions on, 16*f*, 19f

B

background noise, 100
Backman, Jill, 89
Barnhouse, Dorothy J., 139
Bastardi, Anthony, 215
Beers, Kylene, 148, 165
behind-the-scenes moves, 5–6
big picture
keeping track of the, 174–176
stepping back to see, 14
Bird, Betsy, 91, 150
body language, observing, 17
Bomer, Katherine, 34
book choice, 5, 64, 68–93
abandoning books and, 76, 84–85
affirmation of, 37*f*
book collections for, 70, 101–102, 103*f*
classroom library curation and, 87, 90
degree of challenge and, 72–74
disengagement and, 105, 106*f*
engaged reading and, 76, 78, 80
essential questions for, 196*f*
first-grade conference on, 201–203
formative data from imperfect, 87, 92
frustration with, 76, 83–84
helping with, 71–75
importance of, 70–71
language for conferring on, 78, 79*f*, 80
language for extending, 47*f*, 49*f*
leveled texts and, 87, 88–89
note taking on, 188–189, 188*f*
overview of, 66*f*
planning for daily reading and, 101–102
for preemergent readers, 122–123
readers in a rut and, 76, 85–86

readers requiring extra care in, 76, 80–82
Remind and, 54*f*
sample conference on, 210–211
scaffolding for, 81, 82*f*
selection strategies for, 87, 89
signs a student might benefit from a
conference focused on, 76–86, 198*f*
teachers' awareness of great books and,
87, 91
teaching parents about, 75*f*
tools and tips to support, 87–92
using conferring observations in future
teaching on, 58, 59*f*
Wonder questions on, 16*f*, 18*f*
your own, 163
Book Choice Conferring Reference, 67,
92, 93*f*
Book Choice Reflection Tool, 217*f*
Book Choice Tool, 71–73, 72*f*, 74, 75*f*, 83
book lists, 91
bookmarks, 56, 109
boredom, 74
Building Healthy Reading Habits tool, 218*f*
Burkins, Jan M., 130, 138–139
Burns, M. Susan, 119

C

calendars, 178–179, 178*f*
Calkins, Lucy, 28, 29
Carle, Eric, 160
celebration, 14. *see also* Affirm move
Chall, Jeanne, 119
challenge levels
balance in, 93*f*
book choice and, 72–74
books by grade span and, 88*f*
chapter books, 131–132
classroom libraries, 87, 90
Clay, Marie M., 34, 118, 138
Clementine (Pennypacker), 212–213
clipboards, 170
collaboration, 43, 192, 193*f*
commitment, 3–4, 184
Extend and, 43
to health habits, 96
to wonder, 12
compliance-based activities, 148
compliments, 28
comprehension
for early readers, 130
initiating conversations on, 136, 139, 140*f*

for transitional readers, 131–134
Conference Record Sheet, 174–176, 175*f*, 221*f*
conferring
   adjusting based on student needs, 174, 179–182
   authentic response and, 149–159
   benefits of, 2–3
   book choice and, 68–93, 76–86
   building expertise in, 3
   commitment to, 3–4
   connectedness in, 57–58
   definition of, 2, 7
   with early readers, 128–131
   with emergent readers, 124–127
   ensuring transfer beyond, 51–62
   flexibility in, 183–184
   frequency of, 176, 177*f*
   gathering materials for, 6, 10*f*, 168, 169–172
   healthy habits and, 99–107
   from the heart, 4, 43
   the how of, 7–10
   interactive moves for, 5
   joyful, 3–4
   language for, 203–205, 226*f*–227*f*
   to learn, 4, 43
   making time for, 173–184
   organization for, 63–67, 168
   planning for, 167–168
   planning for follow-up in future, 48
   with preemergent readers, 120, 122–125
   priorities in, 66*f*
   with readers showing signs of disengagement, 99, 104–107
   on reading spots, 100–101
   sample of fifth-grade, 210–211
   sample of first-grade, 197–200, 201–203
   sample of fourth-grade, 206–209
   sample of third-grade, 209–210
   setting ambitious yet reasonable goals for, 174, 176–179, 177*f*
   signs a student might benefit from, 67, 119–136, 197, 198*f*
   student discomfort with, 8–9
   teacher moves for, 10*f*
   with tenacity, 4
   with transitional readers, 131–134
confidence, 27, 201
   affirmations and, 31
   public affirmation and, 60–61
confusion, 136, 139–141, 141*f*

connections, 57–58
   authentic response and, 144, 147
   note taking and, 187
   with other readers, 149, 154–156
   planning to make, 158
creativity, 201
curiosity, 13, 16. *see also* Wonder move

D
decision making, 7, 194–216
   the Know question in, 194, 196–200
   the Nurture question in, 194, 200–203
   sample conferences showing, 197–214, 201–203
Decision Making Map, 4–6, 65*f*, 194, 195*f*
   Affirm on, 27*f*
   authentic response on, 145*f*
   book choice on, 69*f*
   Extend on, 39*f*
   guiding questions in, 8
   healthy habits on, 95*f*
   intentional focus on, 23, 24*f*
   note taking on, 186*f*
   Remind on, 52*f*
   strategic process on, 117*f*
   Wonder on, 13*f*
decoding skills, 132
defensiveness, 19–20
demonstrations, 44, 45*f*
digital tools, 171
disengagement, 14, 99, 104–107
disorientation, 139–140, 141*f*
Disrupting Thinking (Beers and Probst), 148
distractions, 102, 103*f*, 182–183
DIY Literacy (Roberts and Roberts), 56
Dorn, Linda J., 119
Dweck, Carol, 33, 74, 128

E
early stage of reading, 119, 121*f*, 128–131
effort, affirming, 33–34, 128
emergent stage of reading, 119, 120*f*, 124–127
   behaviors in, 125
   language to support readers in, 125, 126*f*
   text characteristics for, 125, 127*f*
empowerment, 34
engaged listeners, 22
engagement
   authentic responses and, 156

book choice and, 68, 70, 71, 76, 78, 80
conferring focused on, 199–200
prioritizing, 196–197
readers showing signs of disengagement
    and, 99, 104–107
explanations, 44, 46
Extend move, 5, 8, 10*f*, 38–50, 205*f*, 227*f*
    action, in, 50
    with authentic responses, 154
    book choice and, 79*f*
    definition of, 38
    for early readers, 129*f*
    for emergent readers, 126*f*
    explaining in, 44, 46
    focus selection for, 40–49
    getting the reader involved in, 40, 49, 49*f*
    language for, 44, 46, 47*f*–48*f*
    lightest support possible in, 40, 44, 45*f*
    making it happen, 40–49
    offering partnership in, 40, 43
    for preemergent readers, 123*f*
    reminding in, 44, 45
    responding with, 200–203
    self-help in, 44, 46
    for transitional readers, 133*f*

F

feedback, 30. *see also* Affirm move
flexibility, 6, 183–184, 201, 206–217
Flowchart for Troubleshooting
    Disengagement, 105, 106*f*
fluency
    for early readers, 130
    for transitional readers, 131–134
fluent stage of reading, 119, 121*f*, 134–136
focus
    for extending, 40–43
    for fluent readers' skills, 135–136
    healthy habits and, 94
    intentional, 5, 23, 24*f*
    signs a student might benefit from
        conference based on, 67
    transferable, 42
    Wonder and, 20, 21*f*
Fountas, Irene C., 118, 119, 125
Four Square Conferring Notes template,
    188–189, 188*f*
Four Square Conferring Reference, 115,
    171, 189
Four Square Grid, 192

Four Square Questions for Conferring, 18,
    18*f*–19*f*, 144, 171, 189, 197, 219*f*, 220*f*
frustration, 74, 76, 83–84
Funny Girl. Funniest. Stories. Ever
    (Bird), 150

G

Gabriel, Rachael E., 70, 73
Galdone, Paul, 119, 123
Gallagher, Margaret, 44
goals
    affirming moves toward, 34
    on healthy habits, 110–111, 111*f*
    setting, 98, 177*f*
    setting ambitious yet reasonable, 174,
        176–179
    setting meaningful, 2
    setting with students vs. for students,
        107–109
    strategy reminders for, 56, 57*f*
    visual reminders for, 109
Godin, Seth, 3
Goldberg, Gravity, 27, 150
Goodman, Yetta, 14
gratitude, 15
Griffin, Peg, 119
growth mindset, 33–34, 74, 128
Guthrie, John T., 70, 90

H

habits, healthy, 5, 64, 94–115
    affirmation of, 37*f*
    anchor charts for, 107, 112, 113*f*
    building, 218*f*
    Conferring Reference on, 114–115, 114*f*
    definition of, 94
    essential questions for, 196*f*
    fourth-grade conference on, 206–209
    future reading plans, 98
    importance of, 96–98
    language for extending, 47*f*, 49*f*
    note taking on, 188–189, 188*f*
    nurturing, 99
    overview of, 66*f*
    planning for daily reading, 97–98, 99,
        101–102
    readers showing signs of disengagement
        and, 99, 104–107
    reading spots, 97, 99–101
    Remind and, 54*f*

setting goals, 98, 107–109
signs a reader might benefit from
   conferring focused on, 99–107
signs a student might benefit from a
   conference focused on, 198f
studying your own and others', 107, 112,
   114
teaching with whole-group and
   small-group instruction, 107, 109–111
time for reading, 97, 99, 102–104
tools and tips to support, 107–114
using conferring observations in future
   teaching on, 58, 59f
Wonder questions on, 16f, 18f
Harackiewicz, Judith M., 70
Harvey, Stephanie, 82
Healthy Habits Conferring Reference,
   114–115, 114f
Healthy Reading Habits Goal-Setting Sheet,
   110–111, 111f
Hidi, Suzanne, 70
Humenick, Nicole M., 70

I

inconsistencies, 35–36
independence, 204f–205f
independent choice reading, 148
intentionality
   conferring with, 206–217
   in focus, 5
   healthy habits and, 96, 99
   language and, 29–31, 53–54, 54f
   moving forward with, 23, 24f
   using Wonder to focus, 20, 21f
interest
   book choice and, 76, 80–82
   readers in a rut and, 76, 85–86

J

Johnson, Pat, 118
Johnston, Peter, 27, 53
joyfulness, 215

K

Keier, Katie, 118
Kids Meet the Tractors and Trucks
   (Abramson and Ross), 197, 199
kidwatching, 14
Know and Nurture T-Chart, 189–190, 191f,
   225f

Know question, the, 8, 12, 194, 196–200
Krashen, Stephen, 96, 148

L

language, 203–205, 226f–227f
   for affirmations, 37f
   for affirming new reading behaviors, 32,
      33f
   on authentic responses, 154
   for book choice, 78, 79f
   to encourage trying out learning, 49f
   for extending, 44, 46, 47f–48f
   to foster self-reliance and independence,
      204f–205f
   intentional, in affirmation, 29–31
   for reminding, 53–54, 54f
   student-centered vs. teacher-centered, 30
   to support authentic responses, 160, 161f
   to support early readers, 128, 129f, 130
   to support emergent readers, 125, 126f
   to support fluent readers, 136
   to support preemergent readers, 122, 123f
   to support transitional readers, 132, 133f
   for teaching on healthy habits, 110
   of transfer, 53–54, 54f
leveled texts, 87, 88–89
   early, 128
   emergent, 125, 127, 127f
library book bins, 86
listening, 22

M

Martinelli, Marjorie, 112
materials, gathering, 6, 10f, 168, 169–172
meaning making
   affirming moves toward, 34
   for emergent readers, 124–127
   questions on, 139, 140f
   setting goals and, 2
   strategic process and, 119
Miller, Debbie, 118
Miller, Donalyn, 2, 81–82
Mindsets and Moves (Goldberg), 150
mirroring, 28, 150–151. see also reflection
modeling, 159, 160–161
Moss, Barbara, 118
motivation
   book choice and, 70–71, 72f
   goals and, 107–108
Mraz, Kristine, 112

multisyllabic words, 48*f*, 132
multitext approach, 87, 88

N

naming, 28
narrative picture books, 123
Nerdy Book Club, 91
nonverbal gestures, listening and, 22
note taking, 6, 10*f*, 168, 185–193, 209
    Know and Nurture T-Chart for, 189–190, 191*f*
    making it happen, 187–190
    other tools for, 190
    reflecting on notes and, 190–193
    to support collaboration with colleagues, 192, 193*f*
    template for, 188–189, 188*f*
noticing, 28
Nurture question, the, 8, 194, 200–203

O

observation, 14
    artifacts, 17, 17*f*
    body language, 17
    lenses for, 14, 15*f*
    questions to guide conference, 206, 228*f*
    up close, 17
    using conferring observations in future teaching, 58, 59*f*
    openness, 13, 16. see also Wonder move
organization, 5–6, 63–67
    of classroom libraries, 90
    disengagement and, 105, 106*f*
    language for Extend teaching on, 47*f*
    making time for reading and, 99, 102–104
    teacher moves for, 10*f*
    time for reading and, 97
Our Class Is Going Green (Elkington and Hailes), 160
Owocki, Gretchen, 14

P

paper, 171
parents, book choice and, 75*f*
partnership with readers, 14–15, 40, 43, 61
patience, 20
patterns, creating small groups based on, 109–110, 134
Pearson, P. David, 44

Pennypacker, Sarah, 212–213
persistence, 20
personalized instruction, 118
Pinnell, Gay Su, 118, 119, 125
planning, 5–6, 10*f*, 168, 173–184
    adjusting based on student needs, 174, 179–182, 181*f*, 182*f*
    behind the scenes, 167–168
    daily, 183*f*
    flexibility in, 183–184
    follow-up teaching, 53, 56–60
    future reading, 98
    helping readers with next steps, 149, 156–159
    making it happen, 174–183
    reading time, 97–98, 99, 101–102
    saying no to distractions and, 182–183
    using notes in, 192–193
point of difficulty, learning from, 136, 138–139
preemergent stage of reading, 119, 120*f*, 122–124
    high-quality texts for, 124*f*
    supporting oral language use in, 119, 122–124
preparation, 5–6
Pressley, Michael, 70
    problem-solving, 208
    affirming effort in, 34
    for early readers, 128–131
    for emergent readers, 127
    making reading time and, 99, 103–104
    reading spots and, 101
strategic process and, 119
Probst, Robert, 148
puzzlement, 139, 140*f*

Q

questions
    about disengagement, 107
    about tools for conferring, 172
    for authentic responses, 153
    for directions of conferring, 16*f*, 196*f*
    exploratory, 17–21
    focusing on reader vs. text, 19
    Four Square, for Conferring, 18, 18*f*–19*f*, 220*f*
    guiding, 6, 8
    guiding conference observations, 228*f*
    meaning-making and, 139, 140*f*
    process-focused, 138–139

reading spots and, 101
for Wonder, 11
the Wonder clause in, 20, 20*f*

R
read-alouds
    authentic responses and, 159, 160–161
    for early readers, 130
    listening to students', 136, 138
    supporting book choice with, 87
    for transitional readers, 132
readers
    believing in the capacity of, 15
    communities of, 155
    connections with other, 149, 154–156
    getting to know, 76, 77–78
reading
    affirming new behaviors in, 32, 33*f*
    development stages in, 119, 120*f*–121*f*
    good-fit spots for, 97, 99–101, 105
    inconsistencies in, 35–36
    independent, books by grade for, 88*f*
    independent, daily, 70
    independent choice, 148
    listening to, 23
    misconceptions about the purpose of, 149, 151–152
    relaxed, 73, 93*f*
    stretch, 73–74, 93*f*
    time for, 97, 99, 102–104
    volume of, 96–97
    in the wild, 2
record keeping, 170
    Conference Record Sheet for, 174–176, 175*f*, 221*f*
reflection, 2
    affirming and, 26, 28
    authentic response and, 144, 146
    on disengagement, 107
    as gift, 29
    healthy habits and, 94, 96, 99
    notes and, 190–193
    reading habits and, 107, 112, 114
    reading spots and, 101
    setting goals and, 108
    slowing down for, 153
    on your own reading, 163
Remind move, 5, 8, 10*f*, 31, 51–62, 205*f*, 227*f*
    action and, 61–62
    with authentic responses, 154

    extending and, 44, 45
    follow-up teaching in, 53, 56–60
    for goals, 109
    language of transfer in, 53–54, 54*f*
    public acknowledgment and celebration in, 53, 60–61
    responding with, 200–203
    visual reminders for, 53, 55–56, 55*f*
resilience, 128–131
respect, 204*f*, 208, 226*f*
    affirming and, 28
    tone and, 16
responses. *see* authentic responses
responsive teaching, 7, 183–184
restating, 22
Roberts, Kate, 56
Roberts, Maggie Beattie, 56
Ross, Lee, 215
Ross, Paula Kovacs, 197, 199
running records, 138

S
scaffolding, 14
    self-help and, 44, 46
    temporary, 55
    visual, 81, 82*f*
    within-reach work, 41
scale of gradual release of responsibility, 44
Scholastic Reading Report, 70
self-extending readers, 118
self-help, 44, 46
self-reliance, 204*f*–205*f*
Serravallo, Jennifer, 56
shopping cards, 81, 82*f*
Simple Starts (Yates), 87, 90, 112
small-group instruction, 134
    follow-up with, 58, 59*f*
    instruction on habits with, 107, 109–111
Smarter Charts (Mraz and Martinelli), 112
Snow, Catherine E., 119
Soffos, Carla, 119
sticky notes, 55, 55*f*, 109, 170, 171
strategic process, 5, 64, 116–143
    affirmation of, 37*f*
    affirming, 28
    book selection strategies, 87, 89
    confusion and, 136, 139–141
    continued learning about, 136, 141, 142*f*
    definition of, 116
    for emergent readers, 124–127
    essential questions for, 196*f*

for fluent readers, 134–136
frustration with book choices and, 83–84
importance of, 118
inconsistencies in, 35–36
language for extending, 48*f*, 49*f*
listening to reading and, 23
note taking on, 188–189, 188*f*
overview of, 66*f*
for preemergent readers, 120–125
reading development stages and, 119, 120*f*–121*f*
Remind and, 54*f*
sample conference on, 209–210
signs a reader might benefit from conferring focused on, 119–136
signs a student might benefit from a conference focused on, 198*f*
tools and tips to support, 136–141
transferable strategies in, 36, 42, 53–54, 54*f*
for transitional readers, 131–134
using conferring observations in future teaching on, 58, 59*f*
Wonder questions on, 16*f*, 19*f*
Strategic Process Conferring Reference, 141, 143–144, 143*f*
strategy sheets, individualized, 56
Sulzby, Elizabeth, 123, 120*f*

T

taking action, authentic response and, 148, 158–159
teachers
    awareness of great books, 87, 91
    understanding of strategic reading process by, 136, 140, 141*f*
Teachers College Reading and Writing Project, 27
teaching
    Book Choice Tool in, 74, 75*f*
    confusion and, 136, 139–141
    follow-up, 53, 56–60
    habits with whole-group and small-group instruction, 107, 109–111
    interactive, 7–8
    light support in, 40, 44, 45*f*
    overeagerness to assist or correct in, 136, 138–139
    as partnership, 40, 43
    personalization of, 118
    responsive, 7, 183–184

right-sized, 41–42
teaching assistants, 61
tenacity, 4
texts. *see also* authentic responses
    authentic responses, on, 165*f*
    for early readers, 128
    for emergent readers, 125, 127, 127*f*
    focusing on readers vs., 19
    interaction around, 155, 156*f*
    leveled, 87, 88–89
    for preemergent readers, 124*f*
    recommendations on, 155
    spending time with, 158
    strategic reading process, on, 140, 141*f*
think-alouds, 44, 45
This Week's Conferring Plan, 222*f*, 223*f*
Three Bears, The (Galdone), 119, 123
time management, 173–184
tone
    for offering partnership, 43
    setting, 12, 14–16
    the Wonder clause and, 20
transition stage of reading, 119, 121*f*, 131–134
trust, 14–15, 43, 215–216

U

Uhlmann, Eric Luis, 215

V

variety, in book choice, 93f
Very Hungry Caterpillar, The (Carle), 160
Vinton, Vicki, 139
visualization, 104
VonSecker, Clare, 90
Vygotsky, Lev, 2, 32, 41, 42

W

wait time, 22
Ward, Annie, 82
weekly planning tools, 178–179, 179*f*, 180*f*
We Need Diverse Books, 91
whole-group instruction, 134
    follow-up with, 58, 59*f*
    instruction on habits with, 107, 109–111
Who's Doing the Work? (Burkins and Yaris), 130
Wigfield, Allan, 90
Wiggins, Grant, 42

Willems, Mo, 86
within-reach work, 41
Wonder move, 5, 8, 10*f*, 11–25
action and, 25
book choice and, 79*f*
decision making and, 196–200
definition of, 11–12
for early readers, 129*f*
for emergent readers, 126*f*
empowerment from, 38
engaged listening and, 22
exploratory questions and, 17–21
exploring in more depth, 12, 16–23
guiding questions for, 11
language for, 204*f*, 226*f*
making it happen, 12–23
moving forward with intentional focus from, 23, 24*f*

for preemergent readers, 123*f*
questions for, 16*f*
seeing the big picture and, 12, 14
setting the tone and, 12, 14–16
for transitional readers, 133*f*
writing, 158, 162
writing utensils, 170–171

Y
Yaris, Kim, 130, 138–139
Yates, Kari, 16, 87, 90

Z
zone of proximal development, 32, 32*f*, 41, 41*f*, 42